105 Polework, Flatwork, Cavaletti & Dressage Exercises

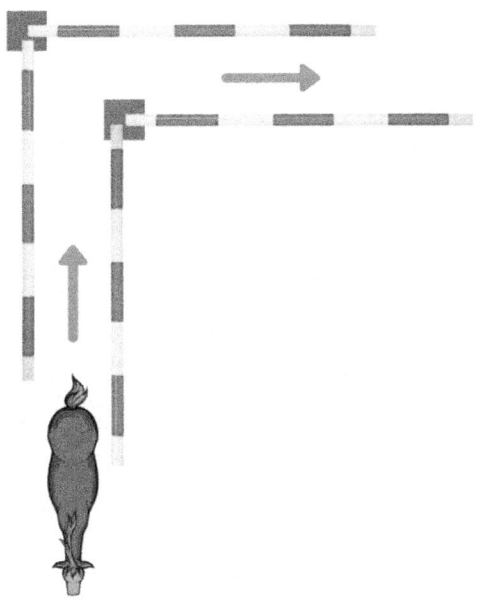

105 Polework, Flatwork, Cavaletti & Dressage Exercises

Elaine Heney

Printer: Amazon Global Publishing, 60 Holborn Viaduct London EC4, UK. Publisher: Elaine Heney, Design Font Apps Ltd, St. Galls House, St. Gall Gardens South, Milltown, Dublin 14, Ireland. www.elaineheneybooks.com This book has been designed and manufactured in accordance with the general safety requirement laid down in Article 5, GPSR. ISBN printed on back cover. EU authorised representative: Elaine Heney. www.elaineheneybooks.com

"The greatest judge in this world is your horse. "

Elaine Heney

Horse books for adults

www.elaineheneybooks.com

The Equine Listenology Guide
Dressage for Beginners
151 Polework Exercises for Horses
The Galway Connemara
The Listenology Guide to Bitless Bridles
Horse Anatomy Colouring Book

Horse books for kids

Listenology for Kids
Horse Care, Riding and Training for Kids
Saddlestone Series for Kids (5 books)

The Coral Cove Series for kids

The Riding School Connemara Pony
The Storm and the Connemara Pony
The Surprise Puppy and the Connemara Pony
The Castle and the Connemara Pony
The Shipwreck the Connemara Pony
The Christmas Connemara Pony

The Connemara Adventure Series for kids

The Forgotten Horse
The Show Horse
The Mayfield Horse
The Stolen Horse
The Adventure Horse
The Lost Horse

Table of contents

Getting started

Bored of the same old arena routine? Discover a fresh world of fun exercises and creative challenges to keep both you and your horse motivated and learning together.

This book is all about having fun with your horse while developing a strong partnership together. From polework inspired flatwork plans to playful cone work and standing cavaletti exercises, there's a world of variety waiting to elevate your training routine.

Every exercise in this book is designed not just to improve your horse's physical skills, but also to enhance your communication and connection. You'll learn how to refine your cues, build trust and create a deeper understanding with your horse, which is essential for a successful partnership.

And the best part? You won't need to stress about competition nerves, dress up in fancy gear, or worry about whether your horse trailer has a flat tire. This is about enjoying your time together, free from the usual pressures that can come with traditional lessons or competition settings way.

Imagine spending quality time with your horse, confidently practicing your skills in a familiar environment where both of you can relax and focus. You'll discover how to create a structured and varied routine that keeps your horse mentally engaged and physically challenged, ensuring you both look forward to every session. The exercises you'll find in this book are designed to be fun and fulfilling, encouraging exploration and creativity while also achieving your training goals.

So, gather your cones, poles and an open mind, and get ready to have fun with your horse.

Let's dive into the exercises that will not only improve your horse's skills but also deepen the bond between you, making each ride a great experience for both you and your horse. Happy riding!

Lessons from the Old Masters

In the 1600s and 1700s in Europe, the old masters of equestrianism laid down the essential principles and techniques that continue to influence modern horse training and riding today.

François Robichon de la Guérinière and Antoine de Pluvinel from France, along with England's William Cavendish were famous horsemen and pioneers from that era who emphasized the importance of understanding horse behaviour, building trust and using humane training methods.

Their teachings offer priceless insights for today's horse riders looking to create strong partnerships with their horses that promote both physical and mental wellbeing.

These old masters also introduced kind and effective training approaches that can be adapted to various disciplines, making their lessons applicable to everything covered in this book. By incorporating their philosophies into contemporary training exercises, you can enhance your horse's overall health while fostering a deeper connection and improving your horse's physical and mental health.

Moreover, blending this traditional wisdom with modern practices allows you to craft well-rounded training programs that are not only effective but also enjoyable for both you and your horse.

Pluvinel's Gentle Approach

Antoine de Pluvinel was a key figure in 17th century France, known for his contributions to classical dressage as an equestrian and horse trainer. His influential work, "L'École de Cavalerie," highlights the importance of kindness, patience, and truly understanding a horse's nature during training. Pluvinel's teachings have laid the groundwork for modern riding techniques, focusing on building trust and communication between horse and rider, which continues to inspire equestrians today. He believed that effective training should foster a bond of trust and open communication, advocating for gentle methods that respect the horse's feelings and instincts.

To apply Pluvinel's teachings in your training, start by observing your horse's body language and reactions to various exercises, ensuring you adapt your approach based on their comfort level. Incorporate positive reinforcement by rewarding small successes, whether through verbal praise, a neck rub or a short rest, to encourage your horse and build their confidence. When working with the exercises in this book, such as pole work, flatwork, dressage tests and cavaletti exercises, consider breaking them down into smaller, manageable steps when you need to. This allows your horse to grasp each concept without feeling overwhelmed. By integrating Pluvinel's principles, you will create a training environment that not only challenges your horse physically but also fosters their mental and emotional well-being, enhancing your partnership and making every session enjoyable and productive.

Cavendish's Creative Mind

William Cavendish, the 1st Duke of Newcastle, was a prominent 17th-century English horseman and equestrian writer known for his impactful contributions to horse training. His influential book, "A General System of Horsemanship," highlighted the importance of understanding horse behaviour and introduced innovative training techniques that blended practicality with creativity. Cavendish's teachings laid the foundation for modern equestrian practices and continue to inspire riders looking to build a harmonious relationship with their horses. Cavendish advocated for a training approach that encourages experimentation and creativity, emphasizing the importance of forming a strong connection between horse and rider. He believed that riders should be open to trying different methods and exercises to find what works best for their horses, fostering a playful and exploratory training environment.

When working with the exercises in this book, channel Cavendish's philosophy by staying adaptable and willing to adjust based on what your horse needs. For example, if a particular exercise isn't resonating with your horse, feel free to modify it or change your approach until you find a method that engages them. Additionally, Cavendish emphasized the importance of observing your horse closely; use their reactions as a guide to adjust your training techniques. By incorporating these principles, you will not only keep your training sessions enjoyable and varied but also cultivate a deeper partnership with your horse based on trust and mutual understanding.

De La Guérinière's Lasting Influence

François Robichon de La Guérinière was a key figure in 18th-century France, known for his influential work in classical dressage and equestrian training. His landmark book, "École de Cavalerie," laid out systematic training methods and stressed the importance of understanding a horse's natural instincts and behaviours.

La Guérinière championed patience, adaptability and humane treatment, principles that have shaped modern equestrian practices and still resonate with riders and trainers today. He believed that training should be compassionate, focusing on each horse's unique characteristics.

Bring La Guérinière's teachings into your practice by maintaining clear, consistent signals that allow your horse to follow your guidance with ease. When incorporating exercises from this book break them down into manageable steps, allowing your horse to master each element before progressing. Don't canter an exercise before you can walk it!

Take the time to assess your horse's response to different exercises; if they seem confused or resistant, adjust your approach to better suit their needs. By integrating La Guérinière's principles into your training sessions, you'll create a supportive environment that promotes confidence and trust.

Create your own exercises

Being creative in horse training is essential for fostering a dynamic and engaging environment that promotes learning and development for both horse and rider. As De La Guérinière emphasized, training should be adaptable and responsive to the needs of the horse, highlighting the importance of understanding individual strengths and weaknesses.

Incorporating creativity into your training regimen not only keeps your horse mentally stimulated but also allows you to explore new ways to build trust, communication, and partnership.

In the spirit of William Cavendish who also recognised the significance of creative training methods, I've included areas in this book where you can design your own dressage tests, flatwork floor plans, and cavaletti exercises. This approach empowers you to take ownership of your training, encouraging innovation while ensuring that each training session remains new and enjoyable.

By embracing creativity in your training, you'll not only enhance your horse's skills but also deepen the bond between you, making every ride a success.

16 Cone Exercises

Using cones in horse training improves agility, balance, coordination and responsiveness by encouraging precise footwork and balance changes. Whether you're working at the walk, trot or canter, cones help improve accuracy, straightness and communication, giving both you and your horse clear visual markers to follow.

Cones are also useful for developing rhythm, impulsion and self-carriage, particularly when incorporated into lateral or backwards movements.

Cones can make sessions more engaging, keeping your horse mentally and physically attentive while adding a bit of variety to prevent boredom. They're an easy and affordable tool that can make a real difference in refining your horse's balance, responsiveness, and overall way of going.

Whether for groundwork, flatwork or jumping preparation, cone exercises are a versatile tool for building a well-rounded, attentive and athletic horse.

What you will need: Between 2 and 8 cones.

Adare Cones

Ride over the cones without knocking any over.
Look straight ahead.

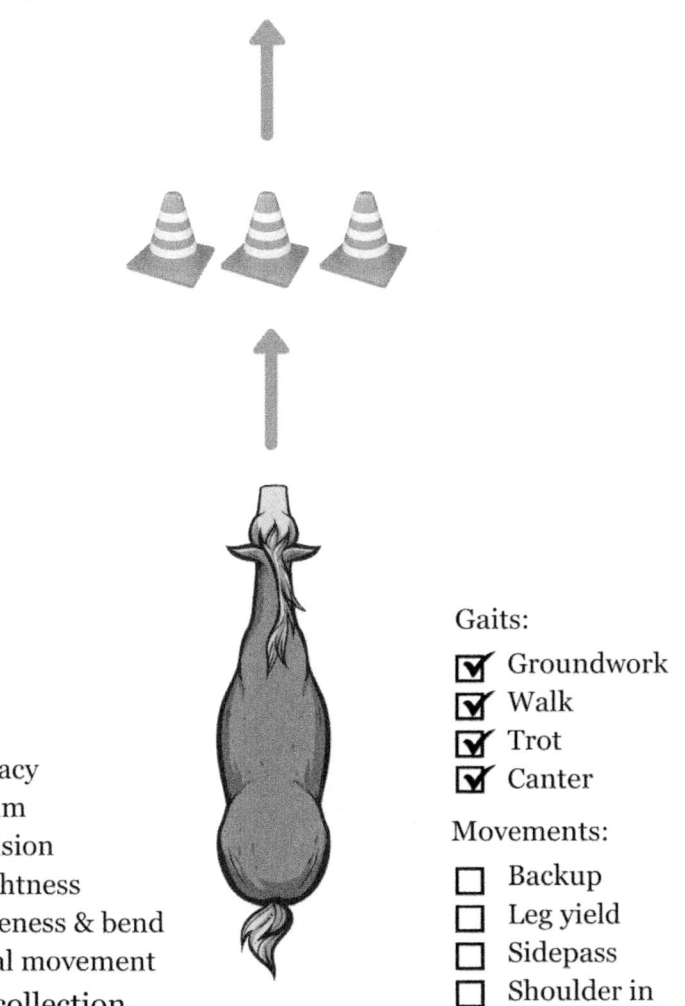

Cones: 3

Level: ★

Benefits:

- ☑ Accuracy
- ☑ Rhythm
- ☑ Impulsion
- ☑ Straightness
- ☐ Suppleness & bend
- ☐ Lateral movement
     & collection

Gaits:

- ☑ Groundwork
- ☑ Walk
- ☑ Trot
- ☑ Canter

Movements:

- ☐ Backup
- ☐ Leg yield
- ☐ Sidepass
- ☐ Shoulder in

Cobh Cones

Ride through the cones without knocking any over. Look straight ahead.

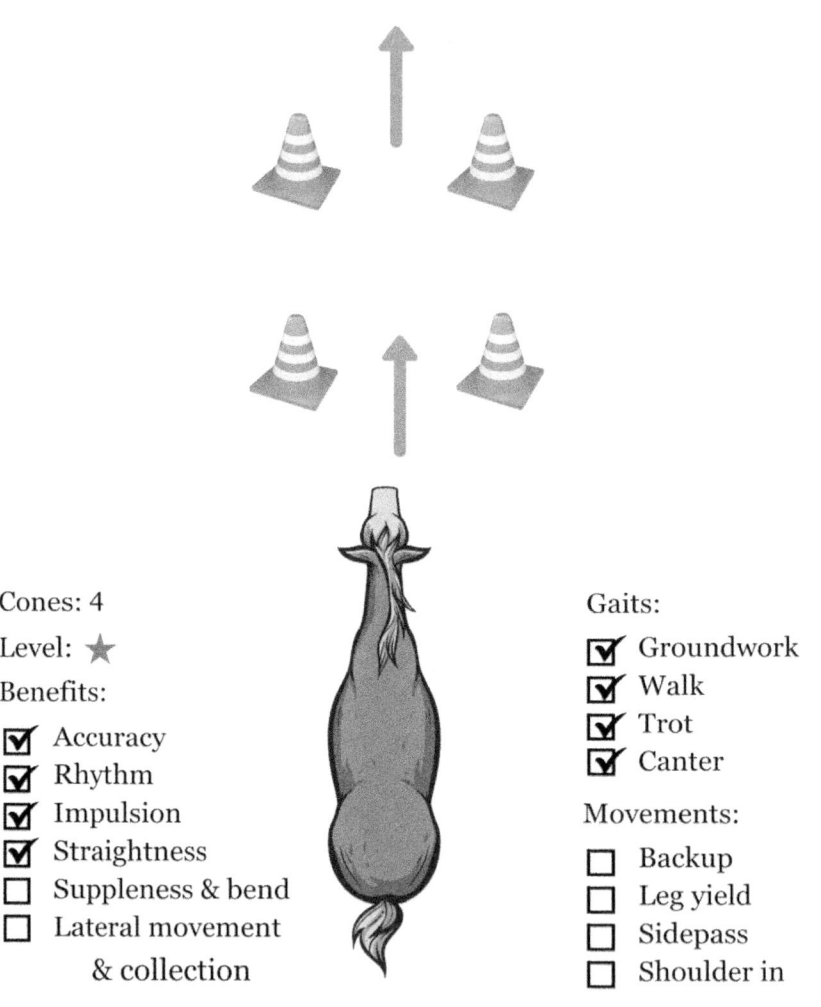

Cones: 4

Level: ⭐

Benefits:

- ☑ Accuracy
- ☑ Rhythm
- ☑ Impulsion
- ☑ Straightness
- ☐ Suppleness & bend
- ☐ Lateral movement
    & collection

Gaits:

- ☑ Groundwork
- ☑ Walk
- ☑ Trot
- ☑ Canter

Movements:

- ☐ Backup
- ☐ Leg yield
- ☐ Sidepass
- ☐ Shoulder in

Emly Cones

Ride a figure of 8 with your horse around the 2 cones. Change the bend in your horse's body before you change direction.

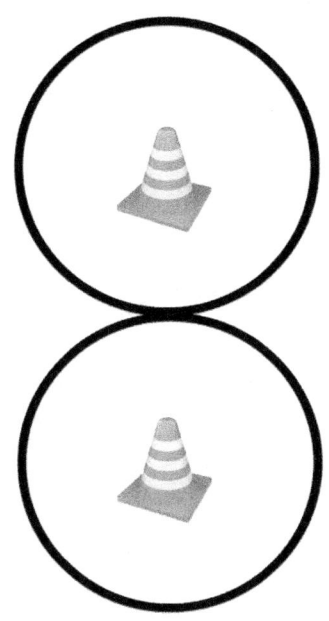

Cones: 2

Level: ★

Benefits:

- ☑ Accuracy
- ☑ Rhythm
- ☑ Impulsion
- ☐ Straightness
- ☑ Suppleness & bend
- ☐ Lateral movement
      & collection

Gaits:

- ☑ Groundwork
- ☑ Walk
- ☑ Trot
- ☑ Canter

Movements:

- ☐ Backup
- ☐ Leg yield
- ☐ Sidepass
- ☐ Shoulder in

Ballywater Cones

Ride a figure of 8 with your horse around the 2 cones. Do a shoulder in movement for half of each circle.

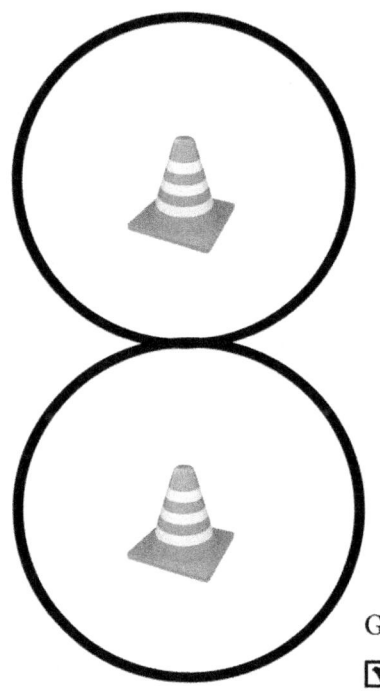

Cones: 2

Level: ★ ★

Benefits:

- ☑ Accuracy
- ☑ Rhythm
- ☑ Impulsion
- ☐ Straightness
- ☑ Suppleness & bend
- ☑ Lateral movement
  & collection

Gaits:

- ☑ Groundwork
- ☑ Walk
- ☑ Trot
- ☑ Canter

Movements:

- ☐ Backup
- ☐ Leg yield
- ☐ Sidepass
- ☑ Shoulder in

Foxrock Cones

Do a figure of 8 with your horse around the 2 cones. Walk 1 circle and then trot the next circle. Change the bend in your horse's body before you change direction.

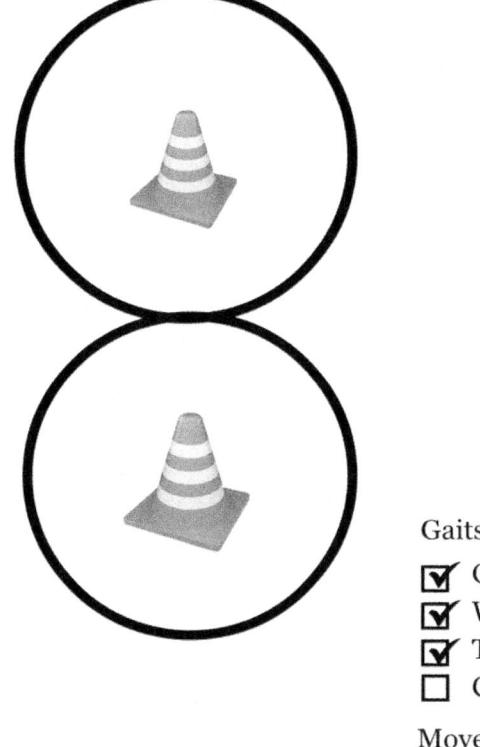

Cones: 2

Level: ★

Benefits:

- ☑ Accuracy
- ☑ Rhythm
- ☑ Impulsion
- ☐ Straightness
- ☑ Suppleness & bend
- ☐ Lateral movement
  & collection

Gaits:

- ☑ Groundwork
- ☑ Walk
- ☑ Trot
- ☐ Canter

Movements:

- ☐ Backup
- ☐ Leg yield
- ☐ Sidepass
- ☐ Shoulder in

Ballycastle Cones

Do a figure of 8 with your horse around the 2 cones. Trot 1 circle and then canter the next circle. Change the bend in your horse's body before you change direction.

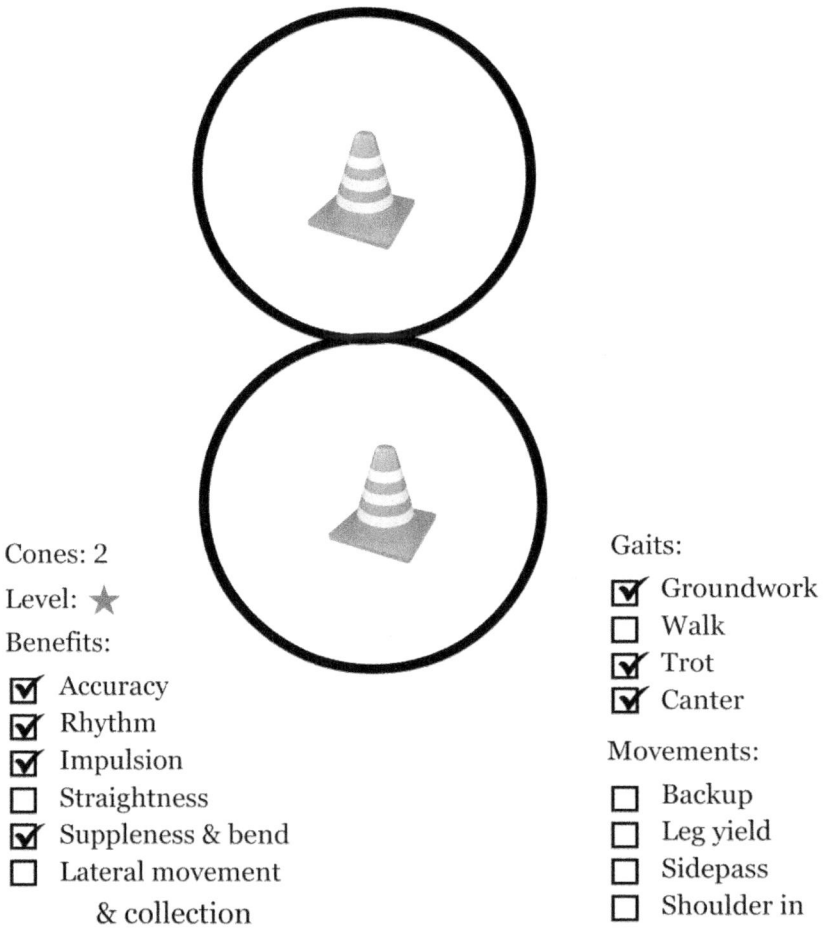

Cones: 2

Level: ★

Benefits:

- ☑ Accuracy
- ☑ Rhythm
- ☑ Impulsion
- ☐ Straightness
- ☑ Suppleness & bend
- ☐ Lateral movement
     & collection

Gaits:

- ☑ Groundwork
- ☐ Walk
- ☑ Trot
- ☑ Canter

Movements:

- ☐ Backup
- ☐ Leg yield
- ☐ Sidepass
- ☐ Shoulder in

Gorteen Cones

Walk serpentines around each cone. Afterwards, do the same in sitting trot. Try to not move your hands, keep them close together at the pommel. Change the bend in your horse's body before you change direction.

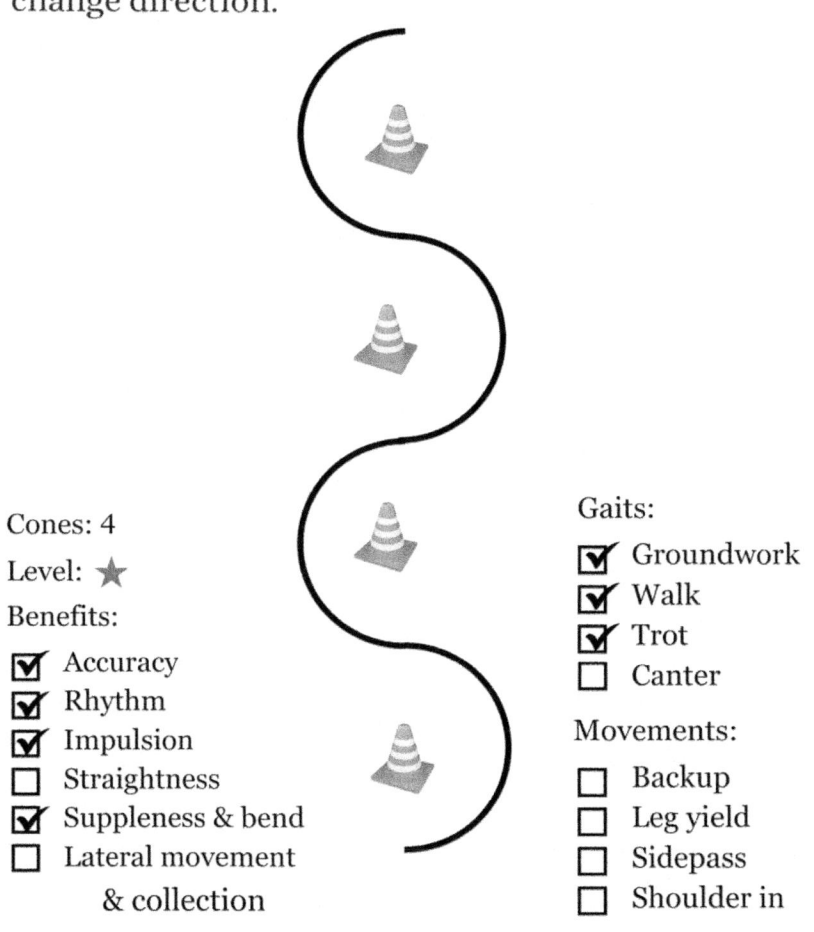

Cones: 4

Level: ★

Benefits:

- ☑ Accuracy
- ☑ Rhythm
- ☑ Impulsion
- ☐ Straightness
- ☑ Suppleness & bend
- ☐ Lateral movement
      & collection

Gaits:

- ☑ Groundwork
- ☑ Walk
- ☑ Trot
- ☐ Canter

Movements:

- ☐ Backup
- ☐ Leg yield
- ☐ Sidepass
- ☐ Shoulder in

Galbally Cones

Canter serpentines around each cone. Use simple changes or flying lead changes. Increase the distance between the cones to make it easier for your horse.

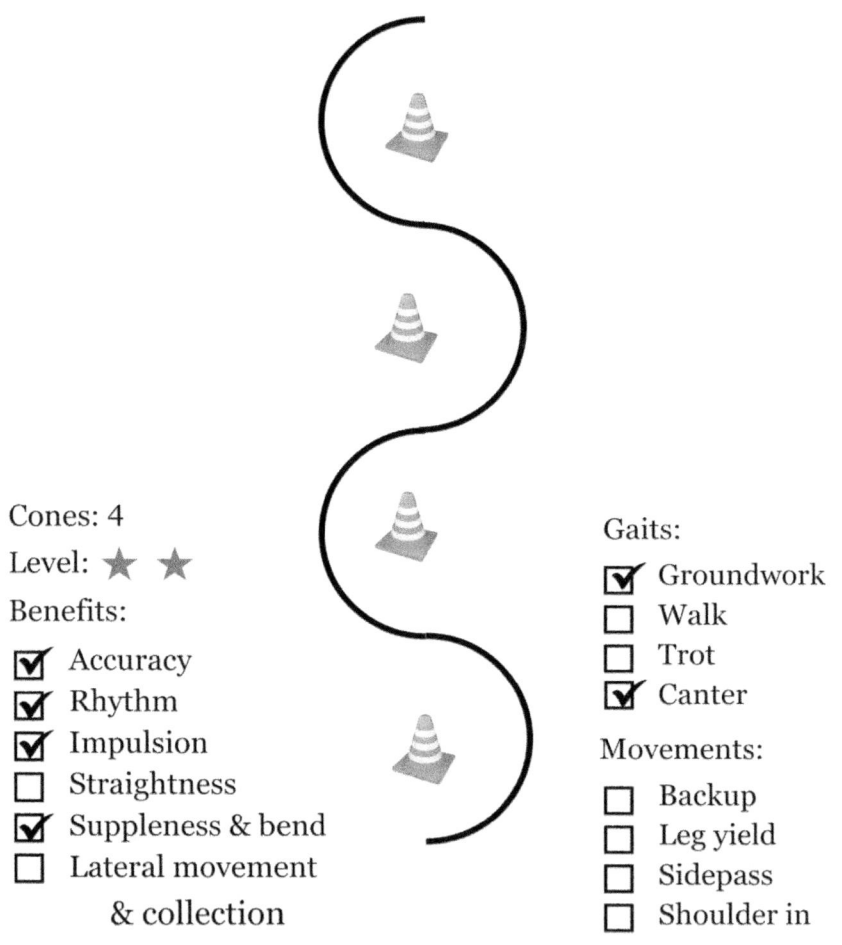

Cones: 4

Level: ★ ★

Benefits:

- ☑ Accuracy
- ☑ Rhythm
- ☑ Impulsion
- ☐ Straightness
- ☑ Suppleness & bend
- ☐ Lateral movement
  & collection

Gaits:

- ☑ Groundwork
- ☐ Walk
- ☐ Trot
- ☑ Canter

Movements:

- ☐ Backup
- ☐ Leg yield
- ☐ Sidepass
- ☐ Shoulder in

Howth Cones

Sidepass in front of the cones without knocking any over, or stepping over them. Do this in both directions. In groundwork. you can stand either beside your horse, or behind the cones. Try both!

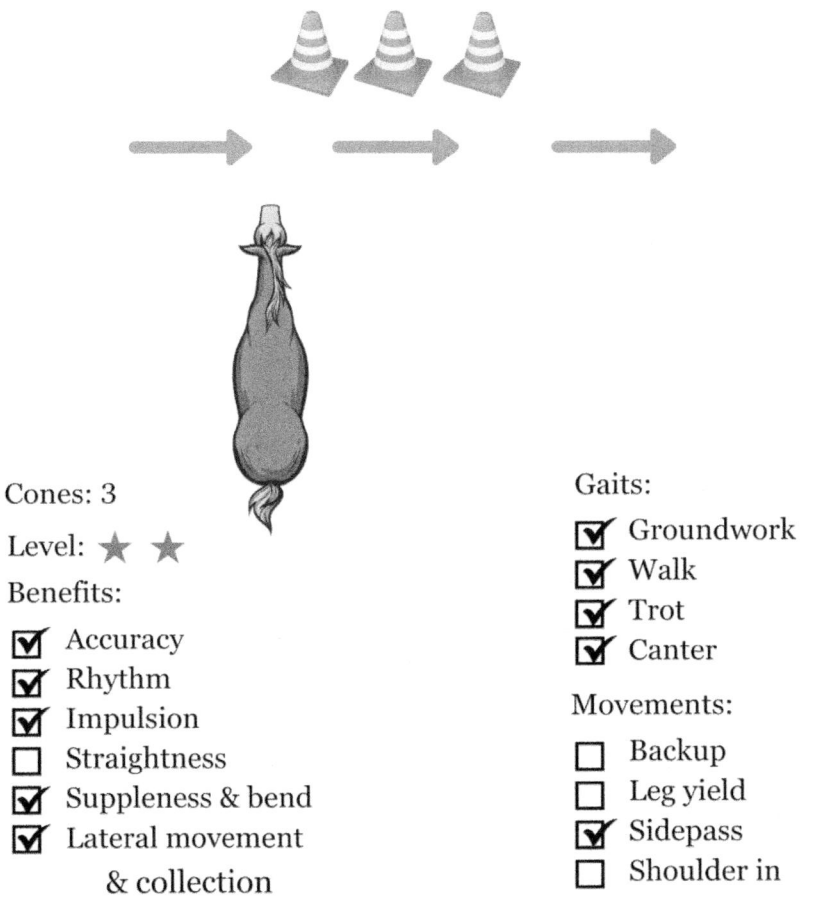

Cones: 3

Level: ★ ★

Benefits:

- ☑ Accuracy
- ☑ Rhythm
- ☑ Impulsion
- ☐ Straightness
- ☑ Suppleness & bend
- ☑ Lateral movement
  & collection

Gaits:

- ☑ Groundwork
- ☑ Walk
- ☑ Trot
- ☑ Canter

Movements:

- ☐ Backup
- ☐ Leg yield
- ☑ Sidepass
- ☐ Shoulder in

Johnstown Cones

Sidepass over the cones in walk without knocking any over. Do this in both directions.

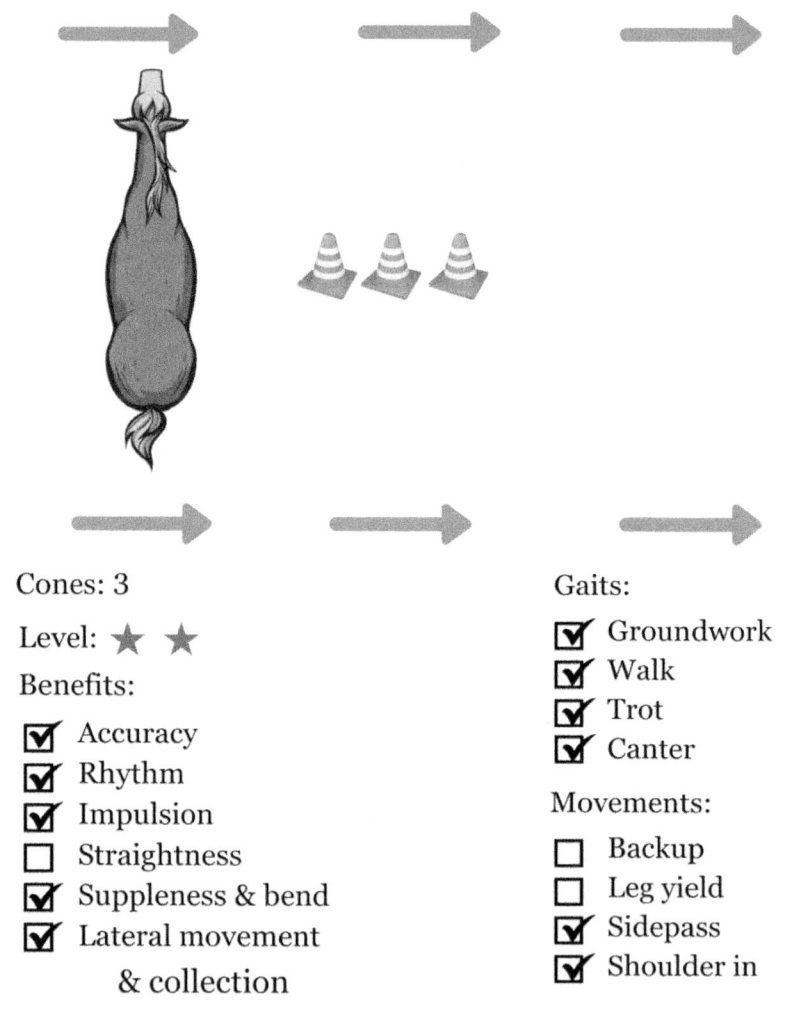

Cones: 3

Level: ★ ★

Benefits:

- ☑ Accuracy
- ☑ Rhythm
- ☑ Impulsion
- ☐ Straightness
- ☑ Suppleness & bend
- ☑ Lateral movement
        & collection

Gaits:

- ☑ Groundwork
- ☑ Walk
- ☑ Trot
- ☑ Canter

Movements:

- ☐ Backup
- ☐ Leg yield
- ☑ Sidepass
- ☑ Shoulder in

Kilconnell Cones

Ride a circle through 4 sets of 2 cones. Do not knock over any cones. Do the same in the opposite direction.

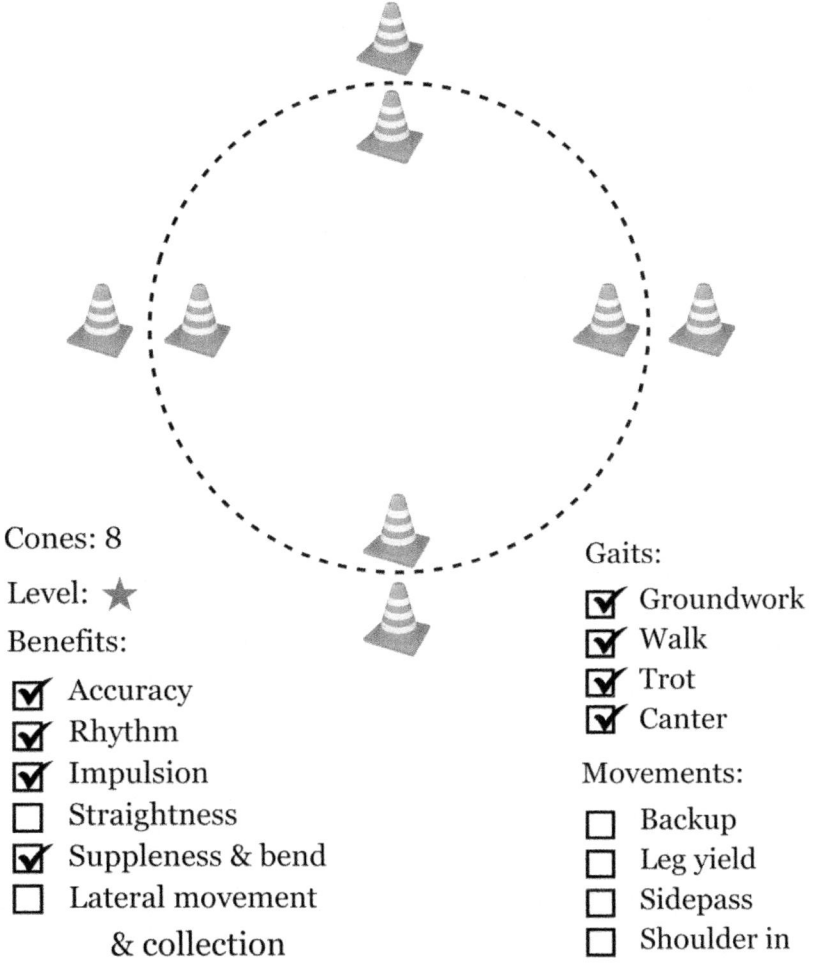

Cones: 8

Level: ★

Benefits:

- ☑ Accuracy
- ☑ Rhythm
- ☑ Impulsion
- ☐ Straightness
- ☑ Suppleness & bend
- ☐ Lateral movement
      & collection

Gaits:

- ☑ Groundwork
- ☑ Walk
- ☑ Trot
- ☑ Canter

Movements:

- ☐ Backup
- ☐ Leg yield
- ☐ Sidepass
- ☐ Shoulder in

Mayfield Cones

Walk in small random circles around every cone you can see. Change direction at each new cone. These are short serpentines. The cones are placed randomly. Use as many cones as you have. Keep your hands close together at the pommel.

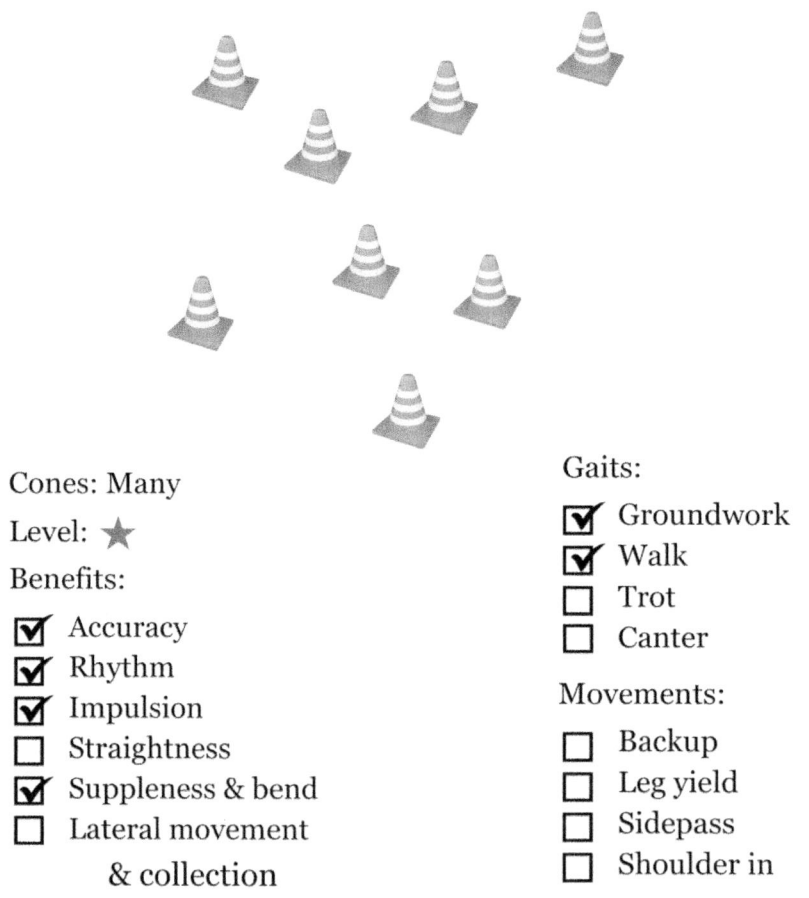

Cones: Many

Level: ★

Benefits:

- ☑ Accuracy
- ☑ Rhythm
- ☑ Impulsion
- ☐ Straightness
- ☑ Suppleness & bend
- ☐ Lateral movement
  & collection

Gaits:

- ☑ Groundwork
- ☑ Walk
- ☐ Trot
- ☐ Canter

Movements:

- ☐ Backup
- ☐ Leg yield
- ☐ Sidepass
- ☐ Shoulder in

Navan Cones

Walk to the cones and ask your horse to step over then with their 2 front feet. Then ask your horse to stand still with 2 feet on either side of the line of the 3 cones. Do not knock the cones.

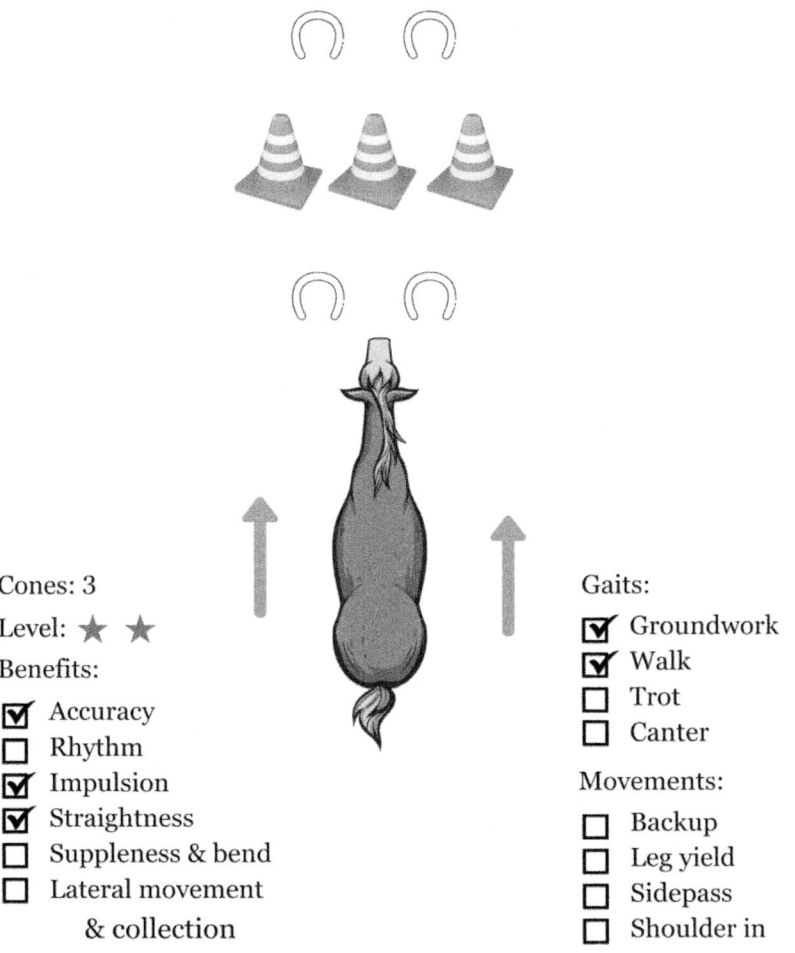

Cones: 3

Level: ★ ★

Benefits:

- ☑ Accuracy
- ☐ Rhythm
- ☑ Impulsion
- ☑ Straightness
- ☐ Suppleness & bend
- ☐ Lateral movement
     & collection

Gaits:

- ☑ Groundwork
- ☑ Walk
- ☐ Trot
- ☐ Canter

Movements:

- ☐ Backup
- ☐ Leg yield
- ☐ Sidepass
- ☐ Shoulder in

Oldcastle Cones

Stand beside the row of cones. Ask your horse to step sideways until they are in position with 2 feet in front and 2 feet behind the cones. Ask your horse to stand still with 2 feet on either side of the line of 3 cones. Do not knock the cones. Do this in both directions.

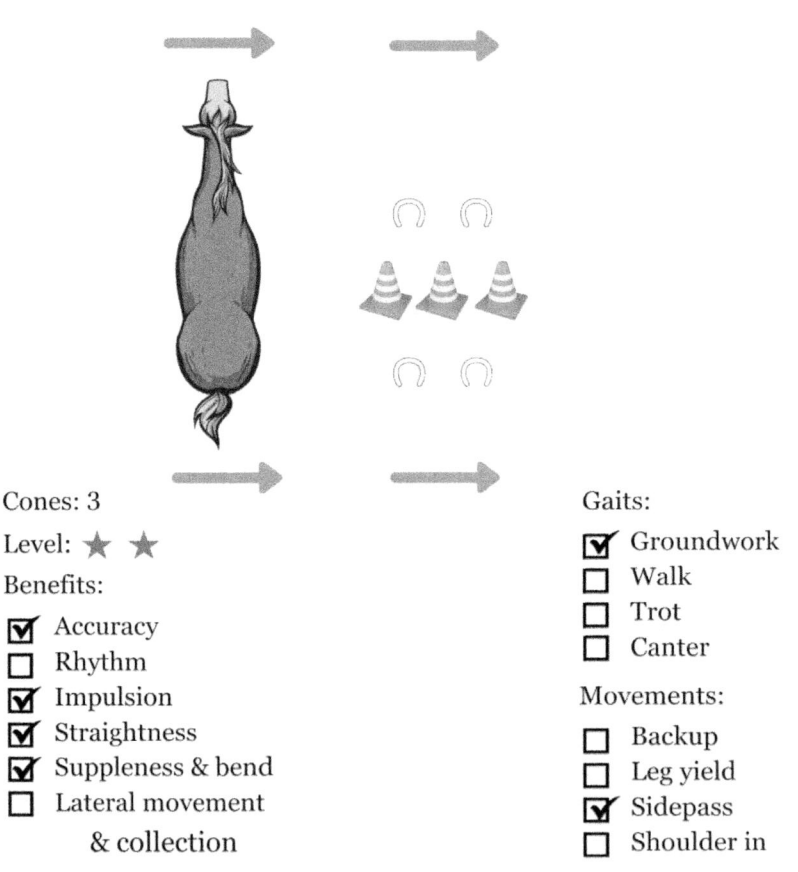

Cones: 3

Level: ★ ★

Benefits:

- ☑ Accuracy
- ☐ Rhythm
- ☑ Impulsion
- ☑ Straightness
- ☑ Suppleness & bend
- ☐ Lateral movement
       & collection

Gaits:

- ☑ Groundwork
- ☐ Walk
- ☐ Trot
- ☐ Canter

Movements:

- ☐ Backup
- ☐ Leg yield
- ☑ Sidepass
- ☐ Shoulder in

Quin Cones

Ask your horse to stand still. Put 1 cone beside each hoof. Walk forwards away from the cones and do a circle. Approach the cones again. Ask your horse to stand still with each hoof beside a cone. Do not knock the cones.

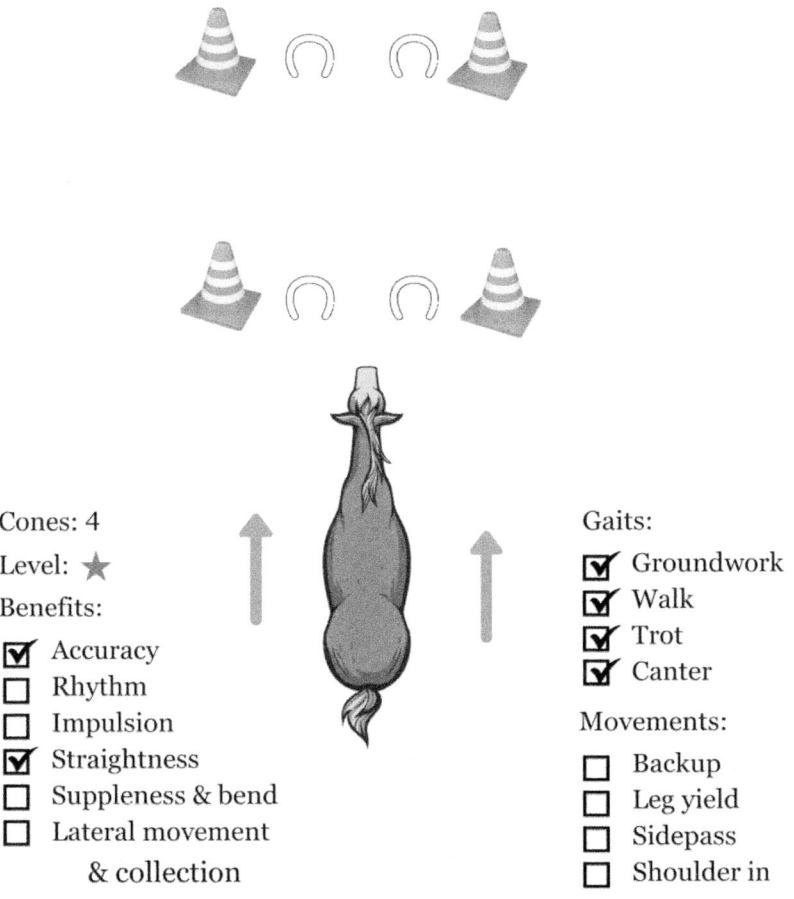

Cones: 4

Level: ★

Benefits:

- ☑ Accuracy
- ☐ Rhythm
- ☐ Impulsion
- ☑ Straightness
- ☐ Suppleness & bend
- ☐ Lateral movement
  & collection

Gaits:

- ☑ Groundwork
- ☑ Walk
- ☑ Trot
- ☑ Canter

Movements:

- ☐ Backup
- ☐ Leg yield
- ☐ Sidepass
- ☐ Shoulder in

Rush Cones

Ask your horse to stand still. Put 1 cone beside each hoof. Walk forwards in a straight line 5 steps out of the cones. Stop. Reverse back into the cones. Ask your horse to stand still with each hoof beside a cone. Do not knock the cones.

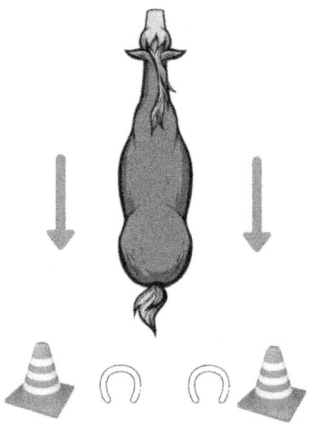

Cones: 4

Level: ★ ★

Benefits:

- ☑ Accuracy
- ☑ Rhythm
- ☑ Impulsion
- ☑ Straightness
- ☐ Suppleness & bend
- ☐ Lateral movement
      & collection

Gaits:

- ☑ Groundwork
- ☐ Walk
- ☐ Trot
- ☐ Canter

Movements:

- ☑ Backup
- ☐ Leg yield
- ☐ Sidepass
- ☐ Shoulder in

Create your own exercises

Create your own cones exercise

Cone exercise name: _____

Goal of exercise:

....

....

....

Benefits of the exercise:

....

....

....

....

....

Notes about the exercise:

....

....

....

....

Important things to remember:

....

....

....

....

Cones:

Level:

Benefits:

- ☐ Accuracy
- ☐ Rhythm
- ☐ Impulsion
- ☐ Straightness
- ☐ Suppleness & bend
- ☐ Lateral movement
    & collection

Gaits:

- ☐ Groundwork
- ☐ Walk
- ☐ Trot
- ☐ Canter

Movements:

- ☐ Backup
- ☐ Leg yield
- ☐ Sidepass
- ☐ Shoulder in

Create your own cones exercise

Cone exercise name: _____

Goal of exercise:

....

....

....

Benefits of the exercise:

....

....

....

....

....

Notes about the exercise:

....

....

....

....

Important things to remember:

....

....

....

....

Cones:

Level:

Benefits:

- ☐ Accuracy
- ☐ Rhythm
- ☐ Impulsion
- ☐ Straightness
- ☐ Suppleness & bend
- ☐ Lateral movement
     & collection

Gaits:

- ☐ Groundwork
- ☐ Walk
- ☐ Trot
- ☐ Canter

Movements:

- ☐ Backup
- ☐ Leg yield
- ☐ Sidepass
- ☐ Shoulder in

Create your own cones exercise

Cone exercise name: _____

Goal of exercise:

....

....

....

Benefits of the exercise:

....

....

....

....

....

Notes about the exercise:

....

....

....

....

Important things to remember:

....

....

....

....

Cones:

Level:

Benefits:

- ☐ Accuracy
- ☐ Rhythm
- ☐ Impulsion
- ☐ Straightness
- ☐ Suppleness & bend
- ☐ Lateral movement
     & collection

Gaits:

- ☐ Groundwork
- ☐ Walk
- ☐ Trot
- ☐ Canter

Movements:

- ☐ Backup
- ☐ Leg yield
- ☐ Sidepass
- ☐ Shoulder in

13 Standing Still Cavaletti Exercises

Using standing still cavaletti exercises in your groundwork and riding training is a fantastic way to refine communication and build a deeper connection with your horse. They provide a clear, structured way to ask for a specific number of steps in an exact direction, helping both horse and rider develop precision and body awareness.

These exercises are especially valuable for teaching patience to the human, rewarding small efforts and encouraging the horse to stay mentally engaged without rushing. For the rider or handler, working with stationary cavaletti helps develop subtle, refined cues, improving clarity and consistency in communication. It's a simple yet powerful tool that strengthens trust, focus, and responsiveness in a way that benefits both horse and human.

What you will need: Up to 4 poles and 2 risers.

Cavaletti: Cavaletti refers to a series of low poles or rails, either set directly on the ground or elevated slightly using riser blocks. These are used in various disciplines, including dressage, jumping, eventing, and rehabilitation, to improve a horse's balance, coordination, strength, and flexibility.

Riser: A cavaletti riser block is a piece of equestrian equipment used to elevate cavaletti poles for horse training. A height of about 6 inches (15 cm) is ideal for walk and rehab work. The green squares in the diagrams indicate that the pole is raised slightly on a cavaletti riser block. You can use your creativity to set up other ways to work with these patterns too. Have fun!

Standing still 1

Stand still with 2 feet either side of the pole.

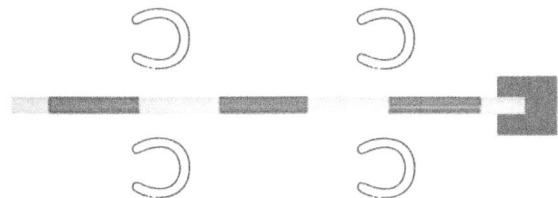

Standing still 2

Stand still with 2 feet either side of the pole.

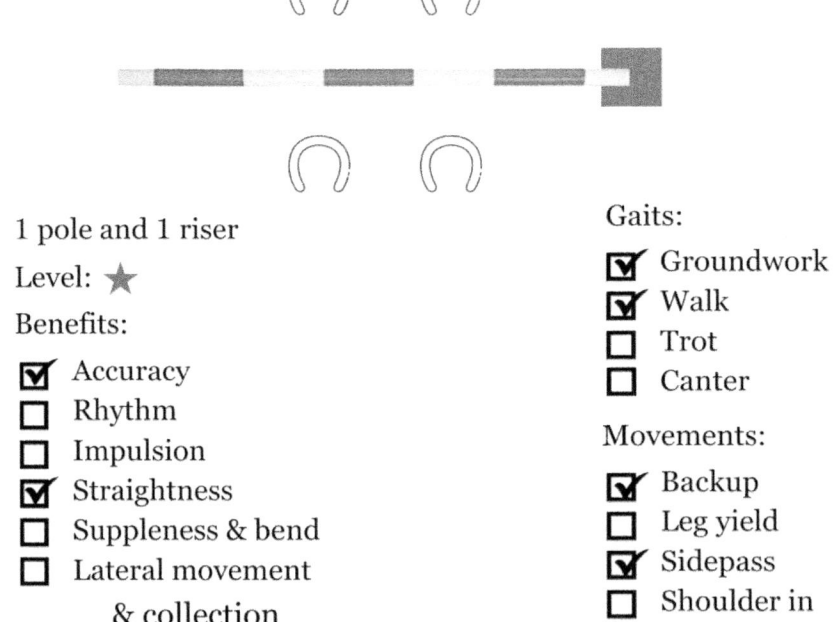

1 pole and 1 riser

Level: ★

Benefits:

- ☑ Accuracy
- ☐ Rhythm
- ☐ Impulsion
- ☑ Straightness
- ☐ Suppleness & bend
- ☐ Lateral movement
        & collection

Gaits:

- ☑ Groundwork
- ☑ Walk
- ☐ Trot
- ☐ Canter

Movements:

- ☑ Backup
- ☐ Leg yield
- ☑ Sidepass
- ☐ Shoulder in

Standing still 3

Stand still with 2 feet either side of the pole.

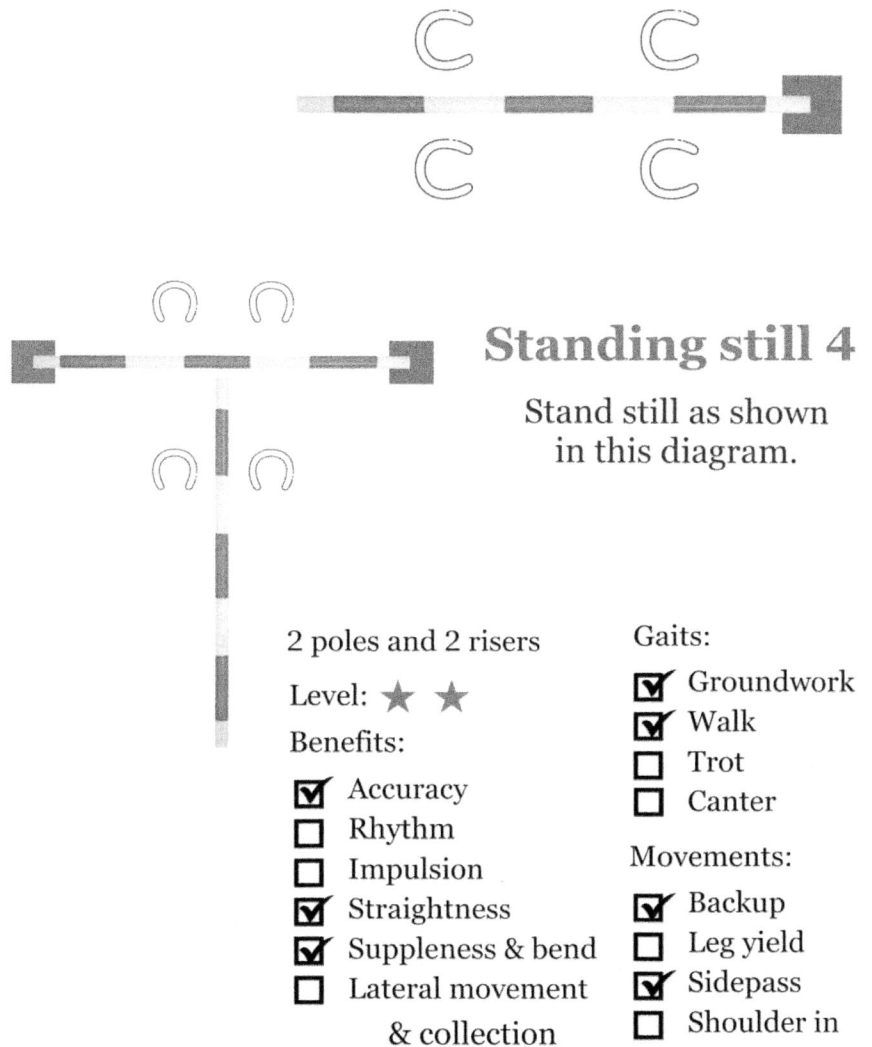

Standing still 4

Stand still as shown in this diagram.

2 poles and 2 risers

Level: ★ ★

Benefits:
- ☑ Accuracy
- ☐ Rhythm
- ☐ Impulsion
- ☑ Straightness
- ☑ Suppleness & bend
- ☐ Lateral movement & collection

Gaits:
- ☑ Groundwork
- ☑ Walk
- ☐ Trot
- ☐ Canter

Movements:
- ☑ Backup
- ☐ Leg yield
- ☑ Sidepass
- ☐ Shoulder in

Standing still 5

Stand still as shown in this diagram.

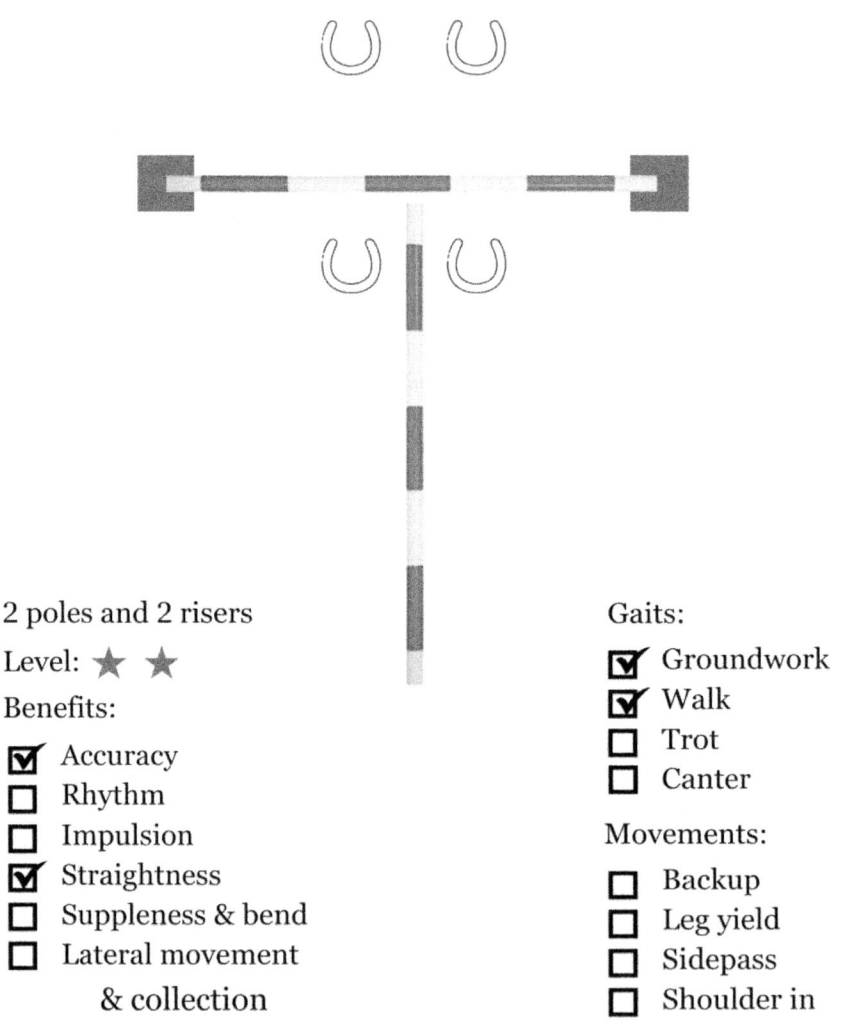

2 poles and 2 risers

Level: ★ ★

Benefits:

- ☑ Accuracy
- ☐ Rhythm
- ☐ Impulsion
- ☑ Straightness
- ☐ Suppleness & bend
- ☐ Lateral movement
  & collection

Gaits:

- ☑ Groundwork
- ☑ Walk
- ☐ Trot
- ☐ Canter

Movements:

- ☐ Backup
- ☐ Leg yield
- ☐ Sidepass
- ☐ Shoulder in

Standing still 6

Stand still with 2 hooves either side of the pole.

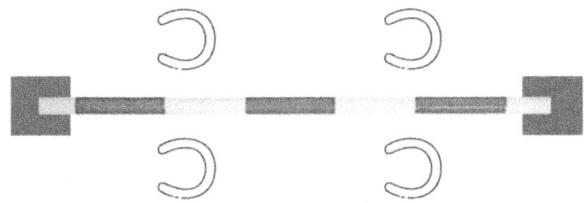

Standing still 7

Stand still with 2 hooves either side of the pole.

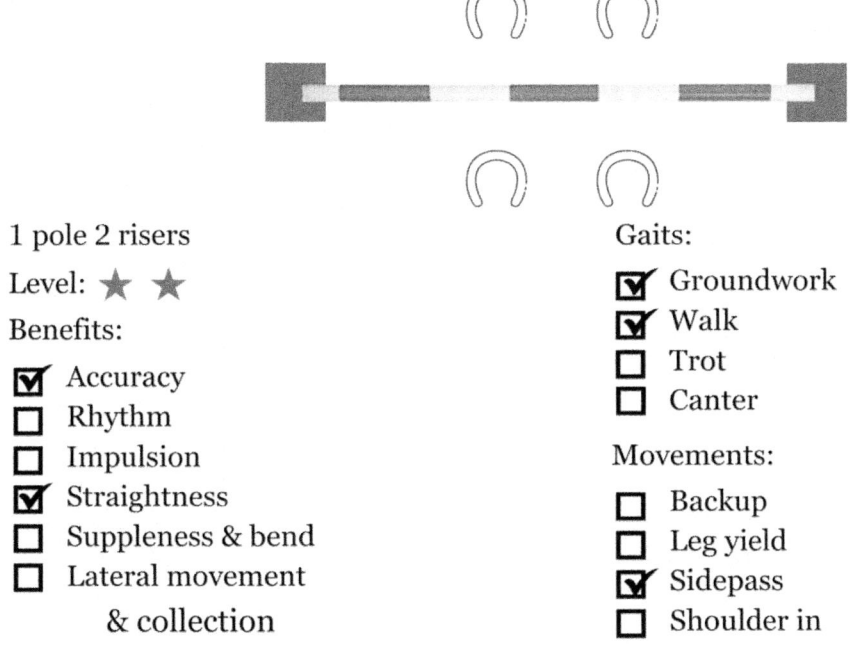

1 pole 2 risers

Level: ★ ★

Benefits:

- ☑ Accuracy
- ☐ Rhythm
- ☐ Impulsion
- ☑ Straightness
- ☐ Suppleness & bend
- ☐ Lateral movement
  & collection

Gaits:

- ☑ Groundwork
- ☑ Walk
- ☐ Trot
- ☐ Canter

Movements:

- ☐ Backup
- ☐ Leg yield
- ☑ Sidepass
- ☐ Shoulder in

Standing still 8

Begin by walking over the pole. Then stand still as shown in this diagram.

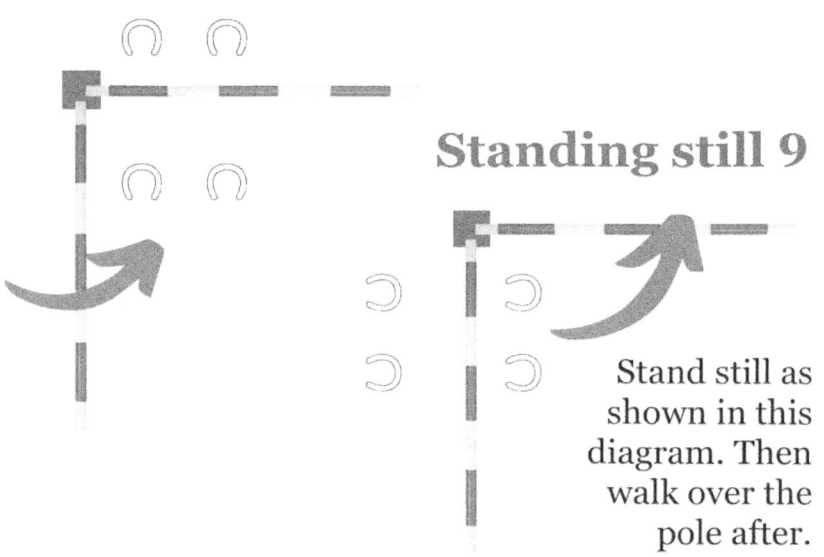

Standing still 9

Stand still as shown in this diagram. Then walk over the pole after.

2 poles and 1 riser

Level: ★ ★

Benefits:

- ☑ Accuracy
- ☐ Rhythm
- ☐ Impulsion
- ☐ Straightness
- ☑ Suppleness & bend
- ☐ Lateral movement & collection

Gaits:

- ☑ Groundwork
- ☑ Walk
- ☐ Trot
- ☐ Canter

Movements:

- ☐ Backup
- ☐ Leg yield
- ☐ Sidepass
- ☐ Shoulder in

Standing still 10

Stand still as shown in this diagram.

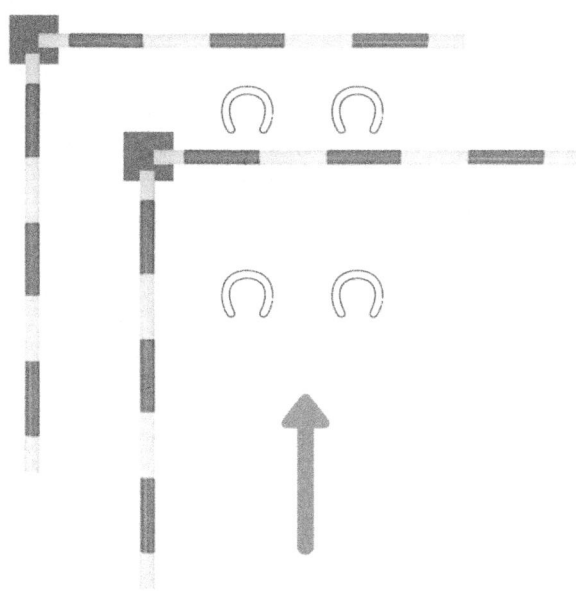

4 poles and 2 risers

Level: ★

Benefits:

- ☑ Accuracy
- ☐ Rhythm
- ☐ Impulsion
- ☑ Straightness
- ☐ Suppleness & bend
- ☐ Lateral movement
      & collection

Gaits:

- ☑ Groundwork
- ☑ Walk
- ☐ Trot
- ☐ Canter

Movements:

- ☐ Backup
- ☐ Leg yield
- ☐ Sidepass
- ☐ Shoulder in

Standing still 11

Stand still as shown in this diagram.

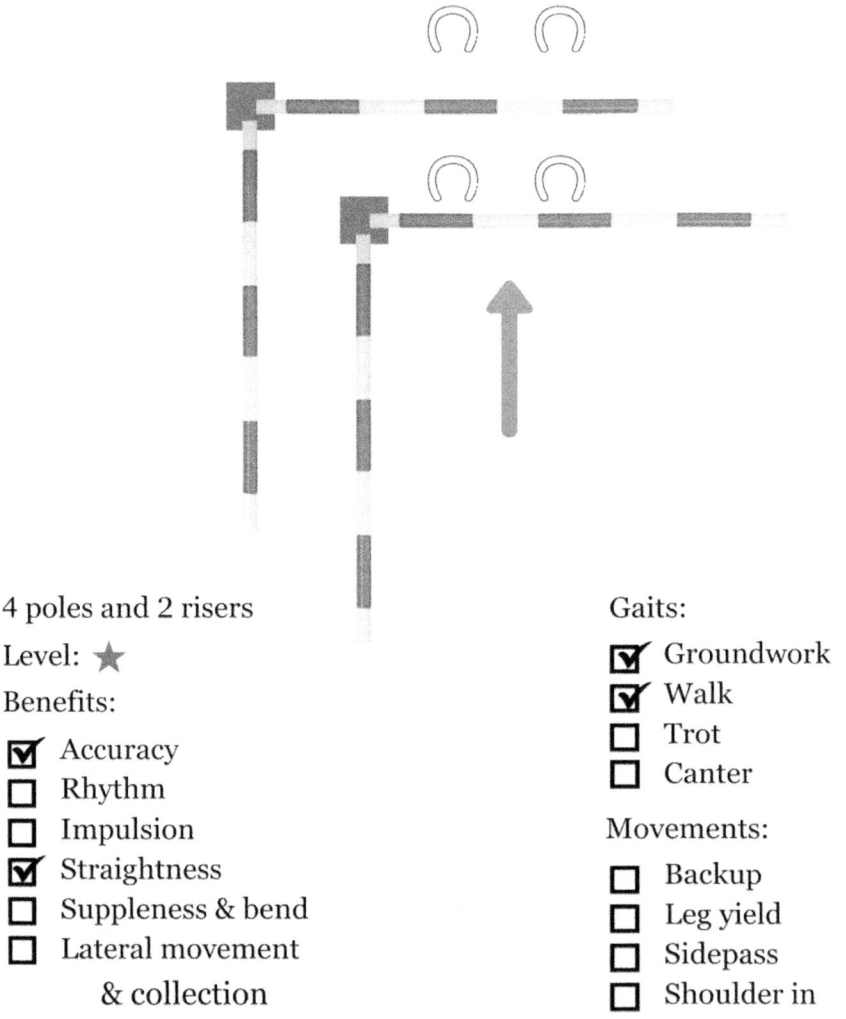

4 poles and 2 risers

Level: ★

Benefits:

- ☑ Accuracy
- ☐ Rhythm
- ☐ Impulsion
- ☑ Straightness
- ☐ Suppleness & bend
- ☐ Lateral movement
     & collection

Gaits:

- ☑ Groundwork
- ☑ Walk
- ☐ Trot
- ☐ Canter

Movements:

- ☐ Backup
- ☐ Leg yield
- ☐ Sidepass
- ☐ Shoulder in

Standing still 12

Reverse backwards & stop as shown in the diagram below.

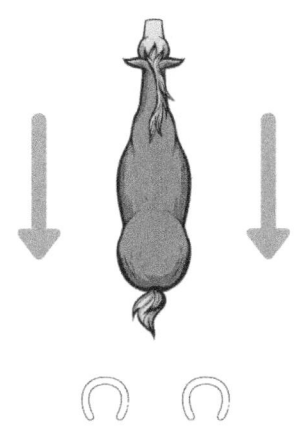

1 pole

Level: ⭐

Benefits:

- ☑ Accuracy
- ☑ Rhythm
- ☑ Impulsion
- ☑ Straightness
- ☐ Suppleness & bend
- ☐ Lateral movement
  & collection

Gaits:

- ☑ Groundwork
- ☑ Walk
- ☐ Trot
- ☐ Canter

Movements:

- ☑ Backup
- ☐ Leg yield
- ☐ Sidepass
- ☐ Shoulder in

Standing still 13

Reverse backwards & stop as shown in the diagram below.

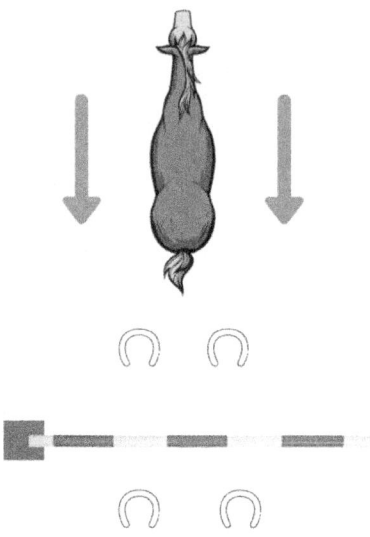

1 pole & 1 riser

Level: ★

Benefits:

- ☑ Accuracy
- ☑ Rhythm
- ☑ Impulsion
- ☑ Straightness
- ☐ Suppleness & bend
- ☐ Lateral movement
    & collection

Gaits:

- ☑ Groundwork
- ☑ Walk
- ☐ Trot
- ☐ Canter

Movements:

- ☑ Backup
- ☐ Leg yield
- ☐ Sidepass
- ☐ Shoulder in

Create your own exercises

Create your own standing still exercise

Standing still exercise name: _____

Goal of exercise:

....

....

....

Benefits of the exercise:

....

....

....

....

....

Notes about the exercise:

....

....

....

....

Important things to remember:

....

....

Cones: Poles:

Level:

Benefits:

- ☐ Accuracy
- ☐ Rhythm
- ☐ Impulsion
- ☐ Straightness
- ☐ Suppleness & bend
- ☐ Lateral movement
  & collection

Gaits:

- ☐ Groundwork
- ☐ Walk
- ☐ Trot
- ☐ Canter

Movements:

- ☐ Backup
- ☐ Leg yield
- ☐ Sidepass
- ☐ Shoulder in

Create your own standing still exercise

Standing still exercise name: _____

Goal of exercise:

....

....

....

Benefits of the exercise:

....

....

....

....

....

Notes about the exercise:

....

....

....

....

Important things to remember:

....

....

Cones: Poles:

Level:

Benefits:

☐ Accuracy
☐ Rhythm
☐ Impulsion
☐ Straightness
☐ Suppleness & bend
☐ Lateral movement
     & collection

Gaits:

☐ Groundwork
☐ Walk
☐ Trot
☐ Canter

Movements:

☐ Backup
☐ Leg yield
☐ Sidepass
☐ Shoulder in

Create your own standing still exercise

Standing still exercise name: _____

Goal of exercise:

....

....

....

Benefits of the exercise:

....

....

....

....

....

Notes about the exercise:

....

....

....

....

Important things to remember:

....

....

Cones: Poles:

Level:

Benefits:

- ☐ Accuracy
- ☐ Rhythm
- ☐ Impulsion
- ☐ Straightness
- ☐ Suppleness & bend
- ☐ Lateral movement
       & collection

Gaits:

- ☐ Groundwork
- ☐ Walk
- ☐ Trot
- ☐ Canter

Movements:

- ☐ Backup
- ☐ Leg yield
- ☐ Sidepass
- ☐ Shoulder in

15 Cavaletti Exercises

Cavaletti exercises, whether ridden or in hand, offer a wide range of benefits for horses by improving strength, balance, coordination, and overall athleticism.

Cavaletti exercises encourage horses to lift their legs with precision, engaging core muscles and promoting better athletic ability. When worked over cavaletti in hand, horses learn to focus, develop body awareness, and build trust with their handler. Under saddle, these exercises help refine rhythm, impulsion, and suppleness while also encouraging a more active hind end.

Cavaletti work is also excellent for improving straightness and developing a horse's ability to adjust stride length, making it beneficial for horses of all disciplines. Plus, it adds variety to training sessions, keeping horses mentally stimulated and engaged.

What you will need: Between 3 and 5 poles and up to 4 risers.

Sligo cavaletti

Walk over the cavaletti.

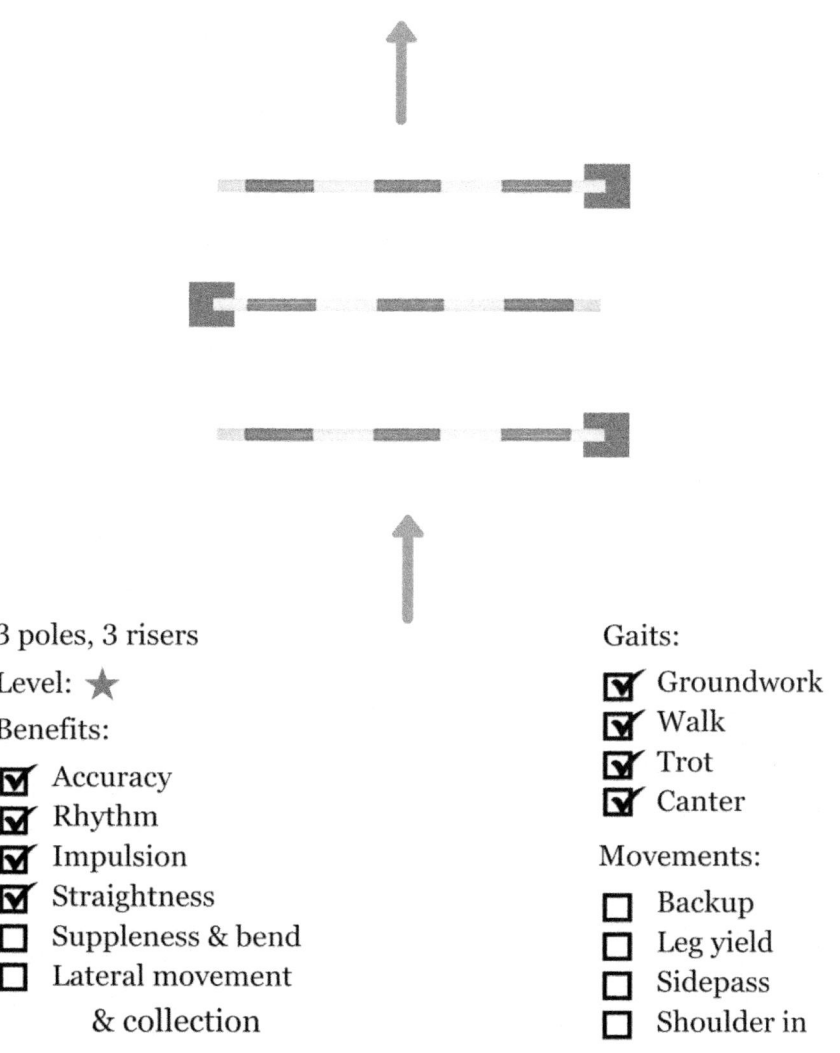

3 poles, 3 risers

Level: ★

Benefits:

- ☑ Accuracy
- ☑ Rhythm
- ☑ Impulsion
- ☑ Straightness
- ☐ Suppleness & bend
- ☐ Lateral movement
  & collection

Gaits:

- ☑ Groundwork
- ☑ Walk
- ☑ Trot
- ☑ Canter

Movements:

- ☐ Backup
- ☐ Leg yield
- ☐ Sidepass
- ☐ Shoulder in

Swords cavaletti

Walk over the cavaletti.

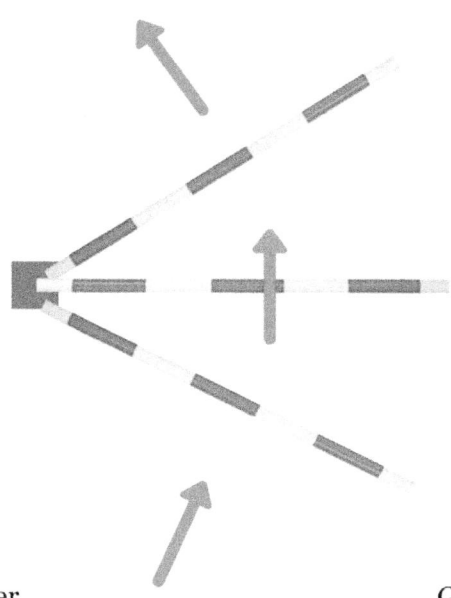

3 poles, 1 riser

Level: ⭐

Benefits:

- ☑ Accuracy
- ☑ Rhythm
- ☑ Impulsion
- ☑ Straightness
- ☑ Suppleness & bend
- ☐ Lateral movement
  & collection

Gaits:

- ☑ Groundwork
- ☑ Walk
- ☑ Trot
- ☐ Canter

Movements:

- ☐ Backup
- ☐ Leg yield
- ☐ Sidepass
- ☐ Shoulder in

Tullow cavaletti

Walk over the cavaletti.

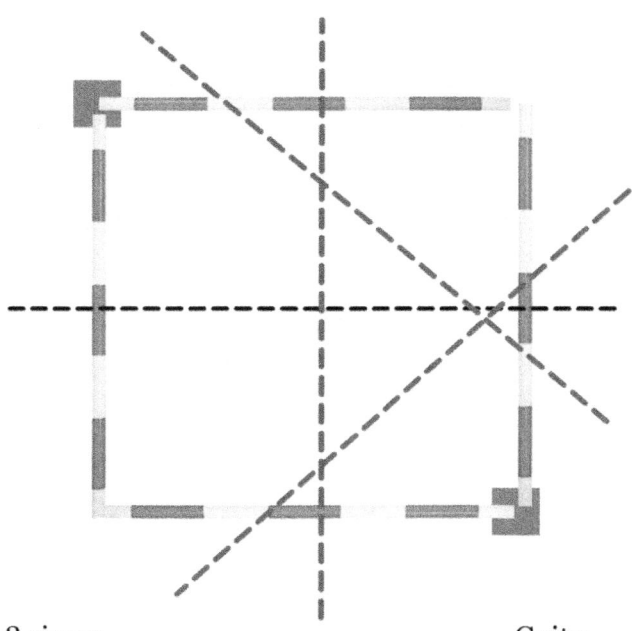

4 poles 2 risers

Level: ★

Benefits:

- ☑ Accuracy
- ☑ Rhythm
- ☑ Impulsion
- ☑ Straightness
- ☐ Suppleness & bend
- ☐ Lateral movement
     & collection

Gaits:

- ☑ Groundwork
- ☑ Walk
- ☑ Trot
- ☑ Canter

Movements:

- ☐ Backup
- ☐ Leg yield
- ☐ Sidepass
- ☐ Shoulder in

Upton cavaletti

Walk over the cavaletti.

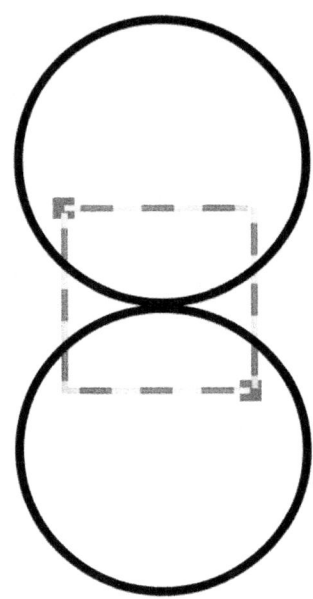

4 poles 2 risers

Level: ★

Benefits:

- ☑ Accuracy
- ☑ Rhythm
- ☑ Impulsion
- ☐ Straightness
- ☑ Suppleness & bend
- ☐ Lateral movement
      & collection

Gaits:

- ☑ Groundwork
- ☑ Walk
- ☑ Trot
- ☑ Canter

Movements:

- ☐ Backup
- ☐ Leg yield
- ☐ Sidepass
- ☐ Shoulder in

Virginia cavaletti

Walk over the cavaletti.

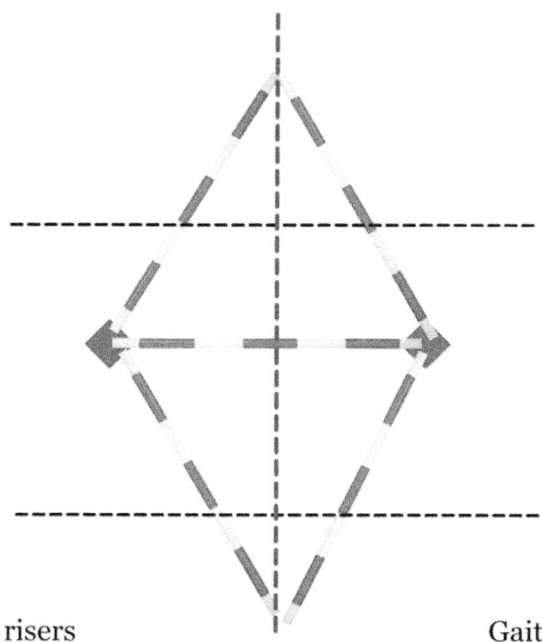

5 poles 2 risers

Level: ★

Benefits:

- ☑ Accuracy
- ☑ Rhythm
- ☑ Impulsion
- ☑ Straightness
- ☐ Suppleness & bend
- ☐ Lateral movement
     & collection

Gaits:

- ☑ Groundwork
- ☑ Walk
- ☑ Trot
- ☑ Canter

Movements:

- ☐ Backup
- ☐ Leg yield
- ☐ Sidepass
- ☐ Shoulder in

Wilton cavaletti

Walk over the cavaletti.

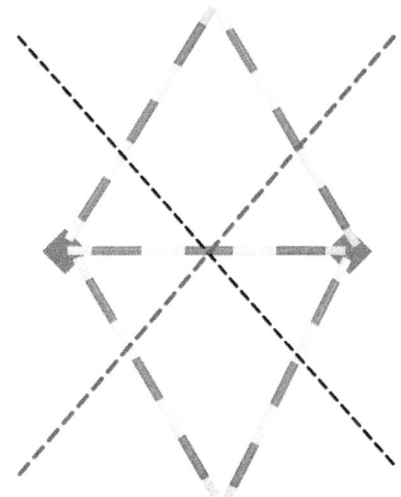

5 poles 2 risers

Level: ★ ★

Benefits:

- ☑ Accuracy
- ☑ Rhythm
- ☑ Impulsion
- ☑ Straightness
- ☐ Suppleness & bend
- ☐ Lateral movement
  & collection

Gaits:

- ☑ Groundwork
- ☑ Walk
- ☑ Trot
- ☐ Canter

Movements:

- ☐ Backup
- ☐ Leg yield
- ☐ Sidepass
- ☐ Shoulder in

Youghal cavaletti

Walk over the cavaletti.

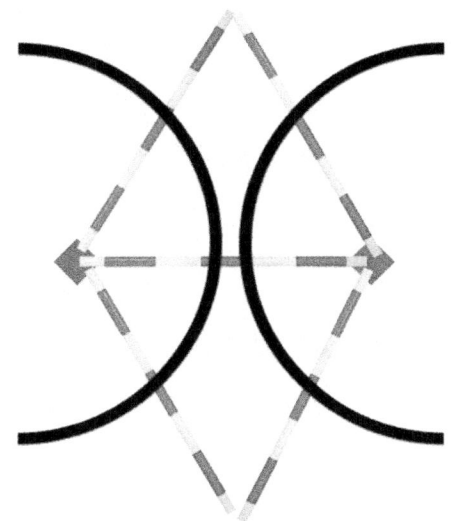

5 poles 2 risers

Level: ★ ★

Benefits:

- ☑ Accuracy
- ☑ Rhythm
- ☑ Impulsion
- ☐ Straightness
- ☑ Suppleness & bend
- ☐ Lateral movement
     & collection

Gaits:

- ☑ Groundwork
- ☑ Walk
- ☑ Trot
- ☑ Canter

Movements:

- ☐ Backup
- ☐ Leg yield
- ☐ Sidepass
- ☐ Shoulder in

Avoca cavaletti

Walk over the cavaletti.

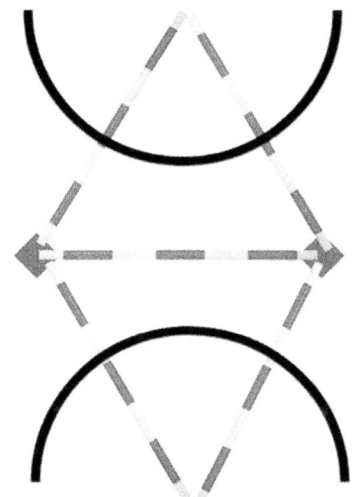

5 poles 2 risers

Level: ★

Benefits:

- ☑ Accuracy
- ☑ Rhythm
- ☑ Impulsion
- ☑ Straightness
- ☑ Suppleness & bend
- ☐ Lateral movement
  & collection

Gaits:

- ☑ Groundwork
- ☑ Walk
- ☑ Trot
- ☑ Canter

Movements:

- ☐ Backup
- ☐ Leg yield
- ☐ Sidepass
- ☐ Shoulder in

Ballyfin cavaletti

Walk through the cavaletti.

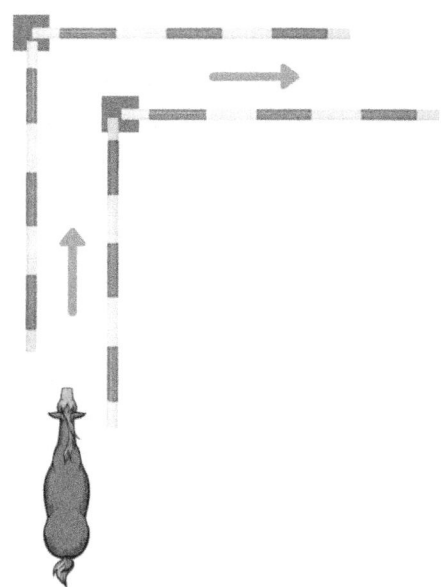

4 poles 2 risers

Level: ★

Benefits:

- ☑ Accuracy
- ☑ Rhythm
- ☑ Impulsion
- ☑ Straightness
- ☑ Suppleness & bend
- ☐ Lateral movement
     & collection

Gaits:

- ☑ Groundwork
- ☑ Walk
- ☐ Trot
- ☐ Canter

Movements:

- ☐ Backup
- ☐ Leg yield
- ☐ Sidepass
- ☐ Shoulder in

Bruff cavaletti

Backup through the cavaletti.

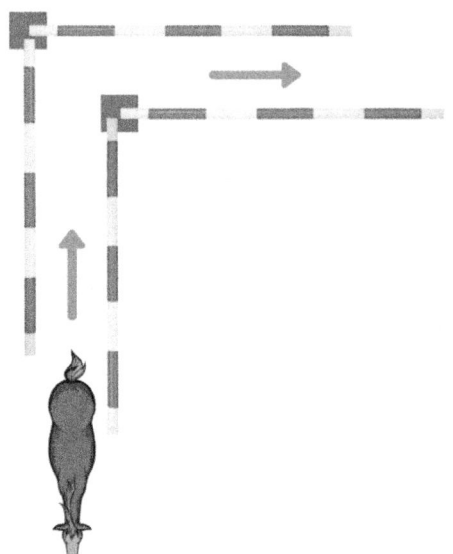

4 poles 2 risers

Level: ★ ★

Benefits:

- ☑ Accuracy
- ☑ Rhythm
- ☑ Impulsion
- ☑ Straightness
- ☑ Suppleness & bend
- ☐ Lateral movement
     & collection

Gaits:

- ☑ Groundwork
- ☑ Walk
- ☐ Trot
- ☐ Canter

Movements:

- ☐ Backup
- ☐ Leg yield
- ☐ Sidepass
- ☐ Shoulder in

Cahir cavaletti

Walk over the cavaletti.

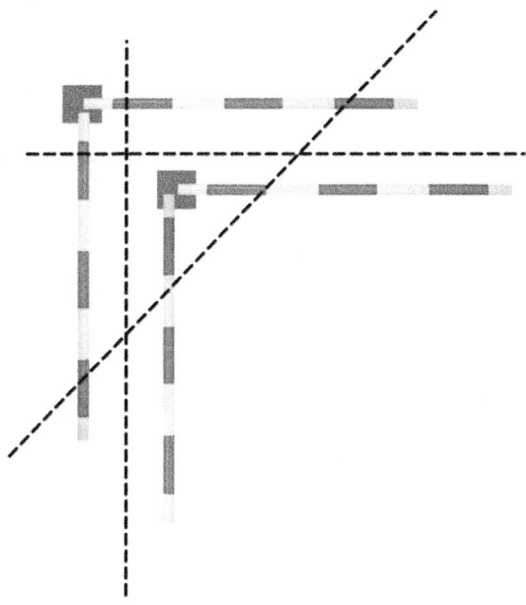

4 poles 2 risers

Level: ⭐

Benefits:

- ☑ Accuracy
- ☑ Rhythm
- ☑ Impulsion
- ☑ Straightness
- ☐ Suppleness & bend
- ☐ Lateral movement
     & collection

Gaits:

- ☑ Groundwork
- ☑ Walk
- ☑ Trot
- ☐ Canter

Movements:

- ☐ Backup
- ☐ Leg yield
- ☐ Sidepass
- ☐ Shoulder in

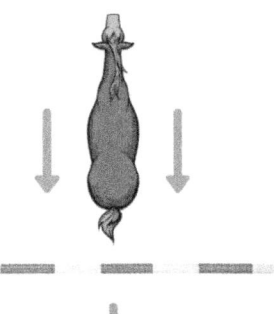

Clane cavaletti
Backup over a pole.

Delvin cavaletti
Backup over the cavaletti.

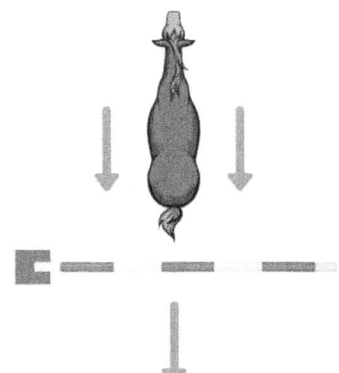

1 pole

Level: ★ ★

Benefits:

- ☑ Accuracy
- ☑ Rhythm
- ☑ Impulsion
- ☑ Straightness
- ☐ Suppleness & bend
- ☐ Lateral movement
     & collection

Gaits:

- ☑ Groundwork
- ☑ Walk
- ☐ Trot
- ☐ Canter

Movements:

- ☑ Backup
- ☐ Leg yield
- ☐ Sidepass
- ☐ Shoulder in

Dunmore cavaletti

Walk over the cavaletti.

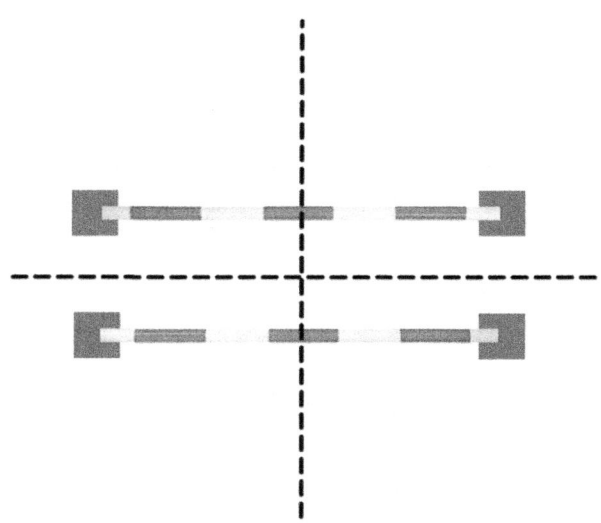

2 poles 4 risers

Level: ★

Benefits:

- ☑ Accuracy
- ☑ Rhythm
- ☑ Impulsion
- ☑ Straightness
- ☐ Suppleness & bend
- ☐ Lateral movement
       & collection

Gaits:

- ☑ Groundwork
- ☑ Walk
- ☑ Trot
- ☑ Canter

Movements:

- ☐ Backup
- ☐ Leg yield
- ☐ Sidepass
- ☐ Shoulder in

Ferns cavaletti

Sidepass in front the cavaletti.

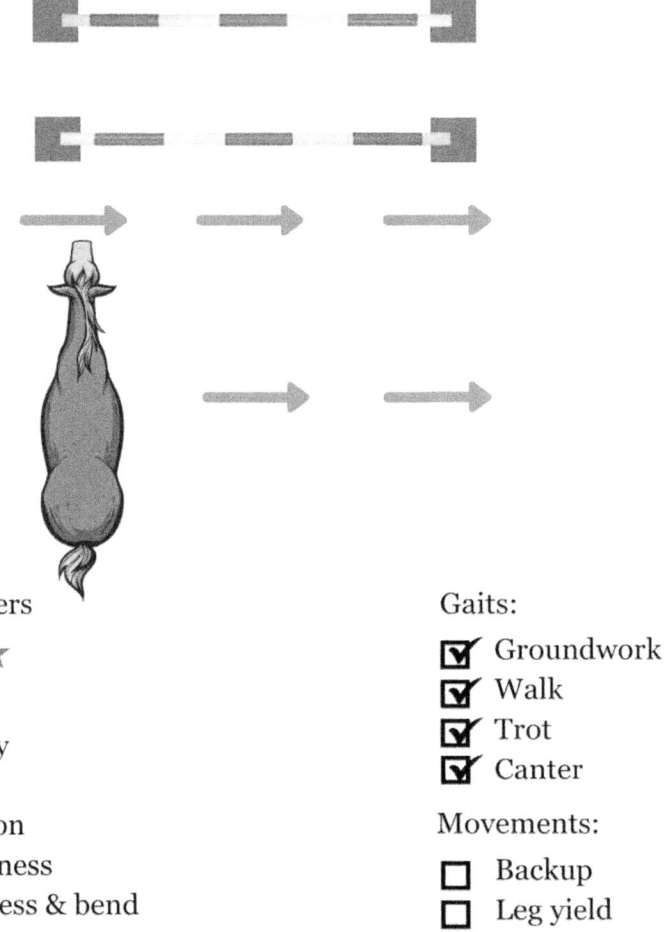

2 cones 4 risers

Level: ★ ★

Benefits:

- ☑ Accuracy
- ☑ Rhythm
- ☑ Impulsion
- ☑ Straightness
- ☑ Suppleness & bend
- ☑ Lateral movement
        & collection

Gaits:

- ☑ Groundwork
- ☑ Walk
- ☑ Trot
- ☑ Canter

Movements:

- ☐ Backup
- ☐ Leg yield
- ☑ Sidepass
- ☐ Shoulder in

Grange cavaletti

Sidepass over the cavaletti.

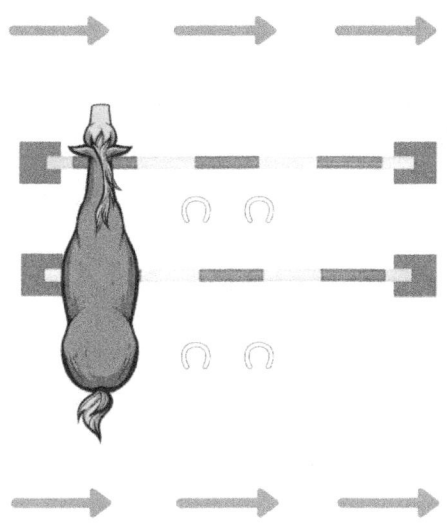

2 poles 4 risers

Level: ★ ★

Benefits:

- ☑ Accuracy
- ☑ Rhythm
- ☑ Impulsion
- ☑ Straightness
- ☑ Suppleness & bend
- ☑ Lateral movement
      & collection

Gaits:

- ☑ Groundwork
- ☑ Walk
- ☑ Trot
- ☐ Canter

Movements:

- ☐ Backup
- ☐ Leg yield
- ☑ Sidepass
- ☐ Shoulder in

Create your own cavaletti exercise

Cavaletti exercise name: _____

Goal of exercise:

....

....

....

Benefits of the exercise:

....

....

....

....

....

Notes about the exercise:

....

....

....

....

Important things to remember:

....

....

....

....

Poles:

Level:

Benefits:

- [ ] Accuracy
- [ ] Rhythm
- [ ] Impulsion
- [ ] Straightness
- [ ] Suppleness & bend
- [ ] Lateral movement
     & collection

Gaits:

- [ ] Groundwork
- [ ] Walk
- [ ] Trot
- [ ] Canter

Movements:

- [ ] Backup
- [ ] Leg yield
- [ ] Sidepass
- [ ] Shoulder in

Create your own cavaletti exercise

Cavaletti exercise name: _____

Goal of exercise:

....

....

....

Benefits of the exercise:

....

....

....

....

....

Notes about the exercise:

....

....

....

....

Important things to remember:

....

....

....

....

Poles:

Level:

Benefits:

☐ Accuracy
☐ Rhythm
☐ Impulsion
☐ Straightness
☐ Suppleness & bend
☐ Lateral movement
    & collection

Gaits:

☐ Groundwork
☐ Walk
☐ Trot
☐ Canter

Movements:

☐ Backup
☐ Leg yield
☐ Sidepass
☐ Shoulder in

Create your own cavaletti exercise

Cavaletti exercise name: _____

Goal of exercise:

....

....

....

Benefits of the exercise:

....

....

....

....

....

Notes about the exercise:

....

....

....

....

Important things to remember:

....

....

....

....

Poles:

Level:

Benefits:

- ☐ Accuracy
- ☐ Rhythm
- ☐ Impulsion
- ☐ Straightness
- ☐ Suppleness & bend
- ☐ Lateral movement
      & collection

Gaits:

- ☐ Groundwork
- ☐ Walk
- ☐ Trot
- ☐ Canter

Movements:

- ☐ Backup
- ☐ Leg yield
- ☐ Sidepass
- ☐ Shoulder in

Flatwork floor plans

Flatwork floor plans

Riders often think that flatwork is boring and repetitive but it doesn't have to be! I've put together lots of exercises here that are designed to keep flatwork fresh, varied and interesting.

Why flatwork? Flatwork is the foundation of all good riding, and it's about so much more than just going in circles! The word dressage comes from the French word meaning "to train," and that's exactly what flatwork does. It trains your horse both physically and mentally. It builds strength, balance and flexibility while also improving focus and concentration. A well-developed horse isn't just athletic; they're confident, responsive and willing. No matter what discipline you ride, good flatwork sets the stage for success and deepens your partnership with your horse.

Creative flatwork exercises are a powerful way to improve key elements of your horse's way of going. By varying your patterns and movements, you can develop greater accuracy, enhance rhythm, build impulsion, and improve straightness. These exercises also encourage suppleness and bend, laying a strong foundation for lateral movements and more advanced collection. The more thoughtfully you ride the flatwork, the more balanced and responsive your horse becomes.

Why do we need an arena? An arena is a safe space where we and our horses can learn. The fences give us some guidelines to work within and help us to be accurate. They also give our horses a visual guide on where they need to be. In an ideal world we might all have access to a perfectly harrowed and watered 20m x 40m fenced and surfaced area marked out with dressage letters to help us to visualise the flatwork patterns. In the real world many of us make do with what we have, be it a different sized arena, or just an area marked out in a field by poles on the ground or fencing. Just use what you have, adapt as you need to, and enjoy learning with your horse.

Any tips for getting started on flatwork? My advice is to keep it simple at first. Do your exercises and patterns at a walk. Literally, don't trot before you can walk! Take your time, don't get too target driven.

If the goal when you went out was to do an exercise at canter, but maybe your horse does it at the most wonderful trot you've ever felt, stop and think for a moment. How about rewarding that big time, getting off, calling it a day or changing the plan and finishing with a short trail ride instead? I bet you anything your horse will remember that feeling just as much as you will and it will set you up for a great canter in the future.

Don't drill yourself and your horse. Make sure that you mix up flatwork with other things like liberty work or riding out.

Most importantly, have fun! If you look at these exercises and think you'd approach them differently or you could create some flatwork patterns of your own – go for it and enjoy!

Arena size: The dressage arena size which these exercises are based upon is 20 metres wide & 40 metres long. If you are riding in an arena that is a different size that is no problem! You are welcome to adapt these exercises to fit your arena. If you are riding in a field or paddock, it can be useful to use some poles on the ground to mark out an arena. These will help you to ride accurately. The letters used around a dressage arena are A, K, E, H, C, M, B, F.

16 Novice Flatwork Floorplans

Flatwork floor plans using poles are a great way to have fun and spice up your training sessions with your horse. They are perfect for groundwork and riding. With groundwork, poles can teach the horse to navigate obstacles, refine their foot placement, and develop trust and communication in their human.

When riding, these ground poles serve as visual markers that promote precision in movements, helping riders focus on maintaining rhythm and straightness throughout transitions and lateral exercises. Overall, using poles in this way adds structure and variety to training sessions, fostering improved communication and connection between horse and rider while making the learning process more engaging and fun.

The floorplans in this book are split into novice, intermediate and advanced levels.

What you will need: Between 2 and 8 poles and a flat area to ride in. This can be an arena or a paddock or part of a field.

The Queenstown

Follow the black lines in the diagram to travel around the arena, passing accurately over the centre of the poles to work in circles. Do the exercise in both directions. Begin in walk.

Goal:

To be able to complete this exercise at the walk, with accurate circles, soft bend and staying straight along the sides of the arena.

Tips:

- Keep your head up.
- Look where you want to go.
- Remember to breathe.

Poles: 4

Level: ⭐

Benefits:

- ☑ Accuracy
- ☑ Rhythm
- ☑ Impulsion
- ☑ Straightness
- ☑ Suppleness & bend
- ☐ Lateral movement
         & collection

Gaits:

- ☑ Groundwork
- ☑ Walk
- ☑ Trot
- ☑ Canter

Movements:

- ☐ Backup
- ☐ Leg yield
- ☐ Sidepass
- ☐ Shoulder in

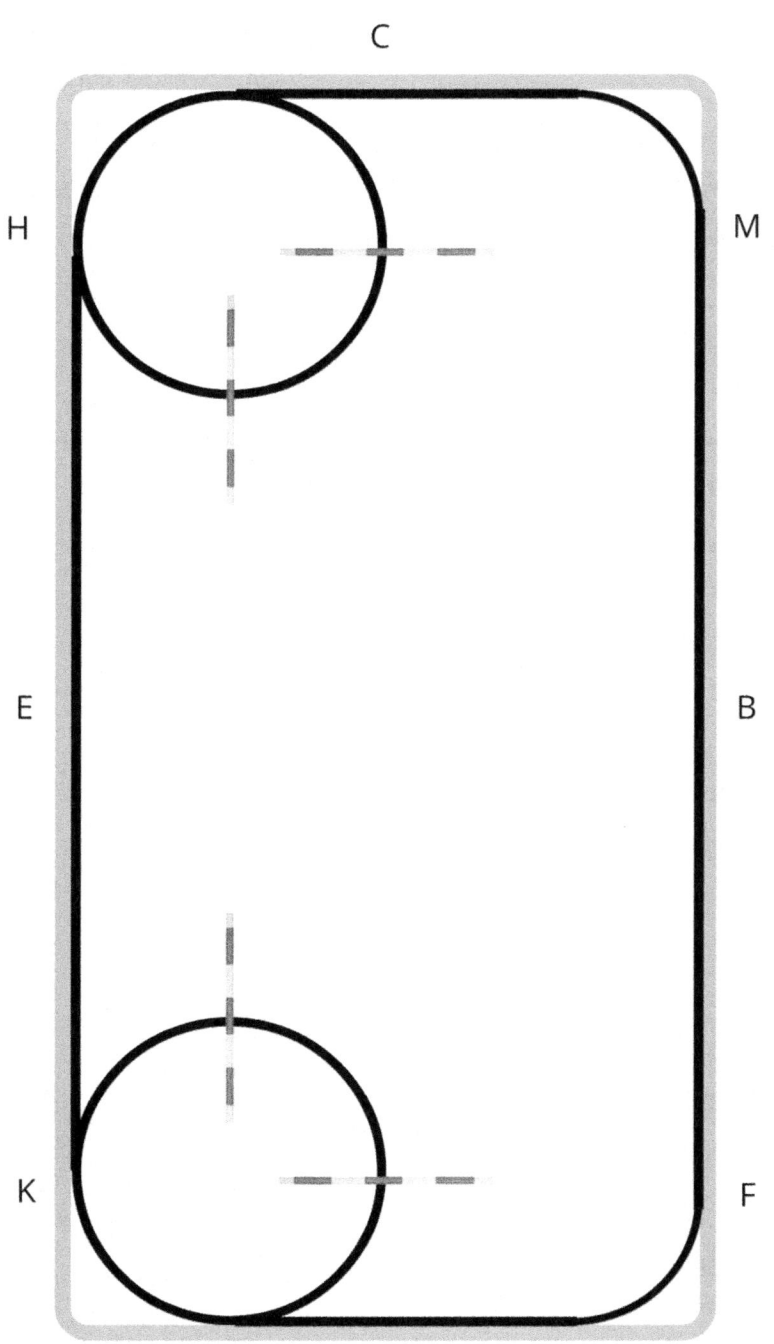

The Wanaka

This exercise develops the previous exercise by introducing upward and downward transitions. Make the transitions where indicated by the stars. Begin with walk and trot transitions.

Goal:

Your goal is to be able to do this exercise accurately with a regular rhythm, a nice bend on the circles and accurate transitions.

Tips:

- If your horse gets tense or starts to rush return to a slower gait until they can relax.
- Remember to breathe and relax your shoulders.
- Smile, it's meant to be fun!

Poles: 4

Level: ★

Benefits:

- ☑ Accuracy
- ☑ Rhythm
- ☑ Impulsion
- ☑ Straightness
- ☑ Suppleness & bend
- ☐ Lateral movement
  & collection

Gaits:

- ☑ Groundwork
- ☑ Walk
- ☑ Trot
- ☑ Canter

Movements:

- ☐ Backup
- ☐ Leg yield
- ☐ Sidepass
- ☐ Shoulder in

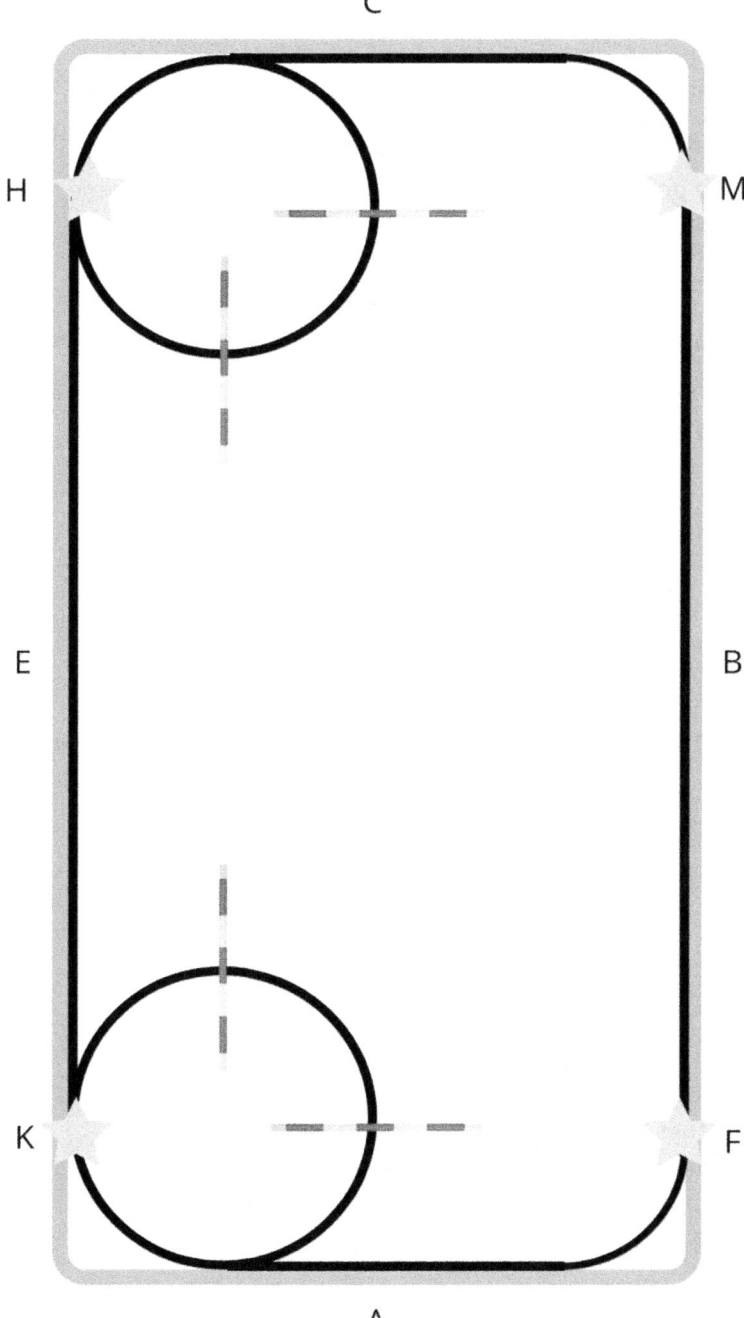

The Kaikōura

Follow the black lines in the diagram to travel around the arena passing accurately over the ground poles. Concentrate on looking up where you are going and having soft bend through your horse's body in the arcs. Ride the exercise in both directions.

Goal: To be able to complete this exercise at the walk, with accurate circles and turns, soft bend and staying straight where indicated in the diagram.

Tips:

- Change the bend in your horse's body before you change direction.
- Allow your hips to move with the swing of your horse's barrel.

Poles: 4

Level: ⭐

Benefits:

- ☑ Accuracy
- ☑ Rhythm
- ☑ Impulsion
- ☑ Straightness
- ☑ Suppleness & bend
- ☐ Lateral movement
        & collection

Gaits:

- ☑ Groundwork
- ☑ Walk
- ☑ Trot
- ☑ Canter

Movements:

- ☐ Backup
- ☐ Leg yield
- ☐ Sidepass
- ☐ Shoulder in

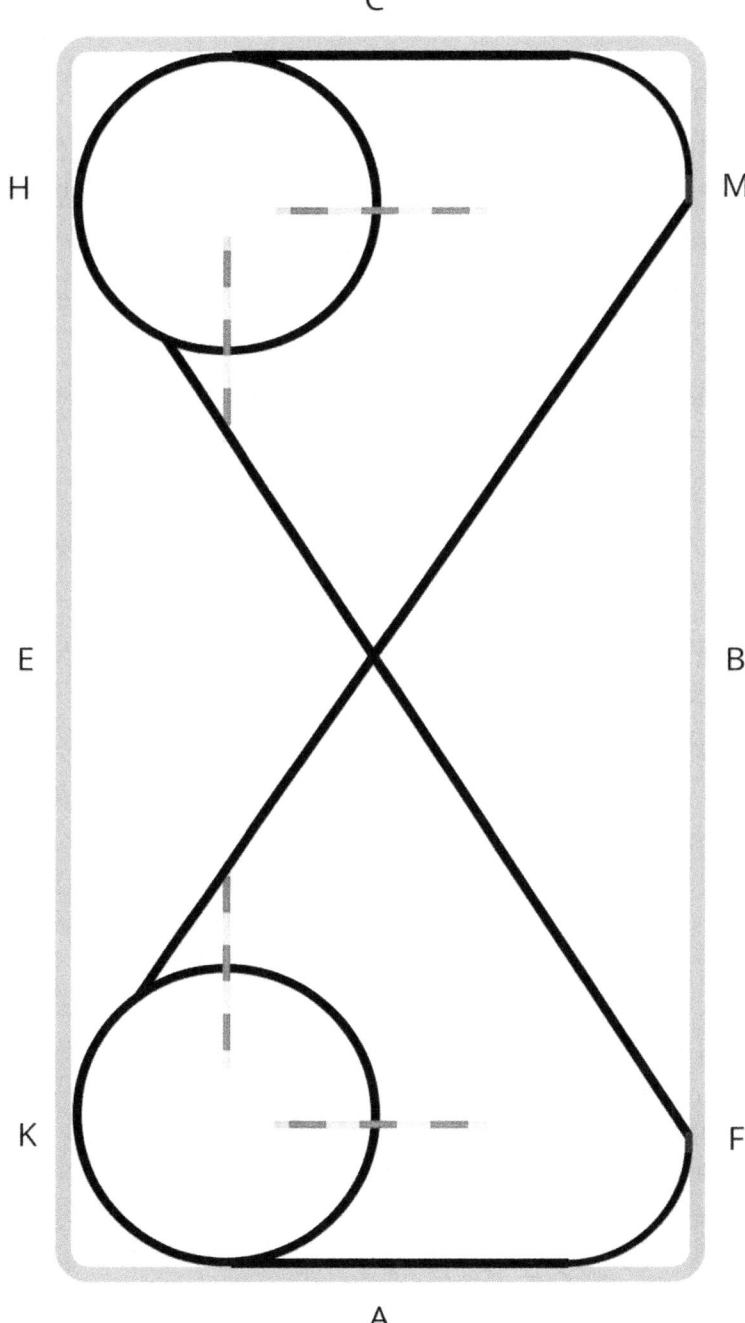

The Christchurch

Ride this at first at the walk. Concentrate on being straight where indicated and having soft bend in the arcs. Make sure that you pass over the poles where indicated. When you are ready add upward and downward transitions as indicated by the position of the stars. Work in both directions.

Goal: Your goal is to be able to do this exercise accurately with smooth and relaxed upward and downward transitions.

Tips:

- Change the bend in your horse's body before you change direction.
- Look where you are going.

Poles: 4

Level: ★

Benefits:

- ☑ Accuracy
- ☑ Rhythm
- ☑ Impulsion
- ☑ Straightness
- ☑ Suppleness & bend
- ☐ Lateral movement & collection

Gaits:

- ☑ Groundwork
- ☑ Walk
- ☑ Trot
- ☑ Canter

Movements:

- ☐ Backup
- ☐ Leg yield
- ☐ Sidepass
- ☐ Shoulder in

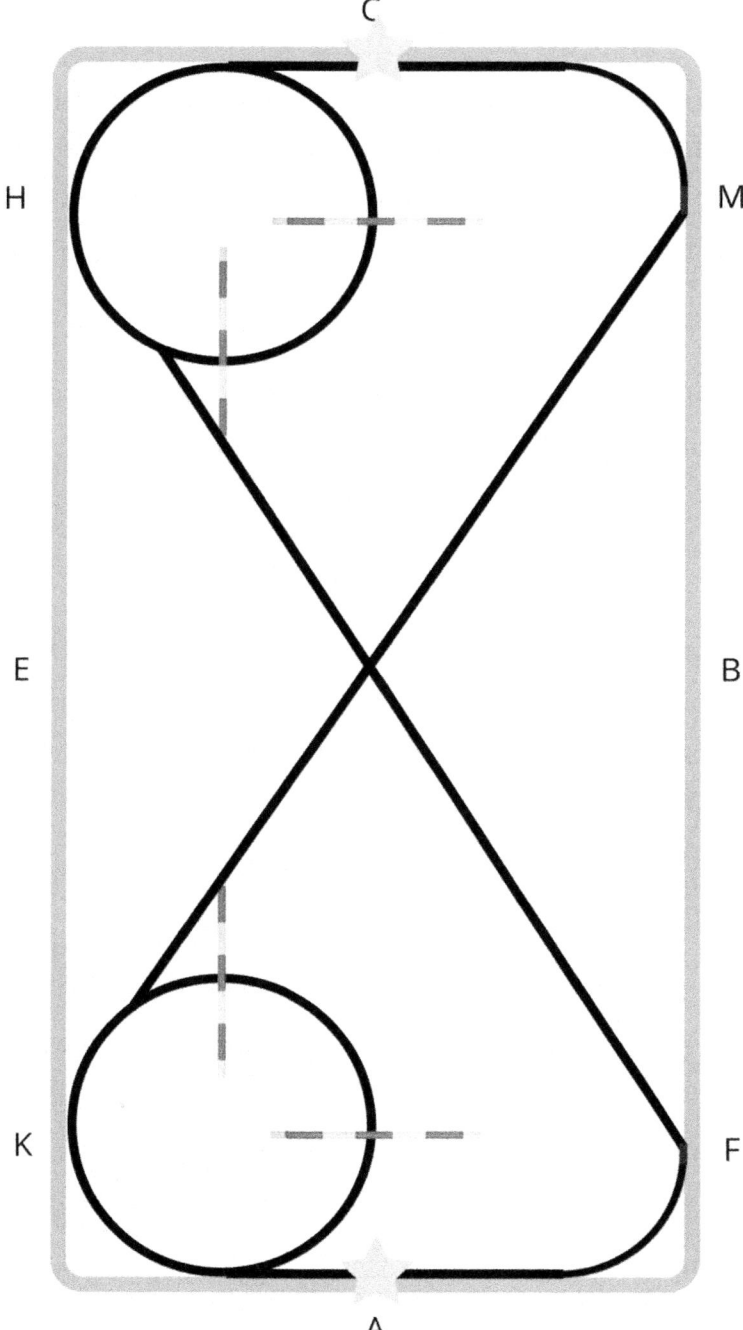

The Invercargill

In this exercise you will work on smaller turns, bends and accuracy. Make sure that you can complete the exercise with your horse working softly at a walk before introducing upward and downward transitions where indicated by the stars.

Goal:

Your bends should be soft and consistent in shape and there should be clear definition between the bends and straightness.

Tips:

- If you need to, break the exercise down at first to learn it.
- Lift your outside hip up slightly to encourage a bend in your horse's body without relying on the reins too much. But keep your shoulders level.

Poles: 4

Level: ⭐

Benefits:

- ☑ Accuracy
- ☑ Rhythm
- ☑ Impulsion
- ☑ Straightness
- ☑ Suppleness & bend
- ☐ Lateral movement
  & collection

Gaits:

- ☑ Groundwork
- ☑ Walk
- ☑ Trot
- ☐ Canter

Movements:

- ☐ Backup
- ☐ Leg yield
- ☐ Sidepass
- ☐ Shoulder in

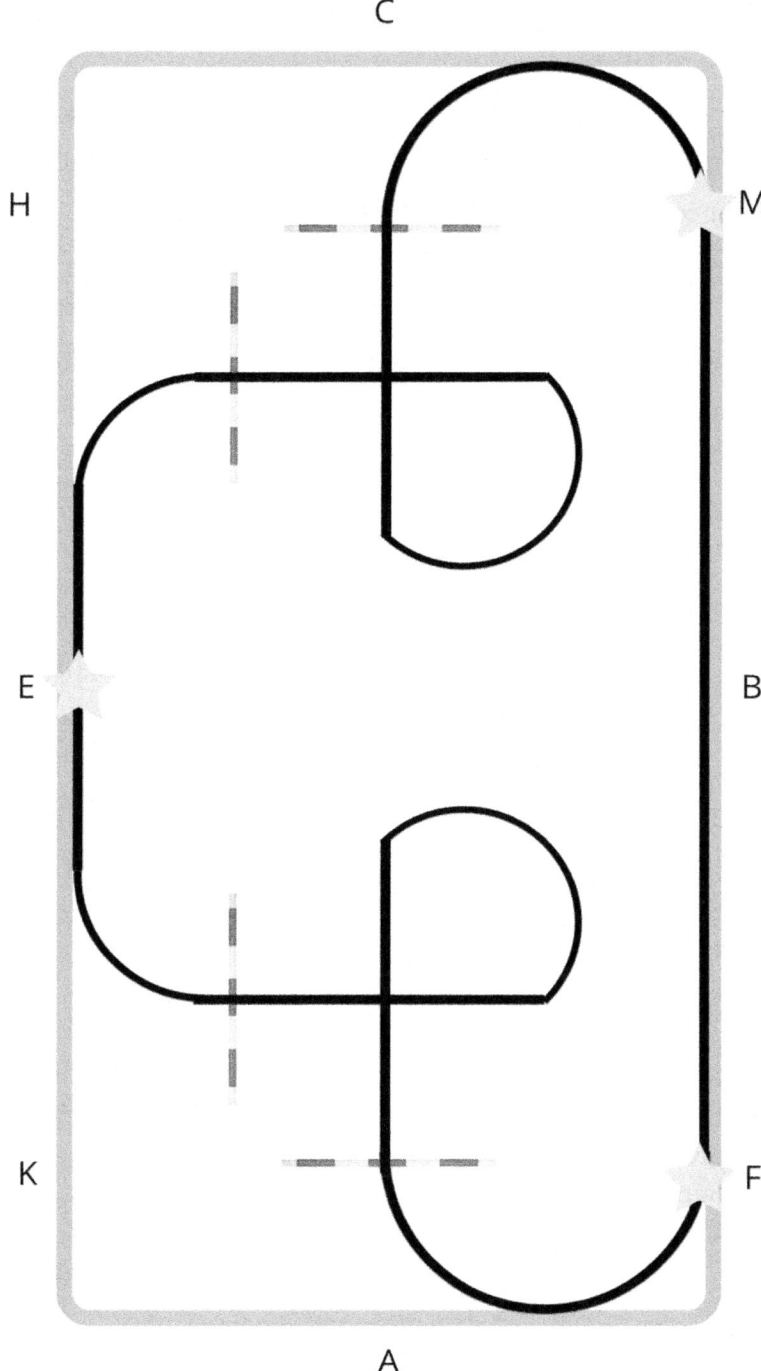

reins.

The Dunedin

This exercise uses the full length of the arena and works on straightness and accurate bends. Work in a walk in both directions and concentrate on softness, rhythm and accuracy.

Goal: The goal is to be working accurately with soft bends, good straight lines and your horse being relaxed. Your horse should maintain a consistent and rhythmic walk.

Tips:

- Remember to breathe.
- Look where you're going to improve your straight lines.
- Allow your hips to move side to side with the swing of your horse's barrel. Keep your shoulders level.

Poles: 3

Level: ★

Benefits:

- ☑ Accuracy
- ☑ Rhythm
- ☑ Impulsion
- ☑ Straightness
- ☑ Suppleness & bend
- ☐ Lateral movement
       & collection

Gaits:

- ☑ Groundwork
- ☑ Walk
- ☑ Trot
- ☑ Canter

Movements:

- ☐ Backup
- ☐ Leg yield
- ☐ Sidepass
- ☐ Shoulder in

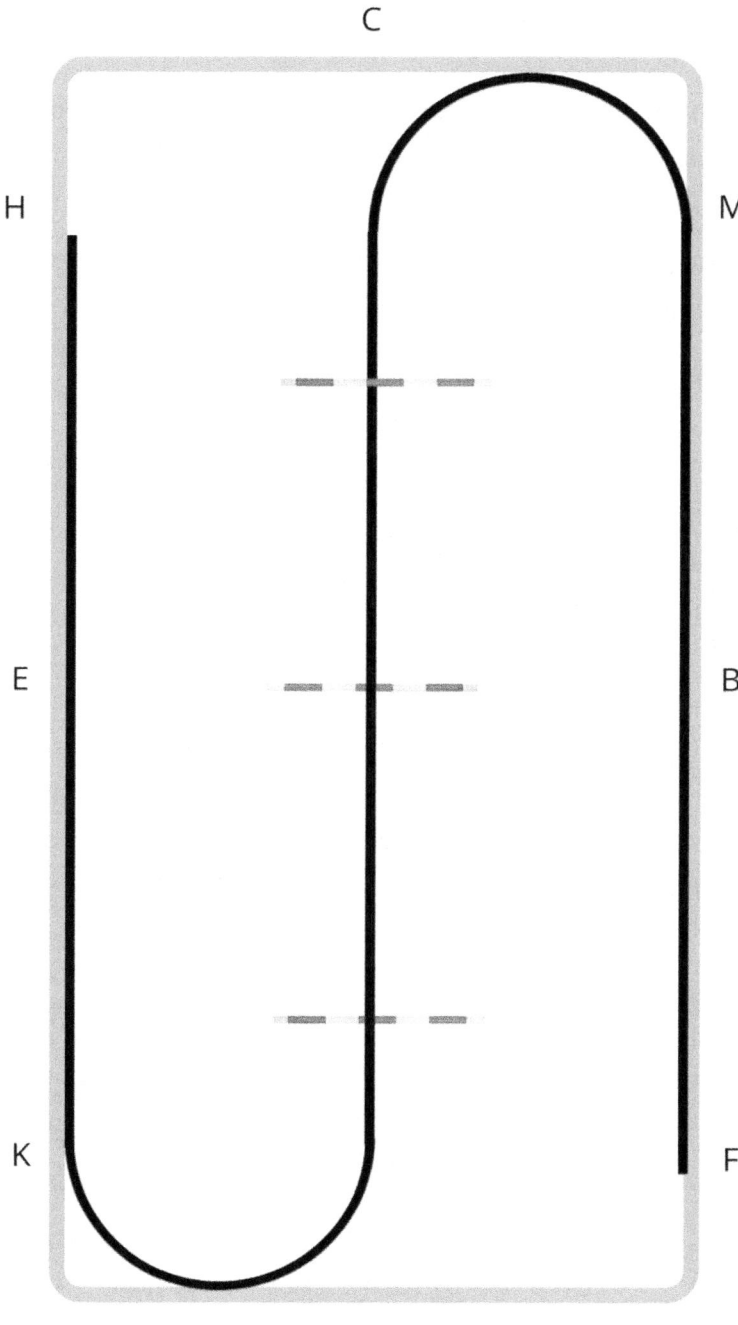

C

H

M

E

B

K

F

A

The Wellington

Building on the previous exercise, introduce upward and downward transitions where indicated by the stars.

Goal: Your goal is to be able to complete the exercise in all gaits, accurately and with your horse staying calm and relaxed.

Tips:

- Remember to breathe regularly.
- How many breaths does this exercise take?
- Smile, it's meant to be fun!

Poles: 3

Level: ★

Benefits:

- ☑ Accuracy
- ☑ Rhythm
- ☑ Impulsion
- ☑ Straightness
- ☑ Suppleness & bend
- ☐ Lateral movement
    & collection

Gaits:

- ☑ Groundwork
- ☑ Walk
- ☑ Trot
- ☑ Canter

Movements:

- ☐ Backup
- ☐ Leg yield
- ☐ Sidepass
- ☐ Shoulder in

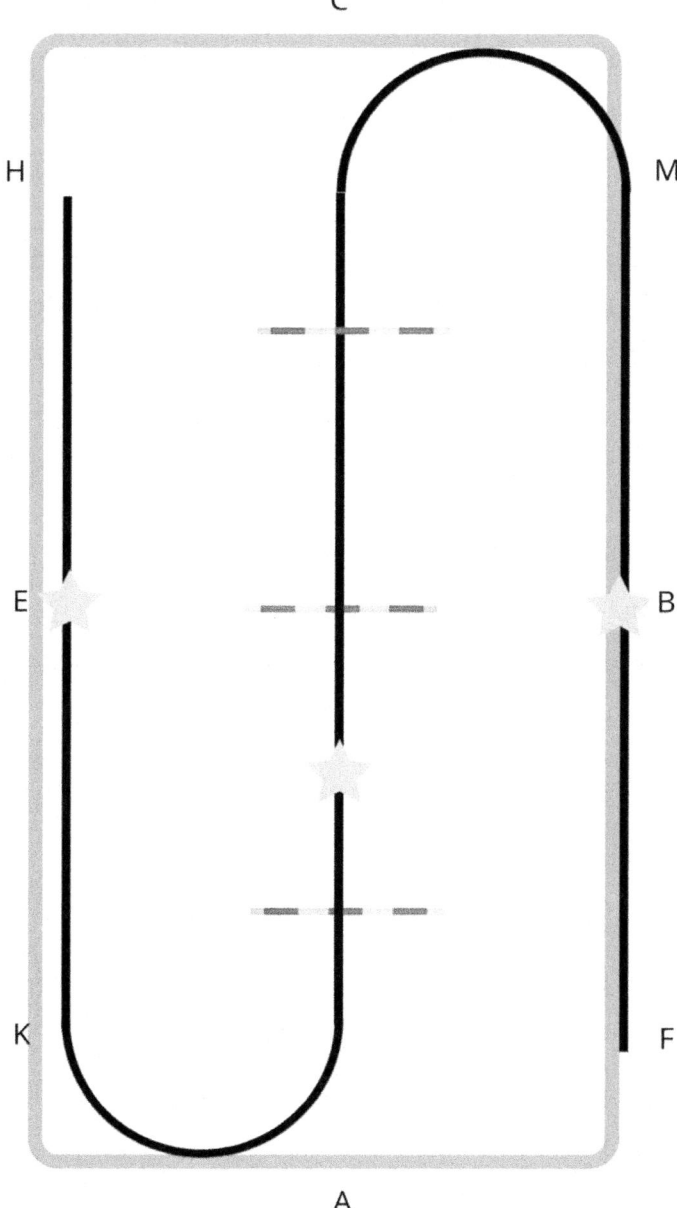

The Taupō

In this exercise you will use the poles as markers to help you to work in accurate serpentines. Work at a walk in both directions.

Goal:

To be able to complete the exercise working in both directions while maintaining a correct and soft bend and a consistent and relaxed walk.

Tips:

- Change the bend in your horse's body before you change direction.
- Lift your outside seat bone up slightly to encourage an inside been in your horse's body. Keep your shoulders level.

Poles: 3

Level: ⭐

Benefits:

- ☑ Accuracy
- ☑ Rhythm
- ☑ Impulsion
- ☑ Straightness
- ☑ Suppleness & bend
- ☐ Lateral movement
  & collection

Gaits:

- ☑ Groundwork
- ☑ Walk
- ☑ Trot
- ☑ Canter

Movements:

- ☐ Backup
- ☐ Leg yield
- ☐ Sidepass
- ☐ Shoulder in

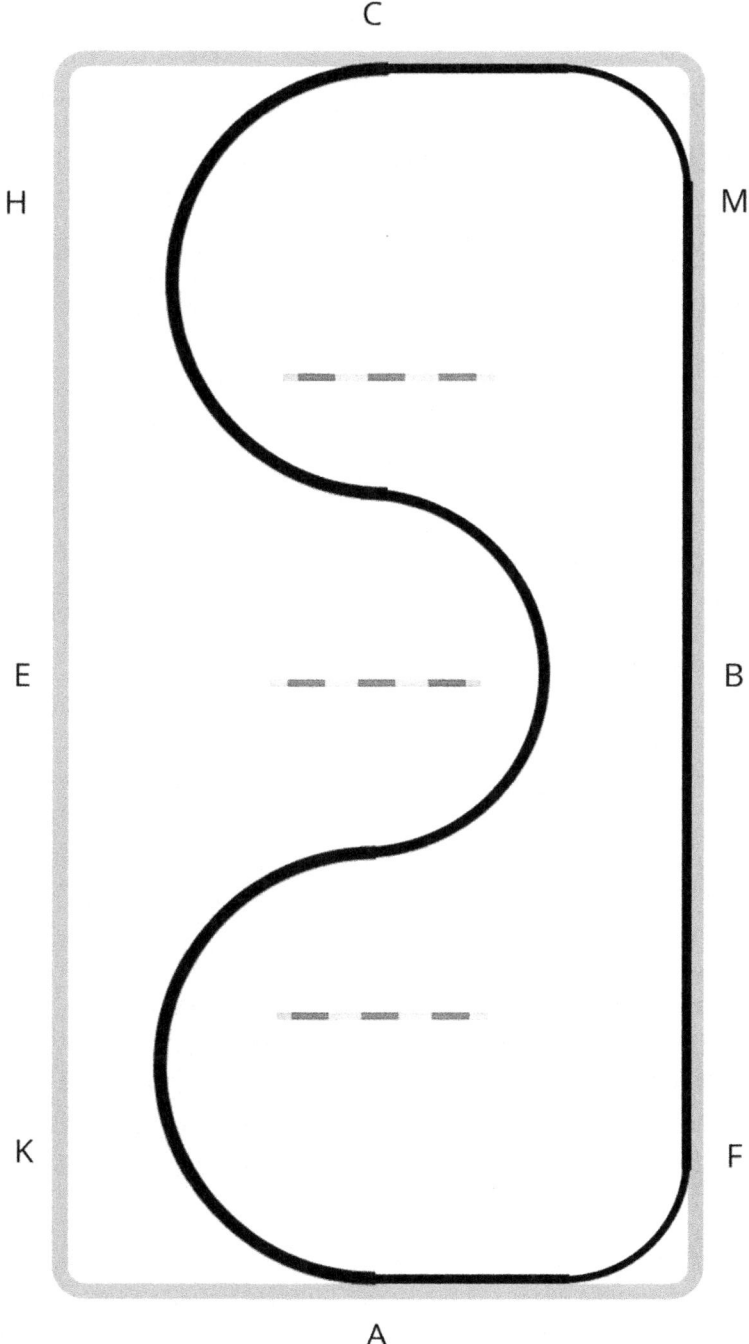

C

H

M

E

B

K

F

A

The Mt. Lyford

This exercise develops the previous one by introducing upward and downward transitions.

Goal: Your goal is to be able to complete the exercise accurately with smooth transitions while your horse stays relaxed.

Tips:

- Remember to breathe.
- Relax your shoulders.
- Allow your hips to move side to side with the swing of your horse's barrel.

Poles: 3

Level: ★

Benefits:

- ☑ Accuracy
- ☑ Rhythm
- ☑ Impulsion
- ☑ Straightness
- ☑ Suppleness & bend
- ☐ Lateral movement
  & collection

Gaits:

- ☑ Groundwork
- ☑ Walk
- ☑ Trot
- ☑ Canter

Movements:

- ☐ Backup
- ☐ Leg yield
- ☐ Sidepass
- ☐ Shoulder in

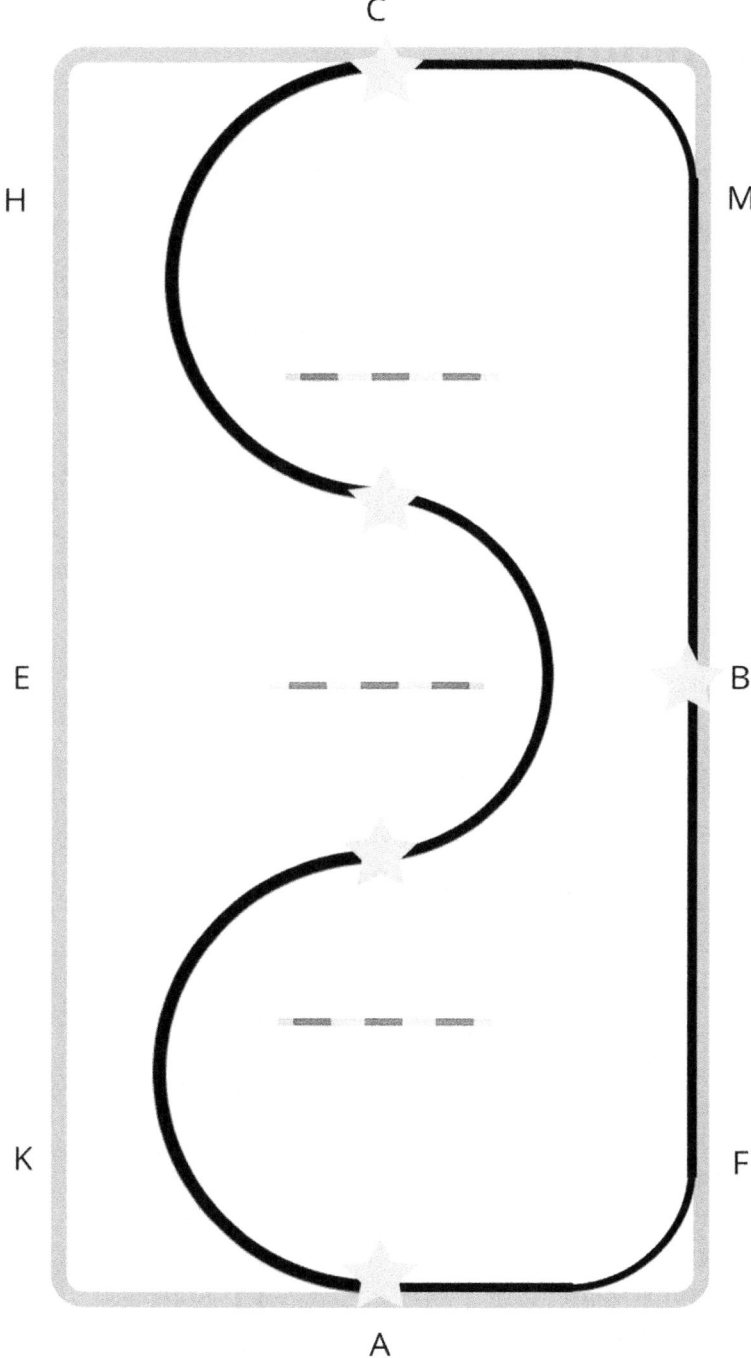

The Rangiora

In this exercise you will use the poles for guidance when riding accurate circles. Work in walk in both directions. Each circle should be a similar size. For the circles, use your inside leg to ask your horse to step their inside hind leg under their body more deeply, to create a gentle bend through their body.

Goal: Your goal is to have accurate circles while your horse works softly in a correct bend.

Tips:

- Look where you want to go.
- Change flexion before you change direction.
- Keep your hands close together at the pommel. No one should be able to see them move.

Poles: 3

Level: ★

Benefits:

☑ Accuracy
☑ Rhythm
☑ Impulsion
☑ Straightness
☑ Suppleness & bend
☐ Lateral movement
       & collection

Gaits:

☑ Groundwork
☑ Walk
☑ Trot
☑ Canter

Movements:

☐ Backup
☐ Leg yield
☐ Sidepass
☐ Shoulder in

C

H

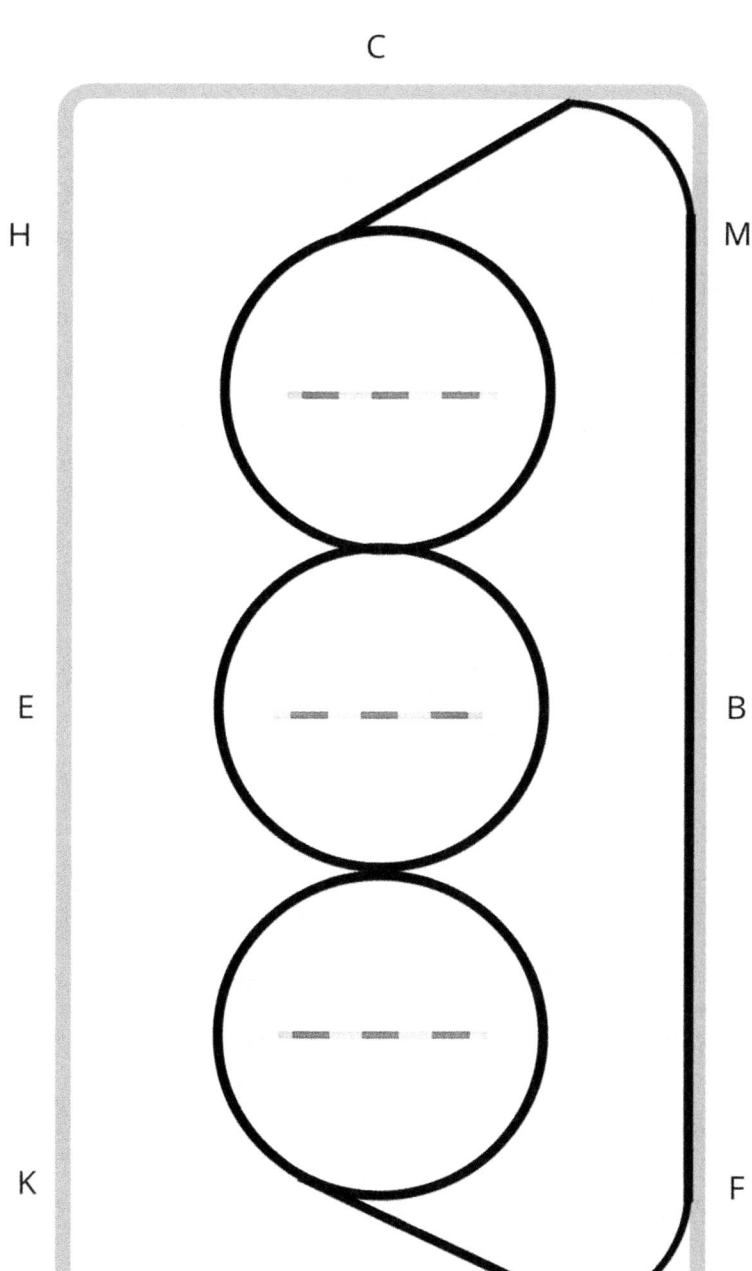

M

E

B

K

F

A

The Waiau

Develop the previous exercises by introducing upward and downward transitions where indicated by the stars. Make sure that you are established in softness, consistency and bend before moving to a faster gait.

Goal: To be able to ride your horse in accurate circles with relaxed transitions in both directions.

Tips:

- Look up and focus on where you are going.
- Smile, it's meant to be fun!

Poles: 3

Level: ★

Benefits:

- ☑ Accuracy
- ☑ Rhythm
- ☑ Impulsion
- ☑ Straightness
- ☑ Suppleness & bend
- ☐ Lateral movement
     & collection

Gaits:

- ☑ Groundwork
- ☑ Walk
- ☑ Trot
- ☑ Canter

Movements:

- ☐ Backup
- ☐ Leg yield
- ☐ Sidepass
- ☐ Shoulder in

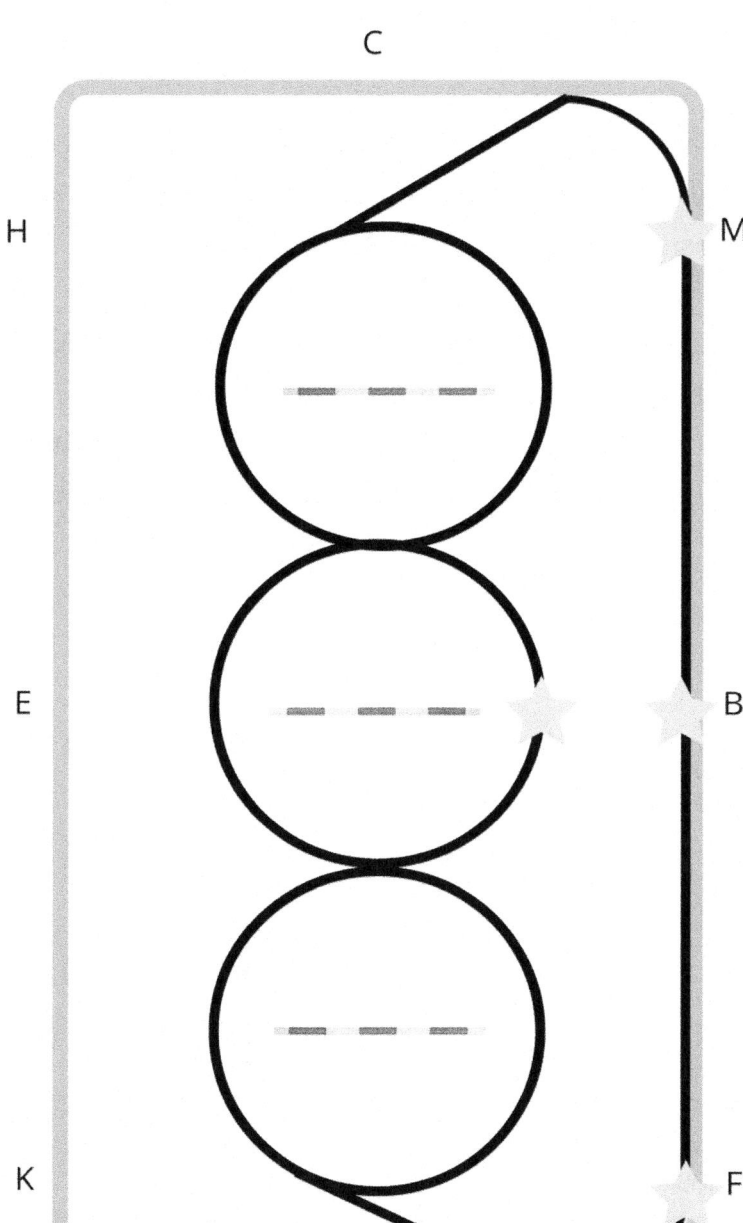

The Rotherham

In this exercise you will work on accurate 10 metre circles and straightness using poles for guidance. Complete it at the walk in both directions. Think about your circles being the same size.

Goal: To be able to complete this pattern accurately at a walk, with your horse's body mirroring the bend of the circle. For the circles, use your inside leg to ask your horse to step their inside hind leg under their body more deeply, to create a gentle bend through their body.

Tips:

- Remember to keep your shoulders relaxed and let them mirror your horse.

Poles: 4

Level: ★

Benefits:

- ☑ Accuracy
- ☑ Rhythm
- ☑ Impulsion
- ☑ Straightness
- ☑ Suppleness & bend
- ☐ Lateral movement
  & collection

Gaits:

- ☑ Groundwork
- ☑ Walk
- ☑ Trot
- ☑ Canter

Movements:

- ☐ Backup
- ☐ Leg yield
- ☐ Sidepass
- ☐ Shoulder in

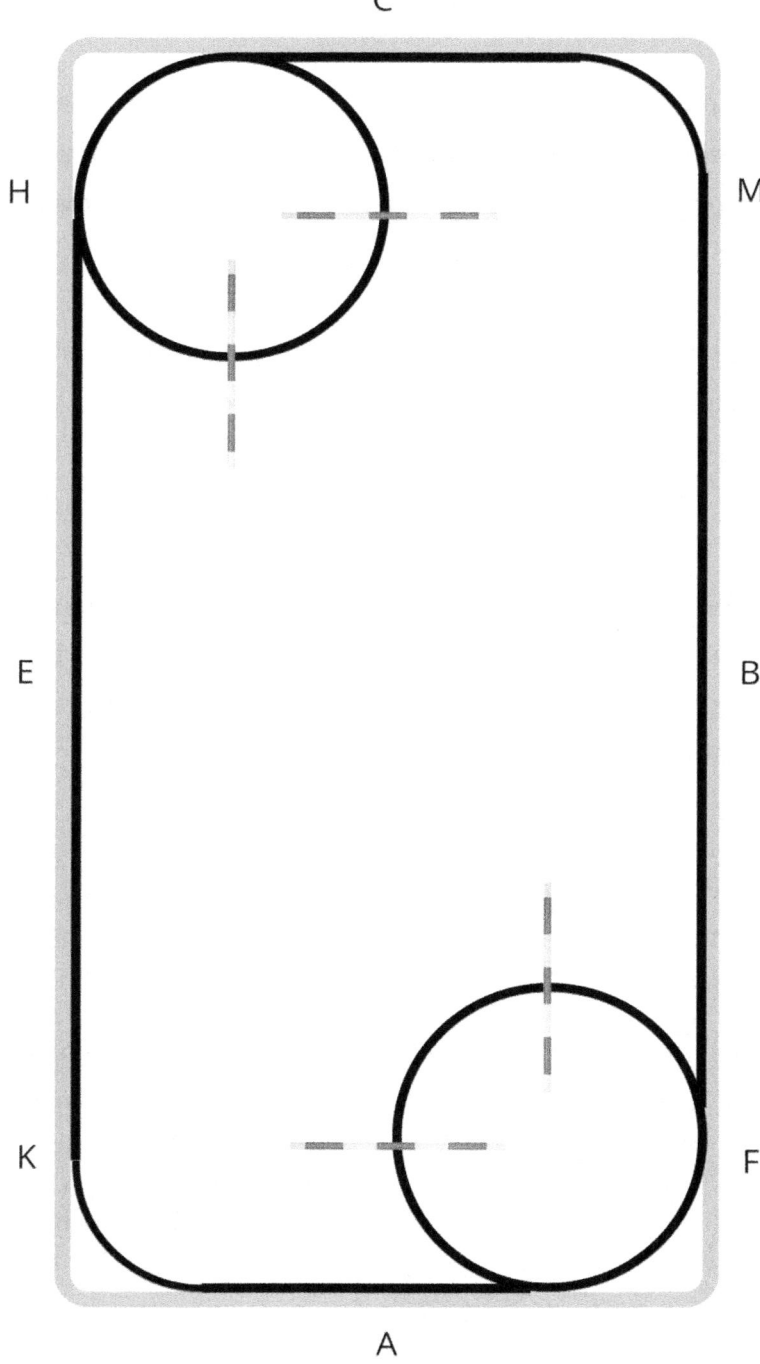

C

H

M

E

B

K

F

A

The Culverden

Develop the previous exercise by introducing upward and downward transitions where indicated by the stars. Start at the walk and only transition up when your horse is relaxed. Pass accurately over the centre of the poles for accurate circles.

Goal: To be able to complete this pattern in both directions while maintaining gait, accurate circles, soft bend and relaxation.

Tip:

- Horses tend to move faster naturally on straight lines and move slower on curves and circles. If your horse has lots of energy, try some extra circles. If your horse is lacking energy, try some more straight lines & look ahead.

Poles: 4

Level: ★

Benefits:

- ☑ Accuracy
- ☑ Rhythm
- ☑ Impulsion
- ☑ Straightness
- ☑ Suppleness & bend
- ☐ Lateral movement
  & collection

Gaits:

- ☑ Groundwork
- ☑ Walk
- ☑ Trot
- ☑ Canter

Movements:

- ☐ Backup
- ☐ Leg yield
- ☐ Sidepass
- ☐ Shoulder in

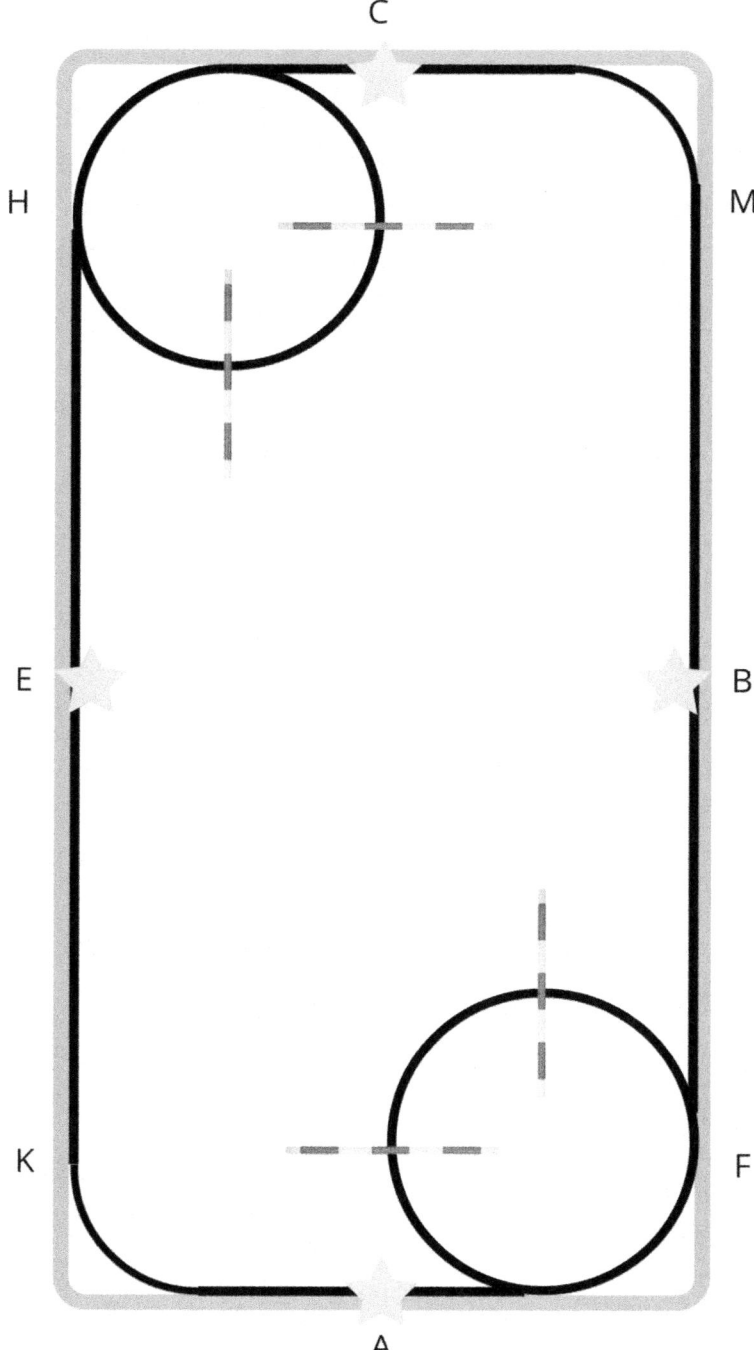

The Hanmer Springs

In this exercise you will work mainly on upward and downward transitions, using poles as guidance for accurate changes of direction in the corners of the arena. Make your transitions where indicated by the stars. Only ask for upward transitions when your horse is relaxed and when you are looking ahead.

Goal: Your goal is to complete the exercise accurately with your horse able to maintain gait and softness throughout.

Tips:

- Look where you want to go.
- Allow your hips to move side to side with the swing of your horse's barrel. Keep your shoulders level.

Poles: 4

Level: ★

Benefits:

- ☑ Accuracy
- ☑ Rhythm
- ☑ Impulsion
- ☑ Straightness
- ☑ Suppleness & bend
- ☐ Lateral movement
  & collection

Gaits:

- ☑ Groundwork
- ☑ Walk
- ☑ Trot
- ☑ Canter

Movements:

- ☐ Backup
- ☐ Leg yield
- ☐ Sidepass
- ☐ Shoulder in

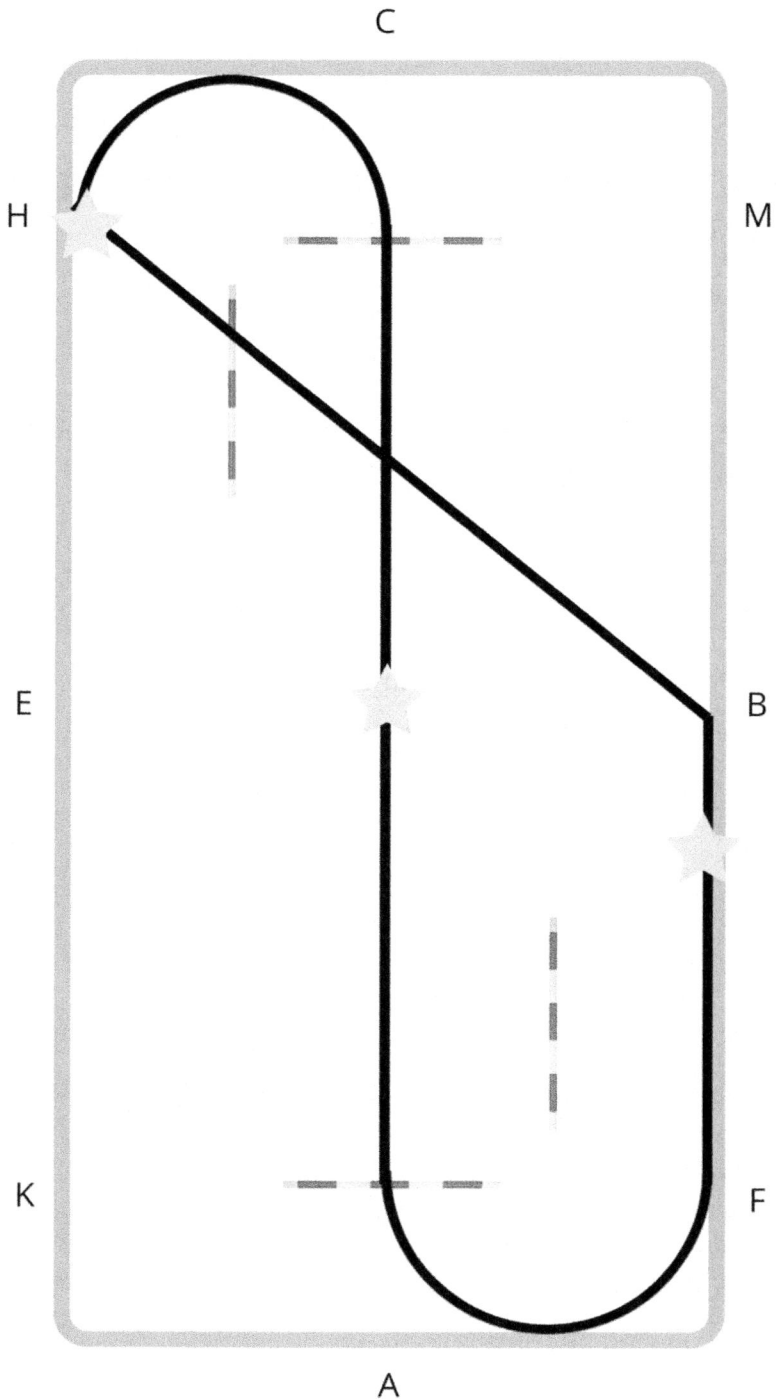

The Amberley

This exercise uses poles as guidance for accurate turns and straight lines across the arena. Practise in walk to begin. Focus on your horse maintaining a consistent gait and softness.

Goal:

To complete the pattern with your horse staying relaxed and in a rhythmic and consistent gait.

Tips:

- Ask for straightness from your body and through your focus, rather than relying on the reins.
- Remember to breathe.

Poles: 4

Level: ⭐

Benefits:

- ☑ Accuracy
- ☑ Rhythm
- ☑ Impulsion
- ☑ Straightness
- ☑ Suppleness & bend
- ☐ Lateral movement
     & collection

Gaits:

- ☑ Groundwork
- ☑ Walk
- ☑ Trot
- ☑ Canter

Movements:

- ☐ Backup
- ☐ Leg yield
- ☐ Sidepass
- ☐ Shoulder in

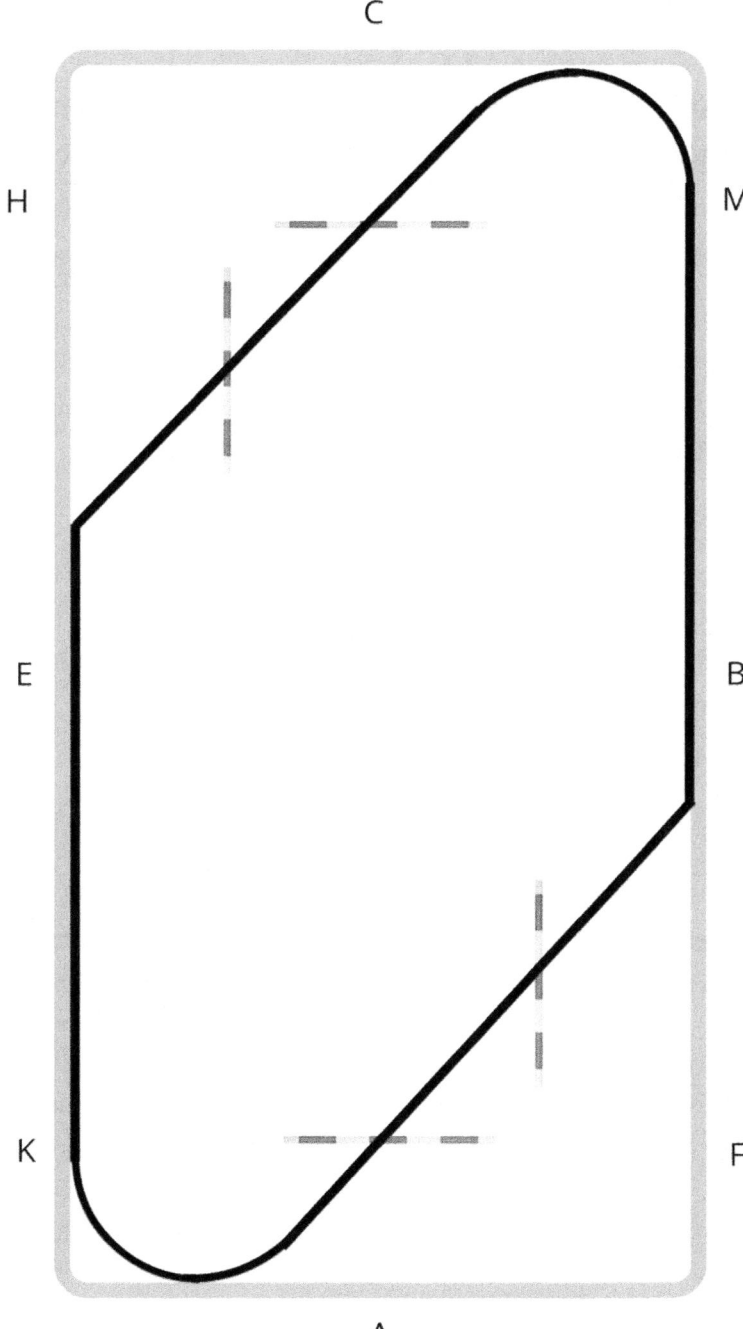

The Hawarden

Develop the previous exercise by introducing upward and downward transitions, accurately as indicated by the stars. If your horse starts to rush, transition down to a slower gait until they can relax. Start at the walk and work up to trot and canter when your horse feels ready.

Goal: Your horse will complete the exercise without rushing, and without the rhythm of your breathing changing.

Tips:

- Think ahead for the change of direction so that your horse is prepared.
- Keep breathing regularly. Do not hold your breath.

Poles: 4

Level: ★

Benefits:

- ☑ Accuracy
- ☑ Rhythm
- ☑ Impulsion
- ☑ Straightness
- ☑ Suppleness & bend
- ☐ Lateral movement
     & collection

Gaits:

- ☑ Groundwork
- ☑ Walk
- ☑ Trot
- ☑ Canter

Movements:

- ☐ Backup
- ☐ Leg yield
- ☐ Sidepass
- ☐ Shoulder in

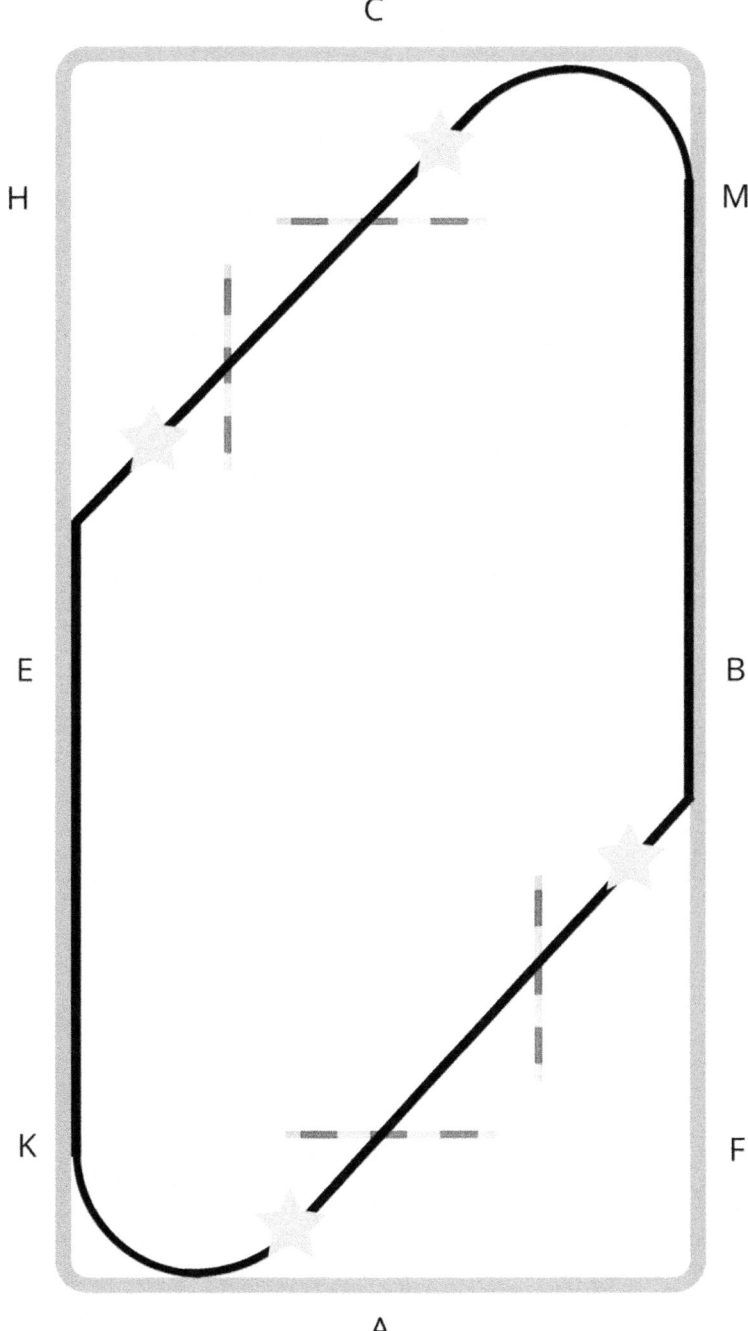

18 Intermediate Flatwork Exercises

The Ballina

In this exercise you will use the poles as guidance to ride accurate circles. Do the exercise at the walk, thinking about working in a soft bend and a good rhythm. If you are using a full sized arena the circles will be 20m and 10m in size.

Goal: To be able to complete this exercise at the walk, with accurate circles, soft bend and without relying too much on your reins.

Tips:

- Lift your outside seat bone slightly to ask for bend.
- Look where you want to go.
- Keep your hands close together at the pommel. No one should be able to see them move.

Poles: 2

Level: ★ ★

Benefits:

- ☑ Accuracy
- ☑ Rhythm
- ☑ Impulsion
- ☑ Straightness
- ☑ Suppleness & bend
- ☐ Lateral movement
     & collection

Gaits:

- ☑ Groundwork
- ☑ Walk
- ☑ Trot
- ☑ Canter

Movements:

- ☐ Backup
- ☐ Leg yield
- ☐ Sidepass
- ☐ Shoulder in

C

H

M

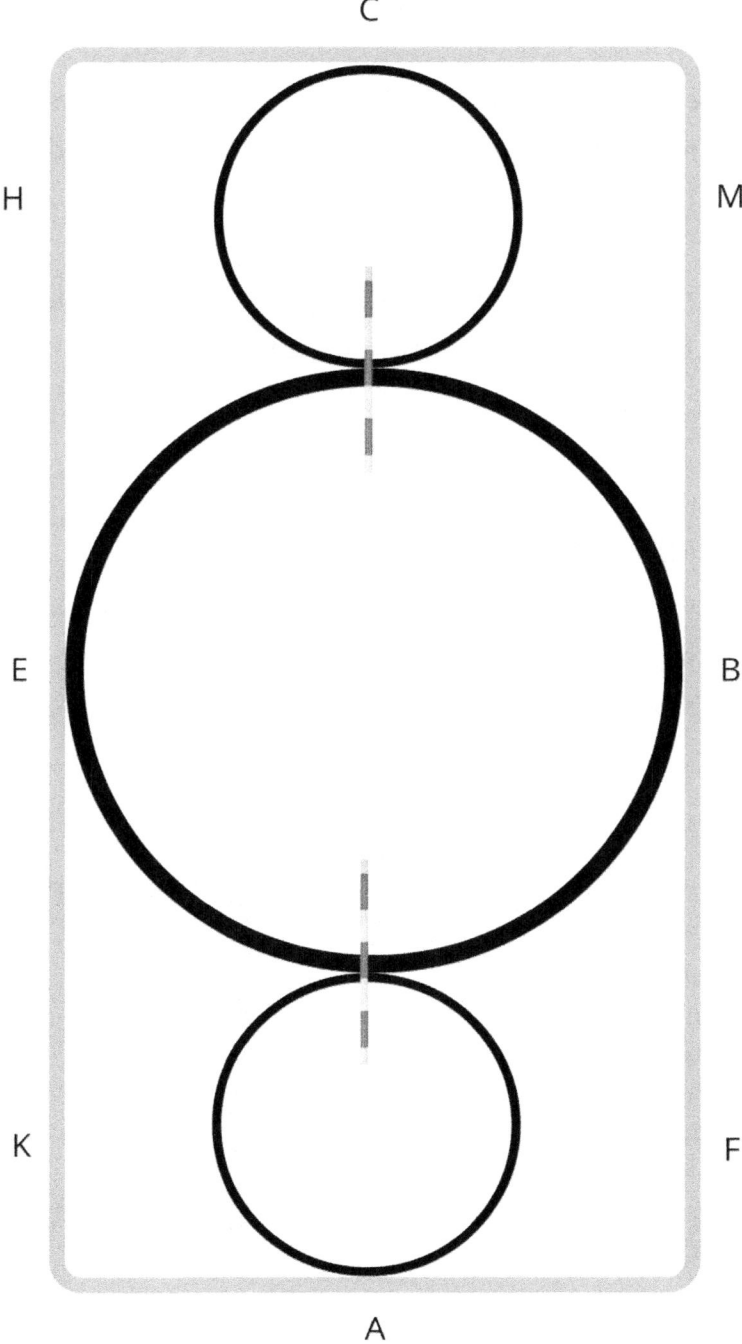

E

B

K

F

A

The Bathhurst

This exercise develops the previous one by introducing upward and downward transitions. Make the transitions where indicated by the stars.

Goal: Your goal is to be able to do this exercise accurately with smooth and relaxed upward and downward transitions.

Tips:

- Remember to breathe.
- Relax your shoulders.
- Allow your hips to move side to side with the swing of your horse's barrel.

Poles: 2

Level: ★ ★

Benefits:

- ☑ Accuracy
- ☑ Rhythm
- ☑ Impulsion
- ☑ Straightness
- ☑ Suppleness & bend
- ☐ Lateral movement
      & collection

Gaits:

- ☑ Groundwork
- ☑ Walk
- ☑ Trot
- ☑ Canter

Movements:

- ☐ Backup
- ☐ Leg yield
- ☐ Sidepass
- ☐ Shoulder in

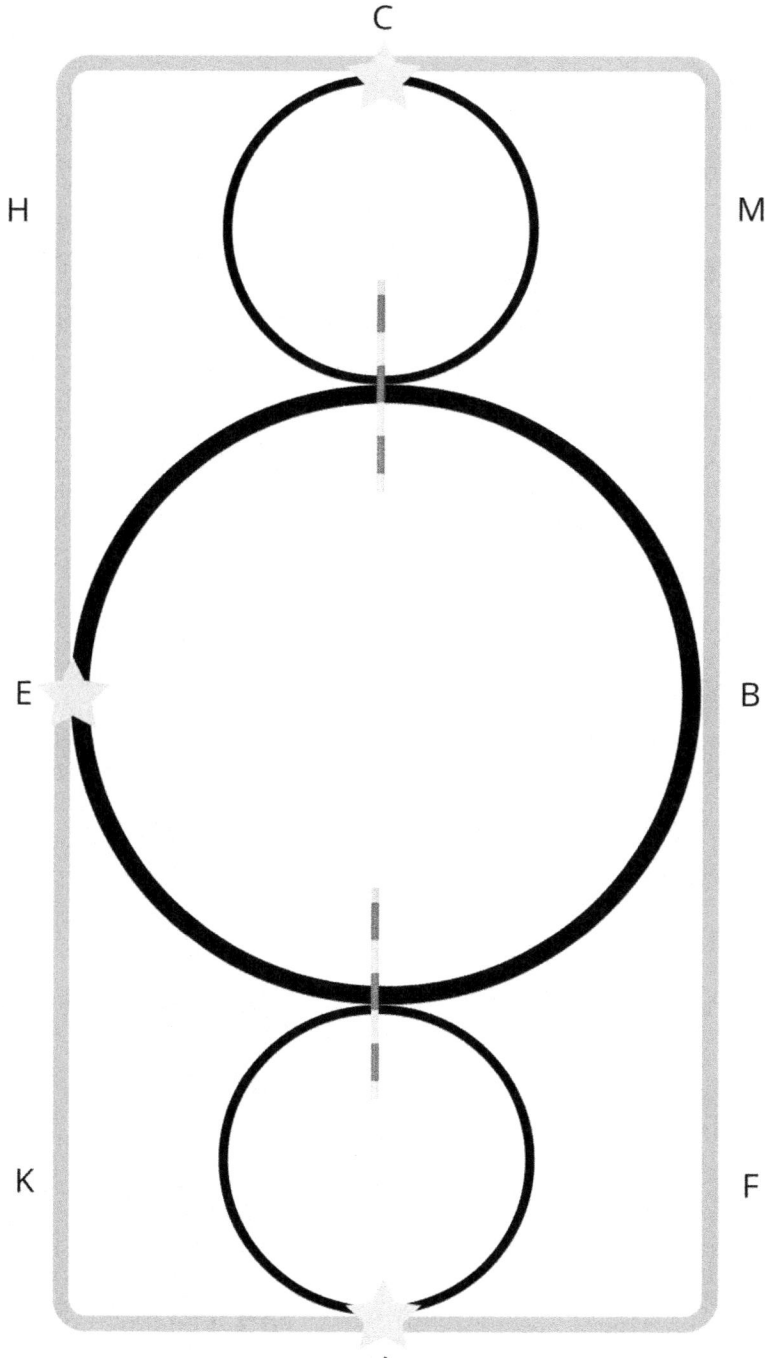

The Byron Bay

At a walk, start at one end of the arena and ride a large circle. As you return to your starting point ride a smaller circle. Then ride the larger circle again. As you reach the middle of the arena (X) change direction to ride the other large circle. Complete a full circle, then as you reach the half way point again ride the smaller circle. When you return to the track complete the larger circle and halt in the middle (X). Do this in both directions.

Goal: Try to ride mainly from your body without relying too heavily on the reins.

Tips:

- For the circles, use your inside leg to ask your horse to step their inside hind leg under their body more deeply, to create a gentle bend through their body.

Poles: 2

Level: ★ ★

Benefits:

- ☑ Accuracy
- ☑ Rhythm
- ☑ Impulsion
- ☑ Straightness
- ☑ Suppleness & bend
- ☐ Lateral movement
  & collection

Gaits:

- ☑ Groundwork
- ☑ Walk
- ☑ Trot
- ☑ Canter

Movements:

- ☐ Backup
- ☐ Leg yield
- ☐ Sidepass
- ☐ Shoulder in

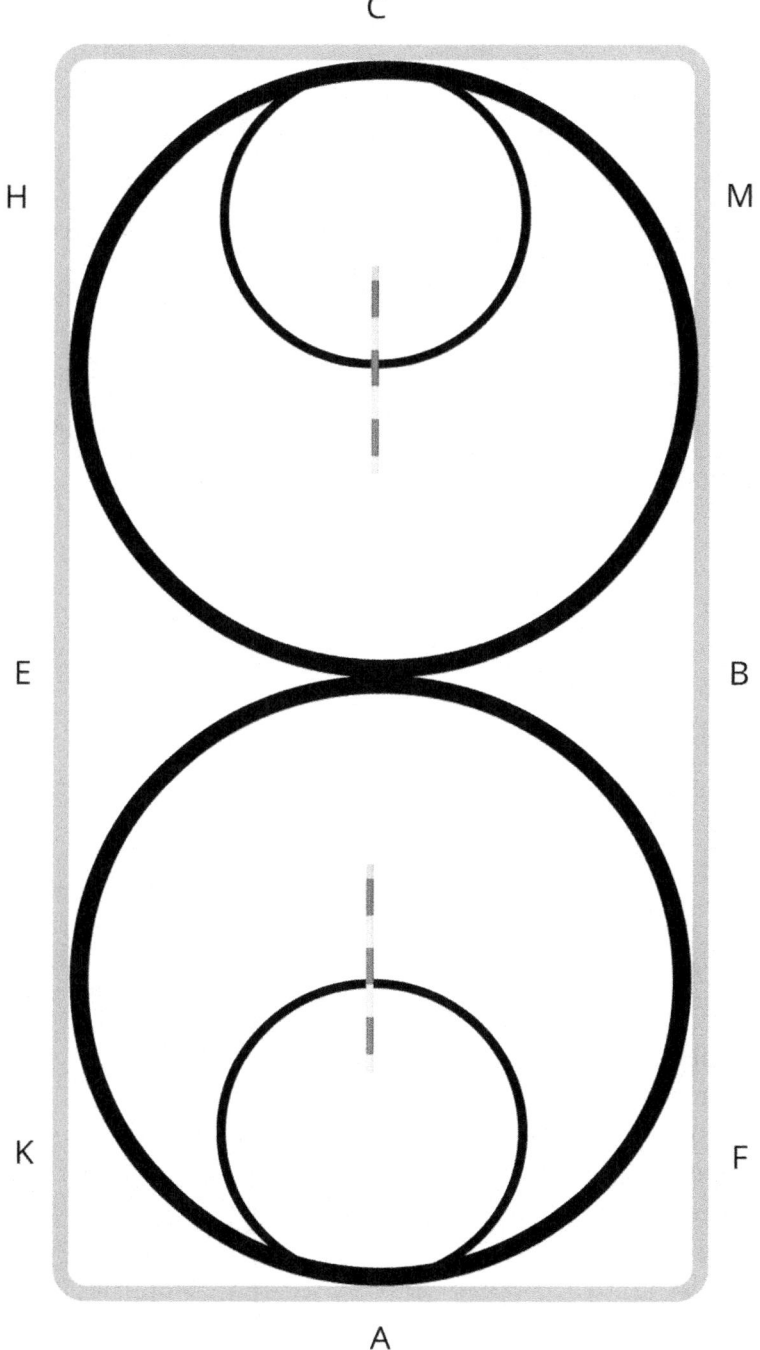

C

H

M

E

B

K

F

A

125

The Melbourne

This adds accurate upward and downward transitions to the previous exercise. Pass over the centre of the poles to help yourself to ride accurate circles. Add canter transitions when you feel your horse is ready. Work in both directions.

Goal: Your goal is to be able to do this exercise accurately with smooth and relaxed upward and downward transitions. Your circles should be consistent in size and shape.

Tips:

- Use smaller cues.
- Change flexion before you change direction.
- Remember to breathe.

Poles: 2

Level: ★ ★

Benefits:

- ☑ Accuracy
- ☑ Rhythm
- ☑ Impulsion
- ☑ Straightness
- ☑ Suppleness & bend
- ☐ Lateral movement
  & collection

Gaits:

- ☑ Groundwork
- ☑ Walk
- ☑ Trot
- ☑ Canter

Movements:

- ☐ Backup
- ☐ Leg yield
- ☐ Sidepass
- ☐ Shoulder in

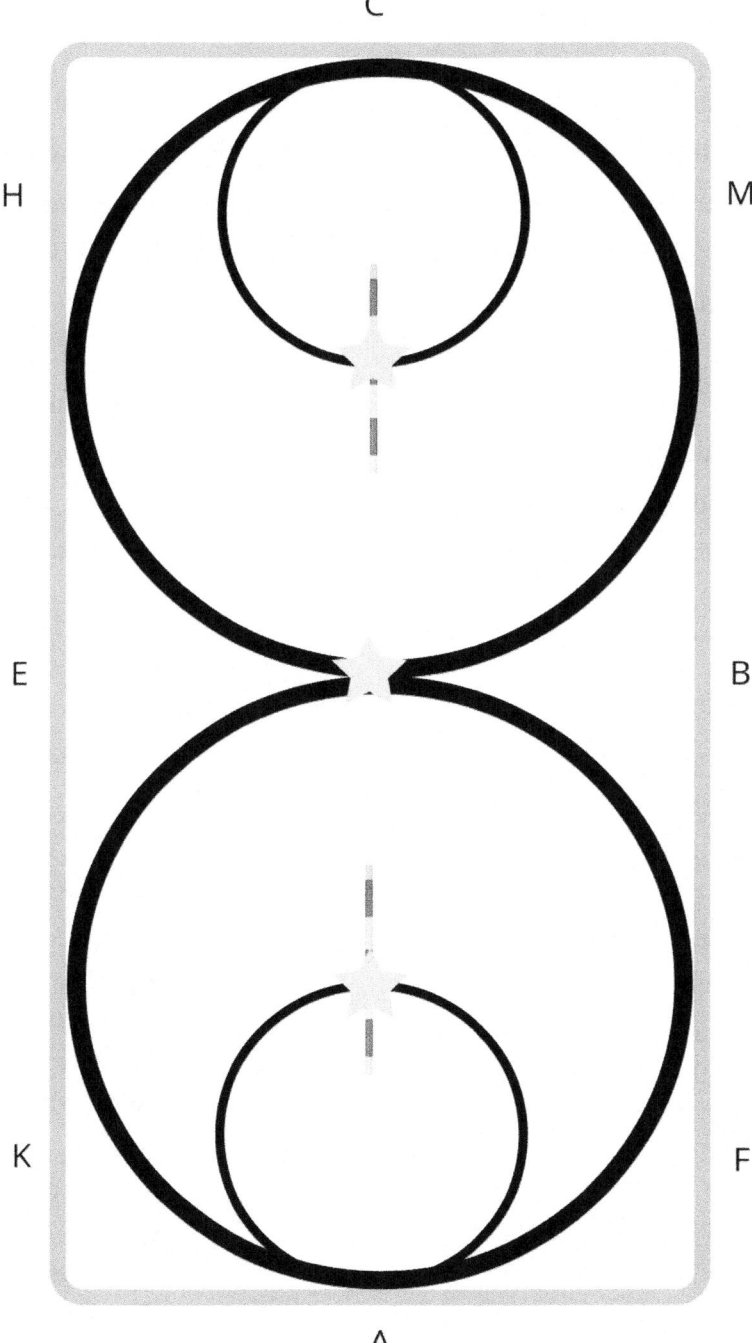

C

H

M

E

B

K

F

A

The Adelaide

In this exercise you will work on smaller circles and accuracy. Work at a walk in both directions to start. Start at the end of the arena and ride your first circle, using the pole as guidance. When you pass over the middle of the pole for the second time change direction and ride the next circle in the opposite direction.

Goal: Your bends should be soft and consistent in shape and your circles should be the same size and shape. You will pass over the poles accurately in the middle.

Tips:

- Keep your head up and look to where you want to go.
- Keep your hands close together at the pommel. No one should be able to see them move.

Poles: 2

Level: ★ ★

Benefits:

- ☑ Accuracy
- ☑ Rhythm
- ☑ Impulsion
- ☑ Straightness
- ☑ Suppleness & bend
- ☐ Lateral movement & collection

Gaits:

- ☑ Groundwork
- ☑ Walk
- ☑ Trot
- ☑ Canter

Movements:

- ☐ Backup
- ☐ Leg yield
- ☐ Sidepass
- ☐ Shoulder in

C

H

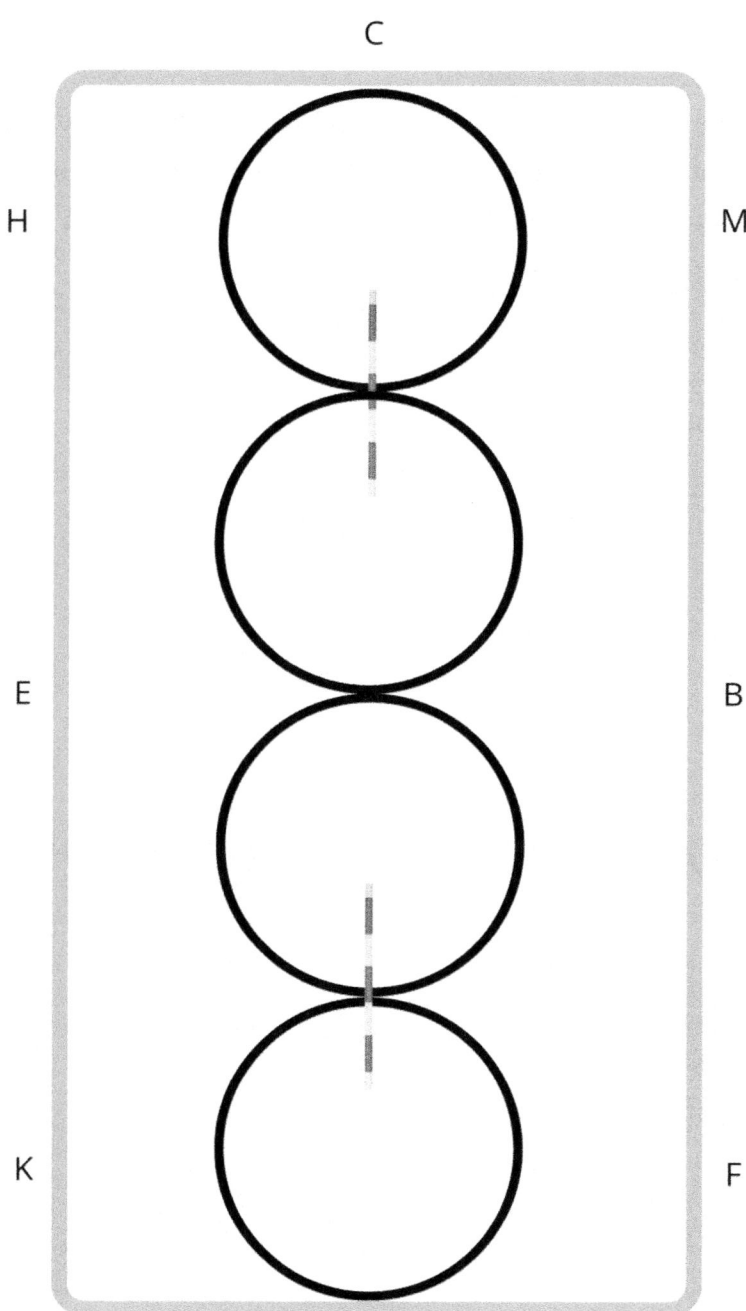

M

E

B

K

F

A

The Brisbane

Add upward and downward transitions to the previous exercise, using the stars as markers. Change direction as you cross over the poles and through the centre of the arena. Start with walk to trot and add canter when your horse feels ready.

Goal: To be able to ride your horse in accurate circles with relaxed transitions in both directions.

Tips:

- Relax your shoulders.
- Allow your hips to move side to side with the swing of your horse's barrel.

Poles: 2

Level: ★ ★

Benefits:

- ☑ Accuracy
- ☑ Rhythm
- ☑ Impulsion
- ☑ Straightness
- ☑ Suppleness & bend
- ☐ Lateral movement
     & collection

Gaits:

- ☑ Groundwork
- ☑ Walk
- ☑ Trot
- ☑ Canter

Movements:

- ☐ Backup
- ☐ Leg yield
- ☐ Sidepass
- ☐ Shoulder in

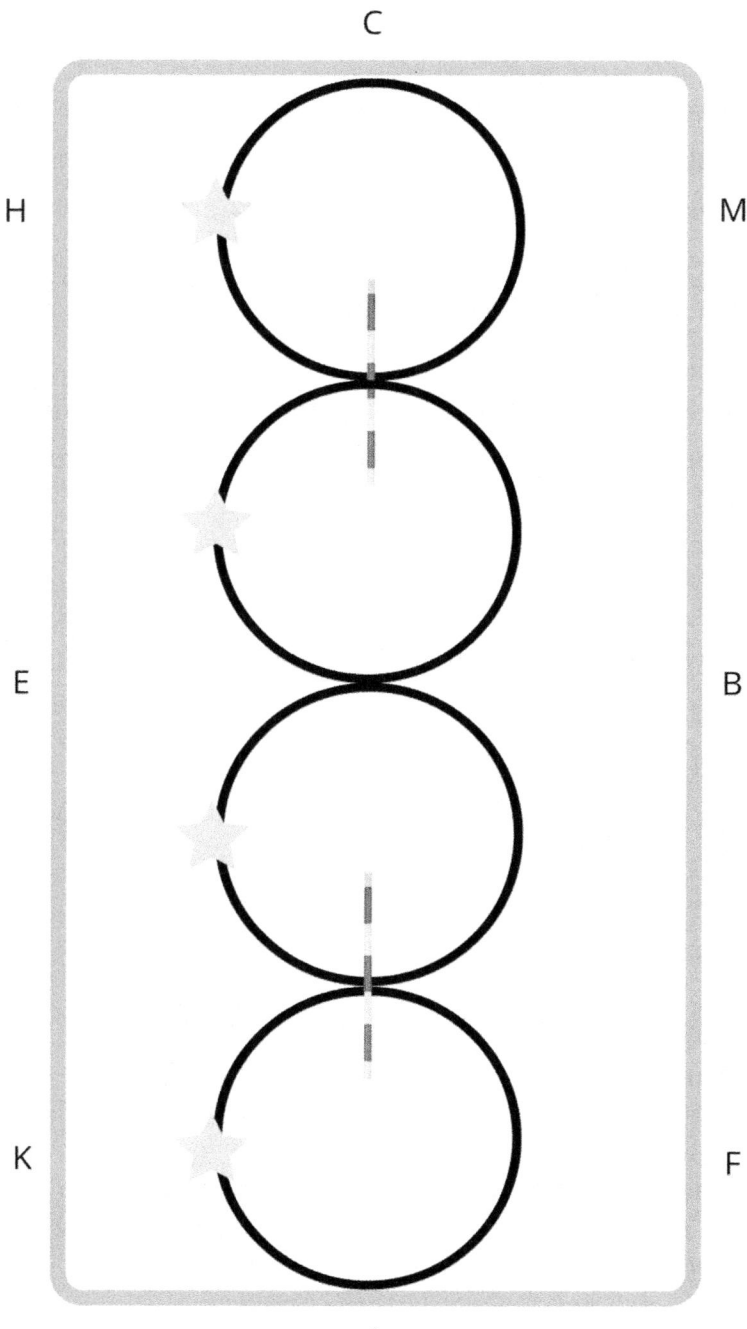

C

H

M

E

B

K

F

A

The Caboolture

This exercise uses poles to encourage you to ride your horse accurately into the corners of the arena. Work at a walk in both directions. Encourage the bend in your horse's body by slightly lifting the weight off your outside seat bone. Avoid trying to pull your horse into the corner with the reins.

Goal: Your goal is to be able to complete the exercise while your horse remains soft and relaxed and maintains gait and rhythm.

Tips:

- Feel your body being straight to encourage your horse to be straight.
- Count your breathing to encourage relaxation.
- Relax your lower back.

Poles: 8

Level: ★ ★

Benefits:

- ☑ Accuracy
- ☑ Rhythm
- ☑ Impulsion
- ☑ Straightness
- ☑ Suppleness & bend
- ☐ Lateral movement
  & collection

Gaits:

- ☑ Groundwork
- ☑ Walk
- ☑ Trot
- ☑ Canter

Movements:

- ☐ Backup
- ☐ Leg yield
- ☐ Sidepass
- ☐ Shoulder in

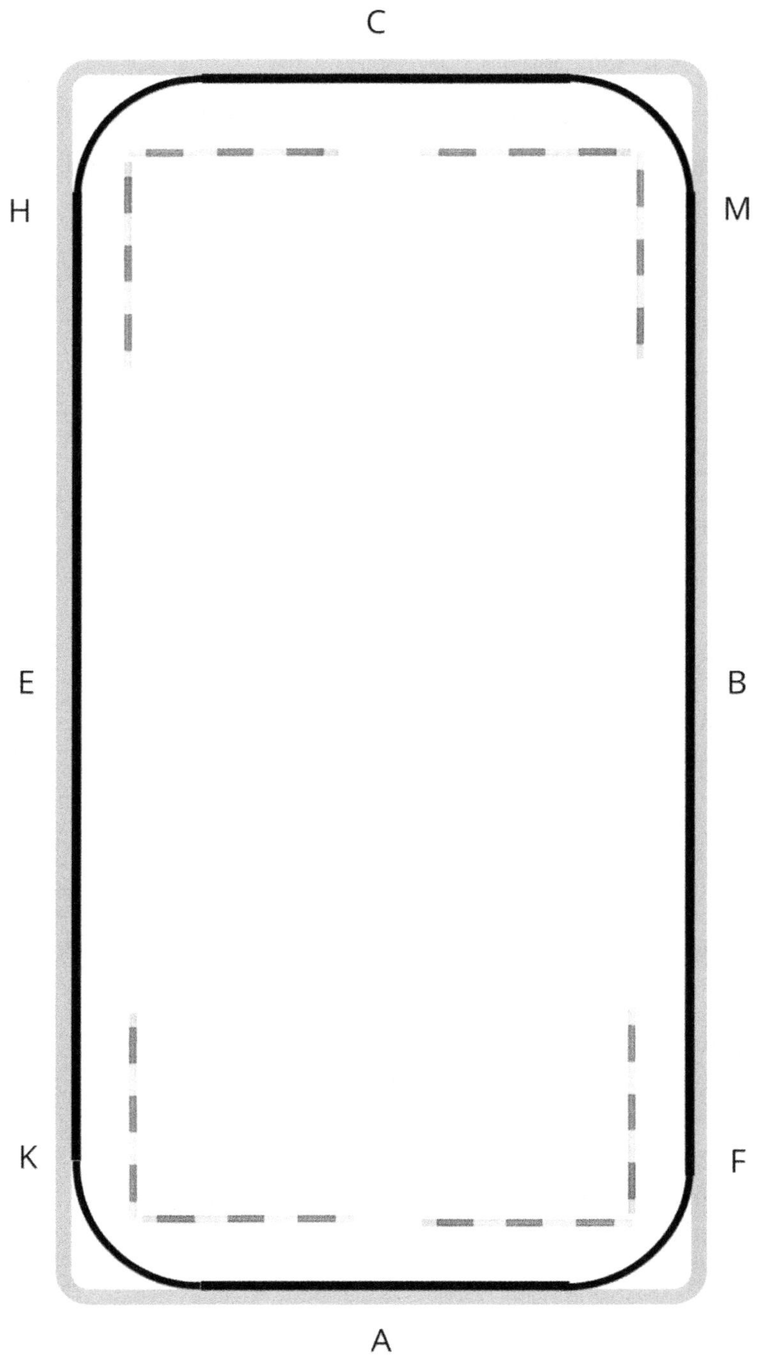

C

H

M

E

B

K

F

A

The Darwin

This exercise develops the previous one by introducing upward and downward transitions. Make the transitions where indicated by the stars. Try first at trot in both directions, then in canter.

Goal:

Your goal is to be able to complete the exercise with soft and relaxed transitions.

Tips:

- Keep your head up and look to where you want to go.
- Think ahead to the transitions to prepare your horse.
- Feel the swing of your horse's barrel from right to left.

Poles: 8

Level: ★ ★

Benefits:

- ☑ Accuracy
- ☑ Rhythm
- ☑ Impulsion
- ☑ Straightness
- ☑ Suppleness & bend
- ☐ Lateral movement
  & collection

Gaits:

- ☑ Groundwork
- ☑ Walk
- ☑ Trot
- ☑ Canter

Movements:

- ☐ Backup
- ☐ Leg yield
- ☐ Sidepass
- ☐ Shoulder in

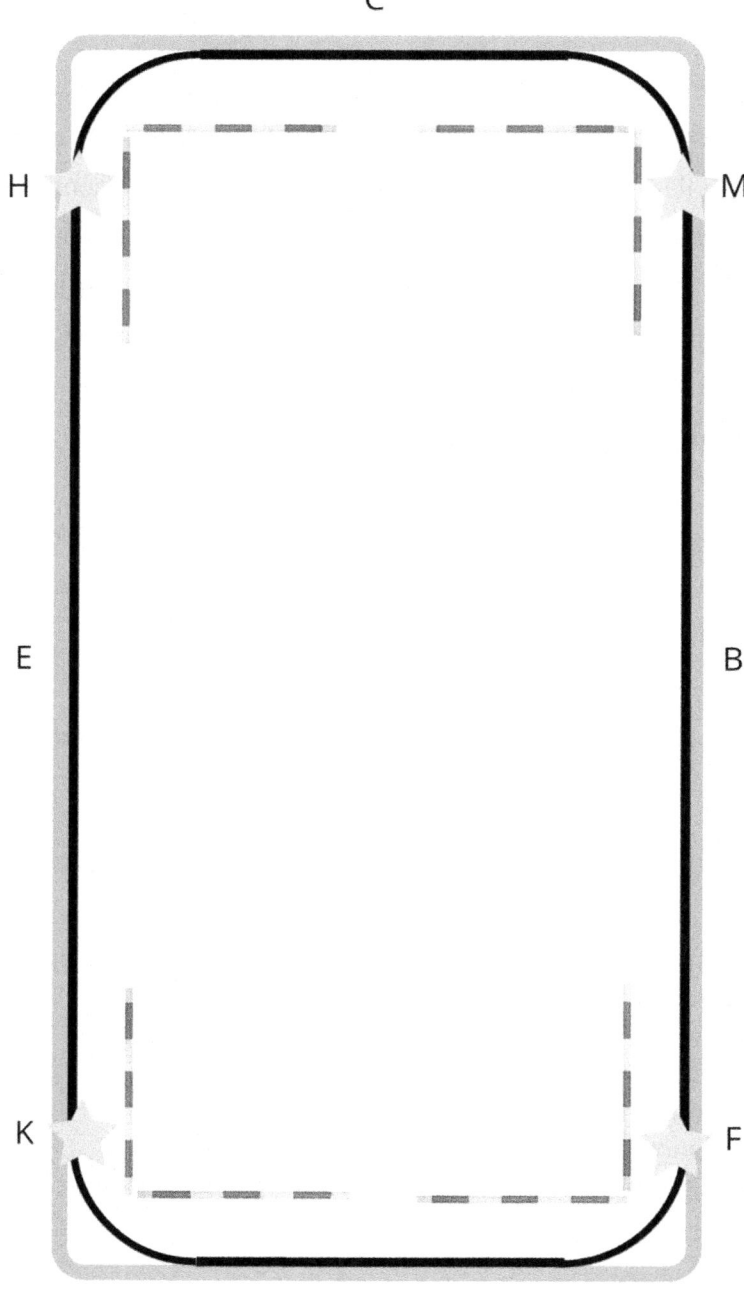

The Cairns

This exercise uses poles to encourage you to ride your horse accurately into the corners of the arena and to have variety by also riding over poles. This will help to develop focus and concentration and also encourage your horse to lift their legs higher. Work at a walk in both directions. Encourage the bend by slightly lifting the weight off your outside seat bone, and by using your inside leg to ask the inside hind leg to step under more deeply. Avoid trying to pull your horse into the corner with the reins.

Goal: Your goal is to be able to complete the exercise accurately while your horse stays relaxed. Your horse should be passing over the poles without touching them.

Tips: Think ahead for the turns so that your horse is prepared.

Poles: 8

Level: ★ ★

Benefits:
- ☑ Accuracy
- ☑ Rhythm
- ☑ Impulsion
- ☑ Straightness
- ☑ Suppleness & bend
- ☐ Lateral movement
  & collection

Gaits:
- ☑ Groundwork
- ☑ Walk
- ☑ Trot
- ☑ Canter

Movements:
- ☐ Backup
- ☐ Leg yield
- ☐ Sidepass
- ☐ Shoulder in

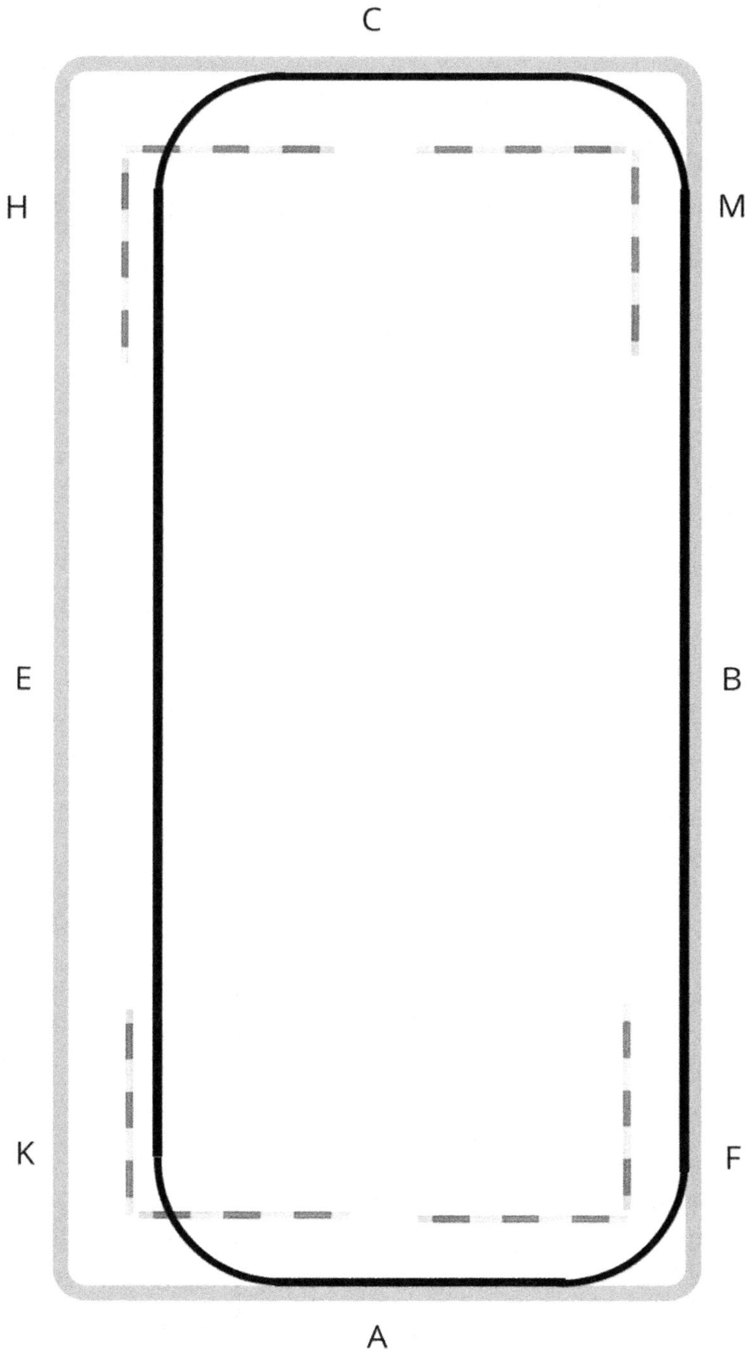

C

H

M

E

B

K

F

A

The Camden

Develop the previous exercise by introducing upward and downward transitions where indicated by the stars. Make sure that you are established in softness, consistency and bend in one gait making an upward transition.

Goal:

To be able to complete this pattern in both directions while maintaining gait, straight lines, soft bend and relaxation.

Tips:

- Keep your head up and look to where you want to be.
- Remember to breathe regularly.
- Keep your hands close together at the pommel.

Poles: 8

Level: ★ ★

Benefits:

- ☑ Accuracy
- ☑ Rhythm
- ☑ Impulsion
- ☑ Straightness
- ☑ Suppleness & bend
- ☐ Lateral movement
     & collection

Gaits:

- ☑ Groundwork
- ☑ Walk
- ☑ Trot
- ☑ Canter

Movements:

- ☐ Backup
- ☐ Leg yield
- ☐ Sidepass
- ☐ Shoulder in

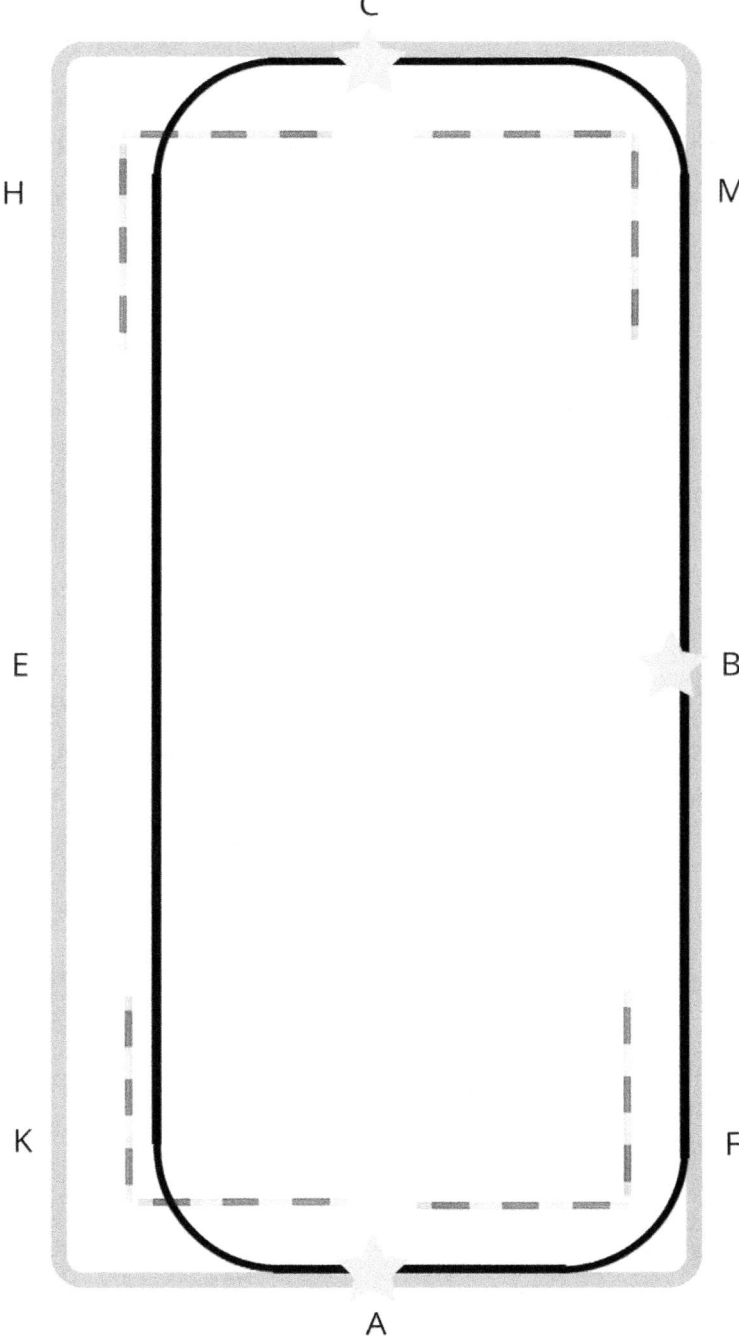

The Forbes

In this exercise you will work on accuracy and straightness in walk. You will be using poles to guide you to keep your horse out on the track in the arena, and make accurate turns. Aim to steer with your body rather than your hands.

Goal:

To be able to complete this pattern accurately in both directions with your horse working with relaxation and soft in your hand.

Tips:

- Look to where you want to go. This will also improve your horse's balance. When you look down you add extra weight to your horse's shoulders and front legs.

Poles: 8

Level: ★ ★

Benefits:

☑ Accuracy
☑ Rhythm
☑ Impulsion
☑ Straightness
☑ Suppleness & bend
☐ Lateral movement
　　& collection

Gaits:

☑ Groundwork
☑ Walk
☑ Trot
☑ Canter

Movements:

☐ Backup
☐ Leg yield
☐ Sidepass
☐ Shoulder in

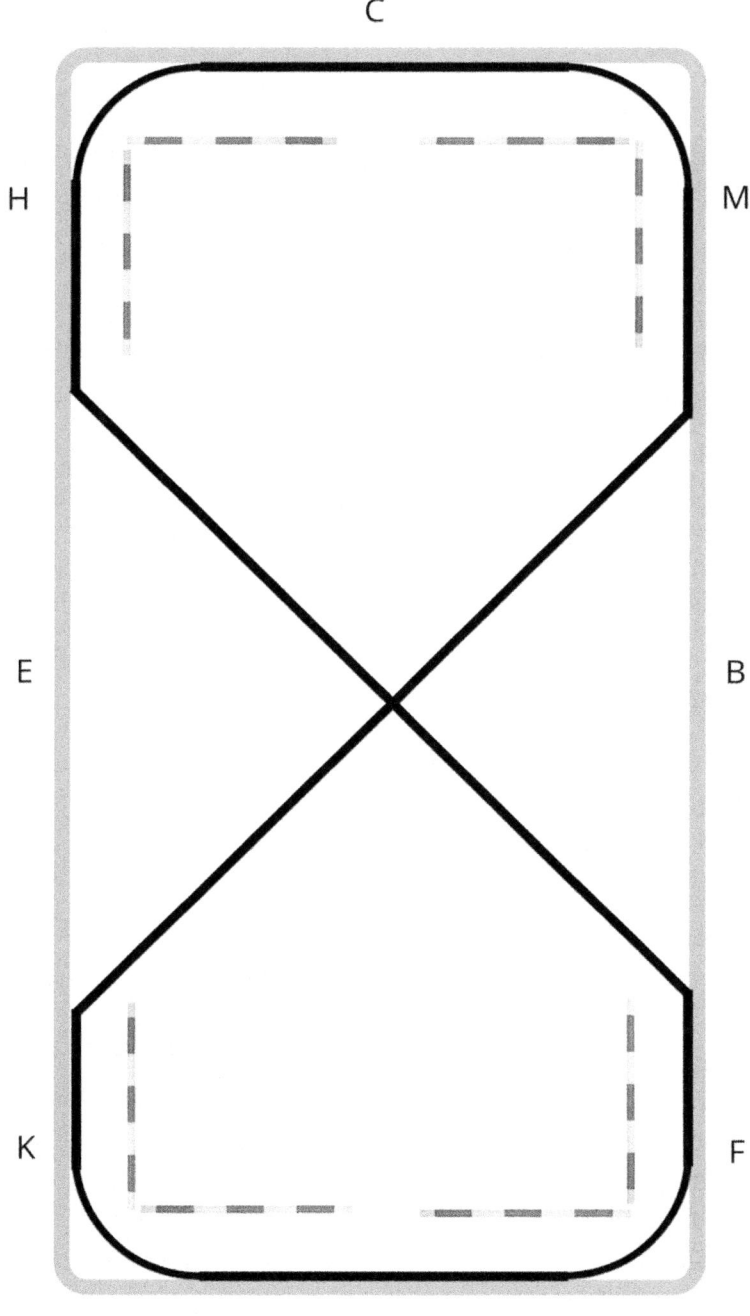

The Katherine

In this exercise you will develop the previous pattern to add transitions up and down. Make your transitions where indicated by the stars. Your horse should feel relaxed and forward before you go up a gait.

Goal: Your goal is to complete this pattern in both directions with relaxed and accurate transitions.

Tips:

- Ask for downward transitions through your body rather than relying on your hands. Breathe out and sit on your back pockets. Add a consistent voice cue.
- Relax your shoulders.

Poles: 8

Level: ★ ★

Benefits:

- ☑ Accuracy
- ☑ Rhythm
- ☑ Impulsion
- ☑ Straightness
- ☑ Suppleness & bend
- ☐ Lateral movement
      & collection

Gaits:

- ☑ Groundwork
- ☑ Walk
- ☑ Trot
- ☑ Canter

Movements:

- ☐ Backup
- ☐ Leg yield
- ☐ Sidepass
- ☐ Shoulder in

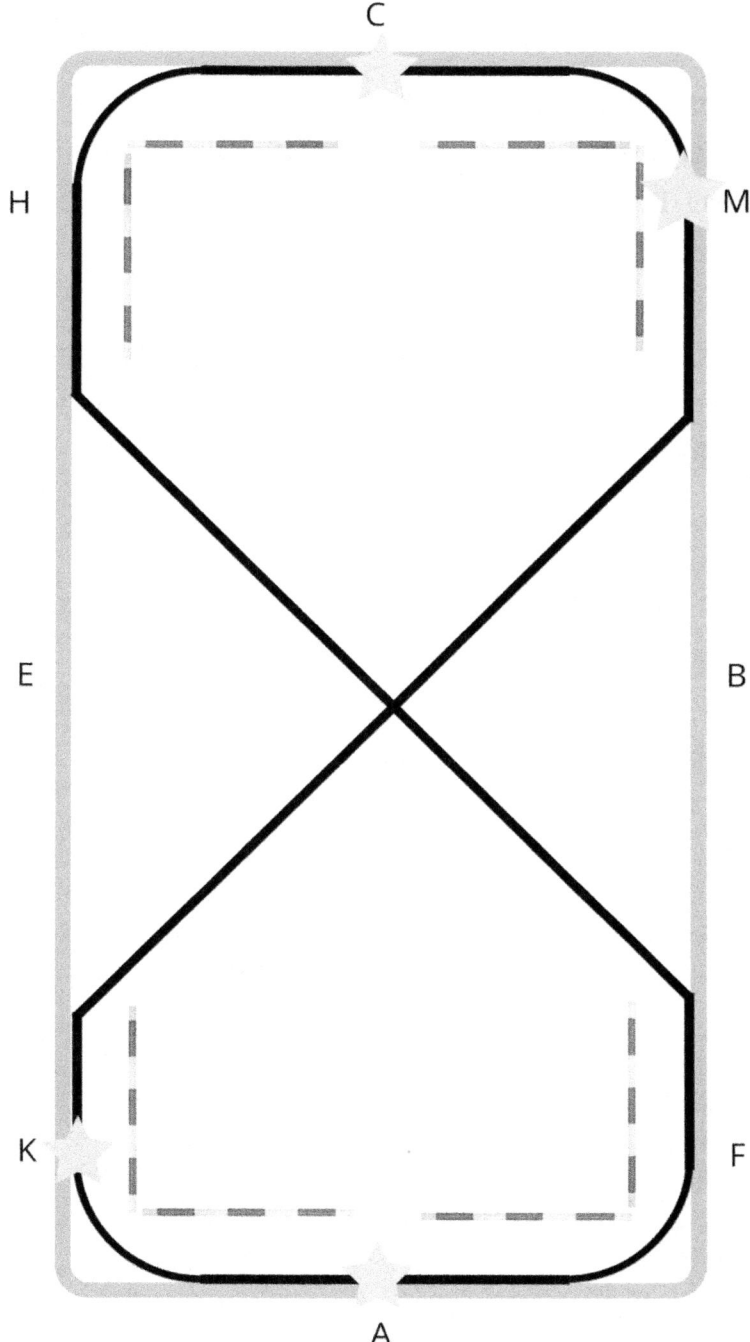

The Sydney

Ride up the centre line, then turn to the right. Then return to the centre line, back to where you started. Optionally you can add a rollback here. Ride up the centre line again and repeat in the opposite direction.

Goal: Your goal is to complete this exercise with your horse maintaining a rhythmic and consistent gait, with soft and correct bend and good straightness.

Tips:

- Look ahead to where you want to be.
- Think about asking for the bends and returning to straightness through your body, rather than with your hands.

Poles: 4

Level: ★ ★

Benefits:

- ☑ Accuracy
- ☑ Rhythm
- ☑ Impulsion
- ☑ Straightness
- ☑ Suppleness & bend
- ☐ Lateral movement
        & collection

Gaits:

- ☑ Groundwork
- ☑ Walk
- ☑ Trot
- ☑ Canter

Movements:

- ☐ Backup
- ☐ Leg yield
- ☐ Sidepass
- ☐ Shoulder in

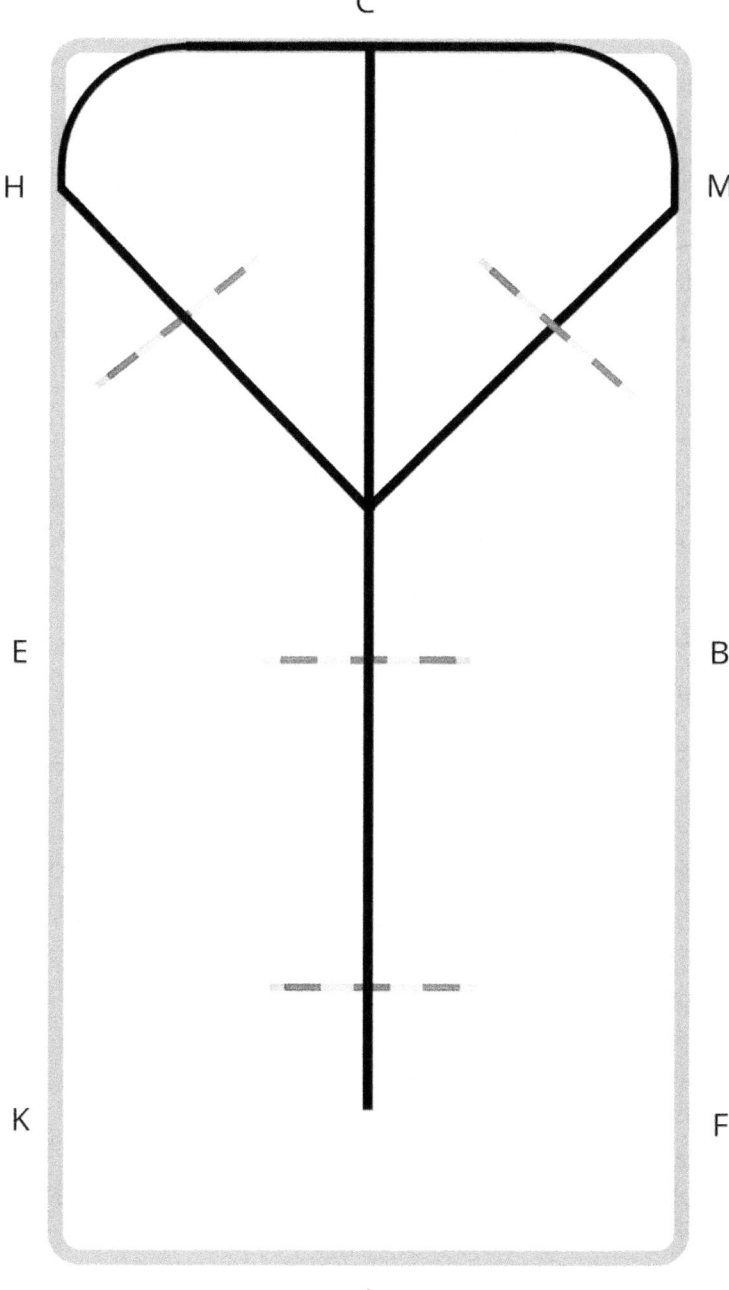

The Alice Springs

In this exercise you will introduce upward and downward transitions to the previous pattern. Make the transitions where indicated on the diagram by a star.

Goal: Your goal is for your horse to be able to complete this exercise in all gaits, maintaining soft and relaxed upward and downward transitions.

Tips:

- Relax your lower back.
- Think ahead to the transitions to prepare your horse.
- Are you still breathing?

Poles: 4

Level: ★ ★

Benefits:

- ☑ Accuracy
- ☑ Rhythm
- ☑ Impulsion
- ☑ Straightness
- ☑ Suppleness & bend
- ☐ Lateral movement
  & collection

Gaits:

- ☑ Groundwork
- ☑ Walk
- ☑ Trot
- ☑ Canter

Movements:

- ☐ Backup
- ☐ Leg yield
- ☐ Sidepass
- ☐ Shoulder in

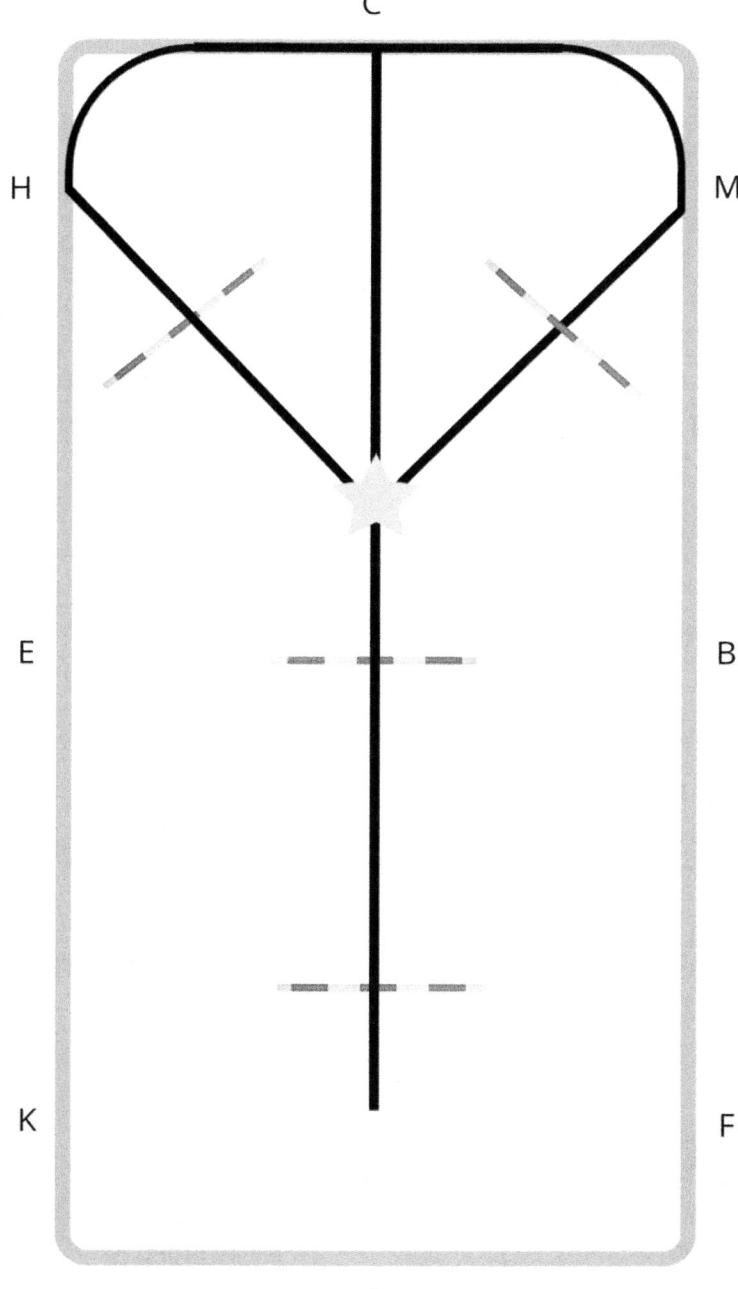

C

H

M

E

B

K

F

A

The Gold Coast

This exercise uses poles as guidance for accurate turns and straight lines across the arena. Practise in walk, focus on your horse maintaining a consistent gait and softness.

Goal:

To complete the pattern with your horse staying relaxed and in a rhythmic and consistent gait.

Tips:

- Ask for straightness from your body and through your focus, rather than relying on the reins.
- Look where you want to go.
- Relax your shoulders.

Poles: 4

Level: ★ ★

Benefits:

- ☑ Accuracy
- ☑ Rhythm
- ☑ Impulsion
- ☑ Straightness
- ☑ Suppleness & bend
- ☐ Lateral movement
  & collection

Gaits:

- ☑ Groundwork
- ☑ Walk
- ☑ Trot
- ☑ Canter

Movements:

- ☐ Backup
- ☐ Leg yield
- ☐ Sidepass
- ☐ Shoulder in

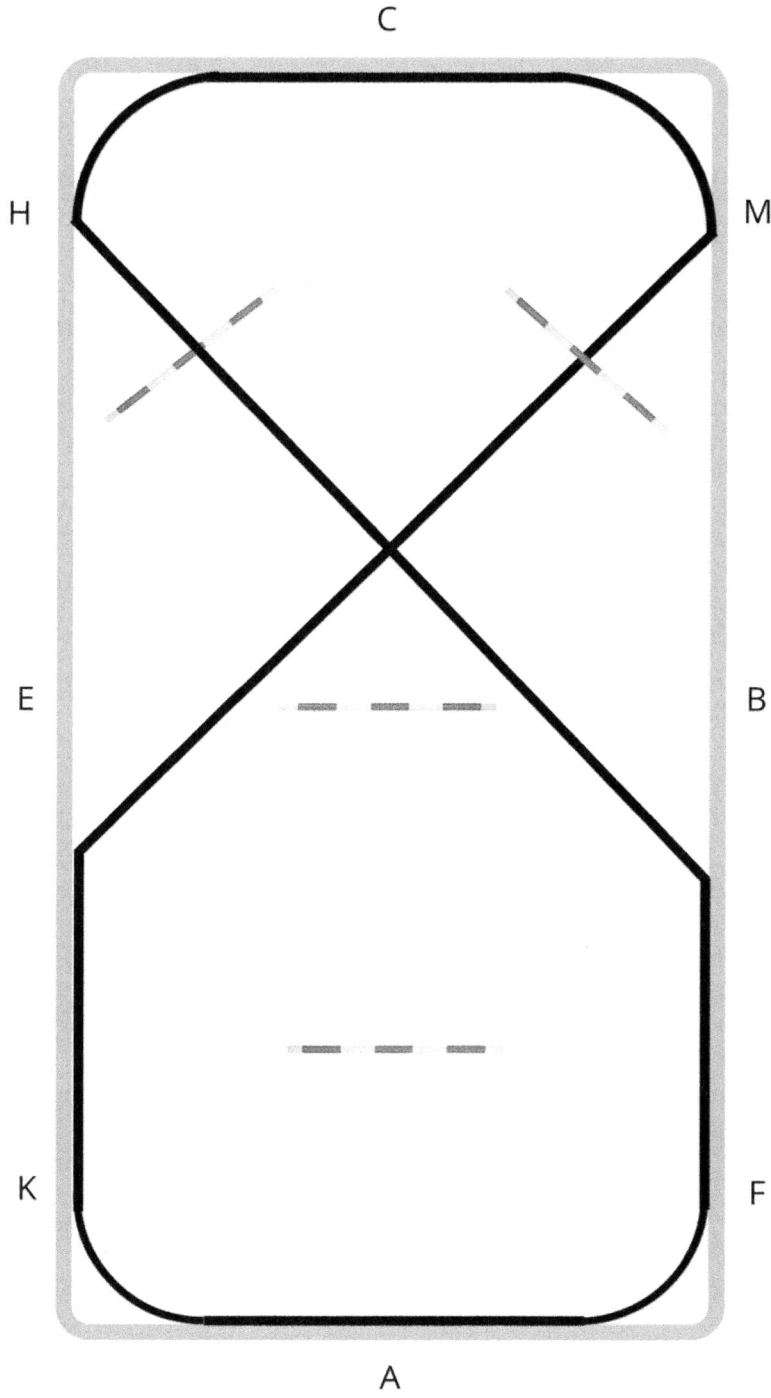

The Rockhampton

Develop the previous exercise by introducing accurate upward and downward transitions, as indicated by the stars. Start at the walk and work up to trot and canter when your horse feels ready.

Goal: Your horse will complete the exercise without rushing, staying soft in your hand and in rhythmic consistent gaits.

Tips:

- Try using the feel through your body to influence a consistent gait.
- Think ahead for the change of gait so that your horse is prepared.
- Don't forget to smile!

Poles: 4

Level: ★ ★

Benefits:

- ☑ Accuracy
- ☑ Rhythm
- ☑ Impulsion
- ☑ Straightness
- ☑ Suppleness & bend
- ☐ Lateral movement
      & collection

Gaits:

- ☑ Groundwork
- ☑ Walk
- ☑ Trot
- ☑ Canter

Movements:

- ☐ Backup
- ☐ Leg yield
- ☐ Sidepass
- ☐ Shoulder in

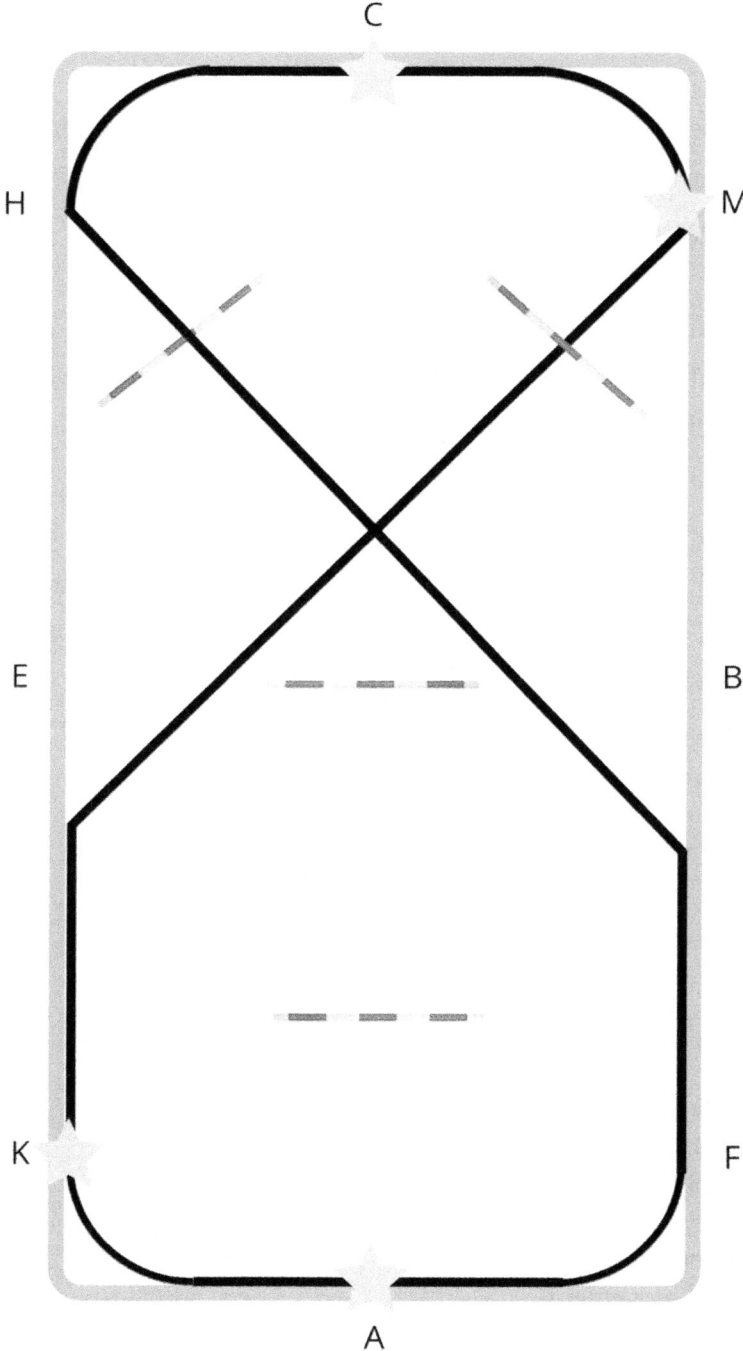

The Barossa

This exercise combines straightness and bend to work on focus and balance. Start between H and M. Then complete the pattern in the opposite direction.

Goal: Your horse will complete the exercise accurately, moving over the centre of the poles and with the correct bend on the corners and half circles.

Tips:

- Aim to use your body to influence turns and straightness rather than relying on the reins.
- Lift your outside hip up slightly to encourage a bend in your horse's body without relying on the reins too much.
- Keep your shoulders level.

Poles: 4

Level: ★ ★

Benefits:

- ☑ Accuracy
- ☑ Rhythm
- ☑ Impulsion
- ☑ Straightness
- ☑ Suppleness & bend
- ☐ Lateral movement
       & collection

Gaits:

- ☑ Groundwork
- ☑ Walk
- ☑ Trot
- ☑ Canter

Movements:

- ☐ Backup
- ☐ Leg yield
- ☐ Sidepass
- ☐ Shoulder in

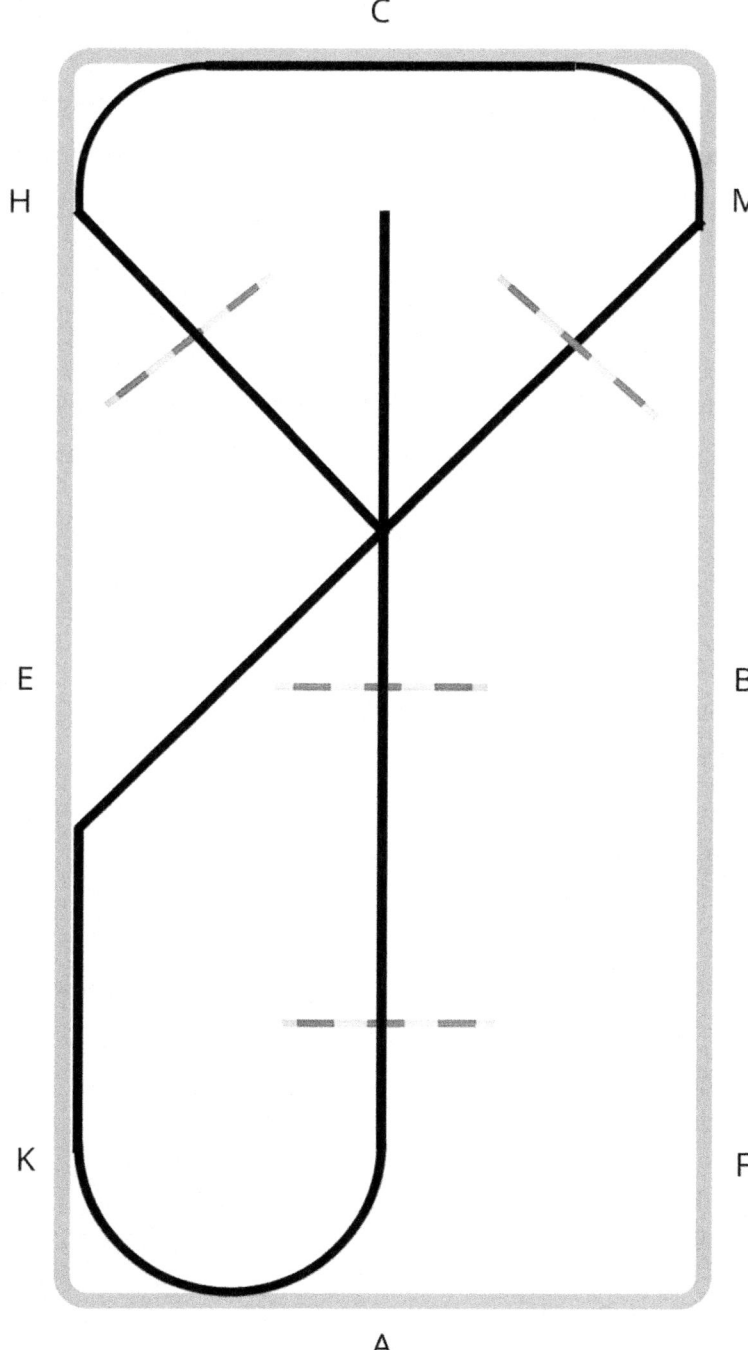

The Hunter Valley

Develop the previous exercise by introducing upward and downward transitions accurately as indicated by the stars. Start at the walk and work up to trot and canter when your horse feels ready.

Goal:

Your horse will complete the exercise accurately, moving over the centre of the poles and with the correct bend on the corners and half circles.

Tips:

- Aim to make downward transitions from your body rather than relying on your hands.
- Keep your hands close together at the pommel. No one should be able to see them move.

Poles: 4

Level: ★ ★

Benefits:

- ☑ Accuracy
- ☑ Rhythm
- ☑ Impulsion
- ☑ Straightness
- ☑ Suppleness & bend
- ☐ Lateral movement
    & collection

Gaits:

- ☑ Groundwork
- ☑ Walk
- ☑ Trot
- ☑ Canter

Movements:

- ☐ Backup
- ☐ Leg yield
- ☐ Sidepass
- ☐ Shoulder in

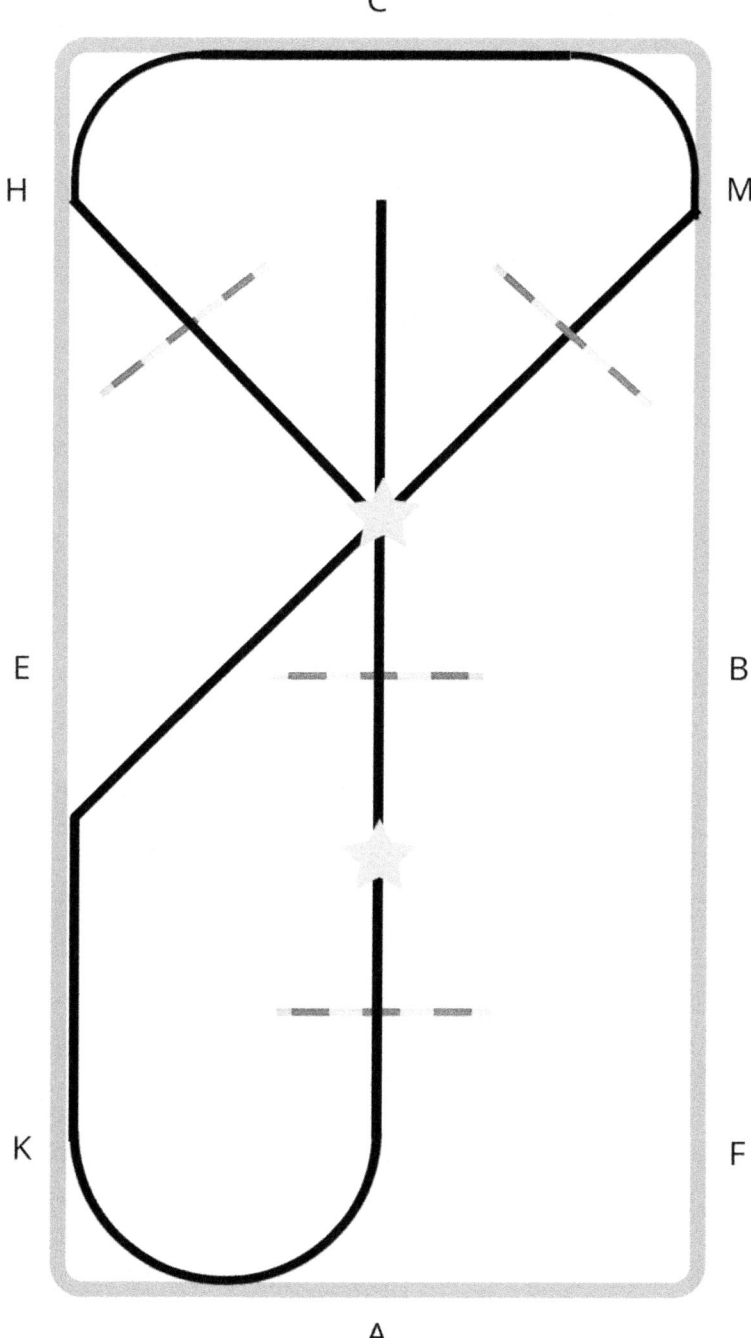

C

H

M

E

B

K

F

A

18 Advanced Flatwork Exercises

The London

In this exercise you will use the poles as guides to ride accurate circles. Do the exercise at the walk, thinking about working in a soft bend and a good rhythm. Start at one end of the arena, ride a circle. Change direction in the middle of the arena while riding over the centre of the pole.

Goal:

Your horse will complete the exercise accurately, moving over the centre of the poles and with the correct bend on the corners and half circles, without relying too much on your reins.

Tips: Lift your outside seat bone slightly to ask for bend. Make sure you pass over the poles accurately, which will help to keep the size of your circles consistent.

Poles: 5

Level: ★ ★ ★

Benefits:

- ☑ Accuracy
- ☑ Rhythm
- ☑ Impulsion
- ☑ Straightness
- ☑ Suppleness & bend
- ☐ Lateral movement
      & collection

Gaits:

- ☑ Groundwork
- ☑ Walk
- ☑ Trot
- ☑ Canter

Movements:

- ☐ Backup
- ☐ Leg yield
- ☐ Sidepass
- ☐ Shoulder in

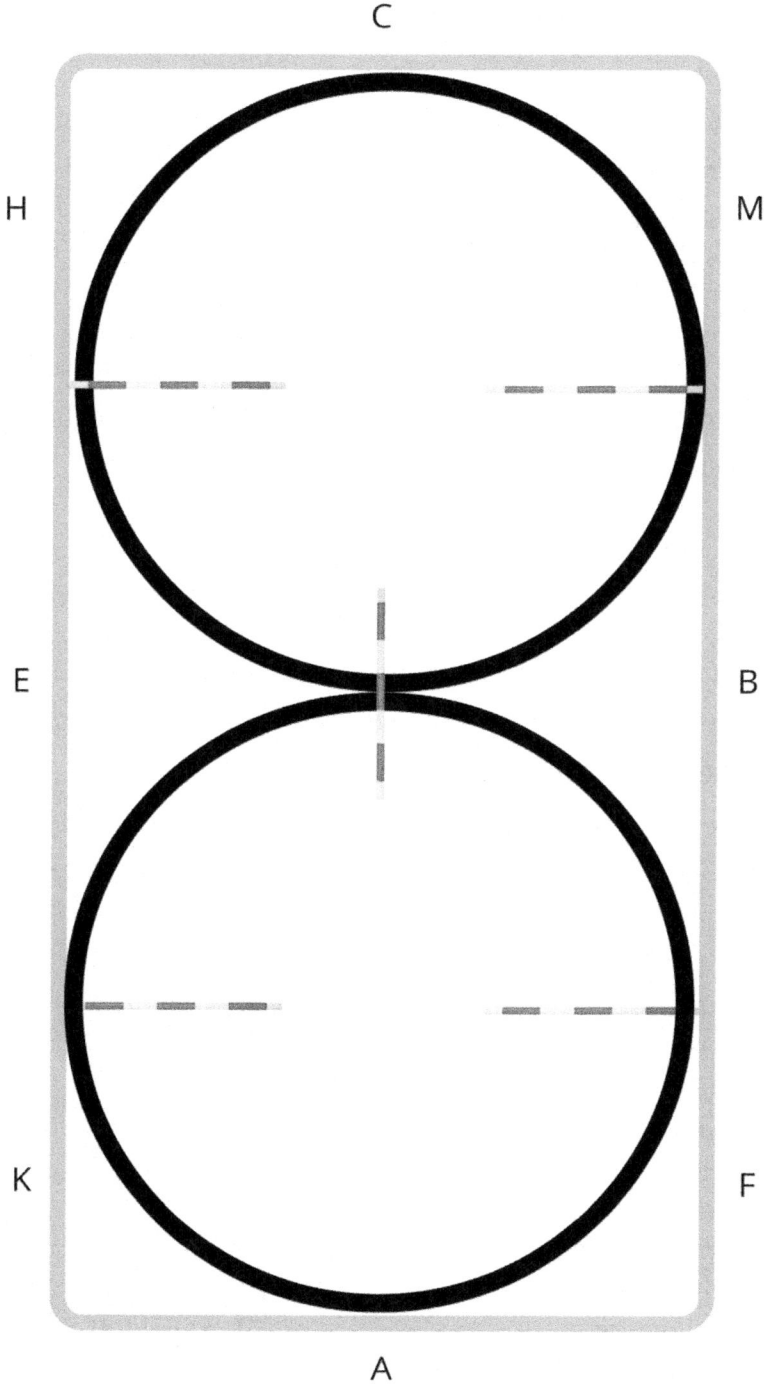

The Mayfield

This exercise develops the previous one by introducing upward and downward transitions. Make the transitions where indicated by the stars. Try first at trot in both directions, then in canter.

Goal:

Your goal is to be able to do this exercise accurately with smooth and relaxed upward and downward transitions.

Tips:

- Ask for downward transitions through your body rather than relying on your hands. Breathe out and sit on your back pockets. Add a consistent voice cue.
- Look where you want to go.

Poles: 5

Level: ★ ★ ★

Benefits:

- ☑ Accuracy
- ☑ Rhythm
- ☑ Impulsion
- ☑ Straightness
- ☑ Suppleness & bend
- ☐ Lateral movement
    & collection

Gaits:

- ☑ Groundwork
- ☑ Walk
- ☑ Trot
- ☑ Canter

Movements:

- ☐ Backup
- ☐ Leg yield
- ☐ Sidepass
- ☐ Shoulder in

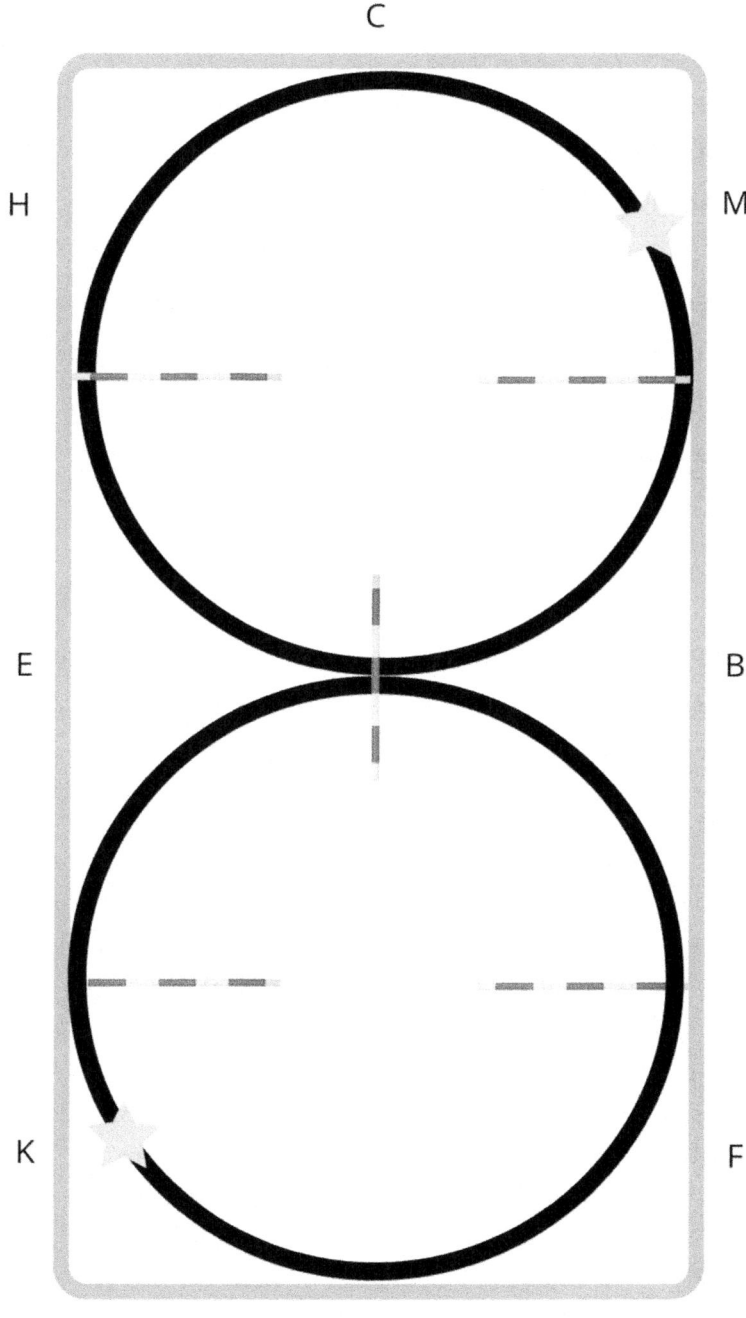

The Gatwick

Ride this pattern at the walk. Make sure that you ride accurately over the centre of the poles. Aim to turn from your body without relying too much on your reins.

Goal: Your goal is to be able to complete this exercise accurately at the walk, with your horse having a consistent and rhythmic gait. You should be riding mainly from your body without relying too heavily on the reins.

Tips:

- Smile you are having fun!
- Allow your hips to move side to side with the swing of your horse's barrel.
- Keep your shoulders relaxed and level.

Poles: 5

Level: ★ ★ ★

Benefits:

- ☑ Accuracy
- ☑ Rhythm
- ☑ Impulsion
- ☑ Straightness
- ☑ Suppleness & bend
- ☐ Lateral movement
        & collection

Gaits:

- ☑ Groundwork
- ☑ Walk
- ☑ Trot
- ☑ Canter

Movements:

- ☐ Backup
- ☐ Leg yield
- ☐ Sidepass
- ☐ Shoulder in

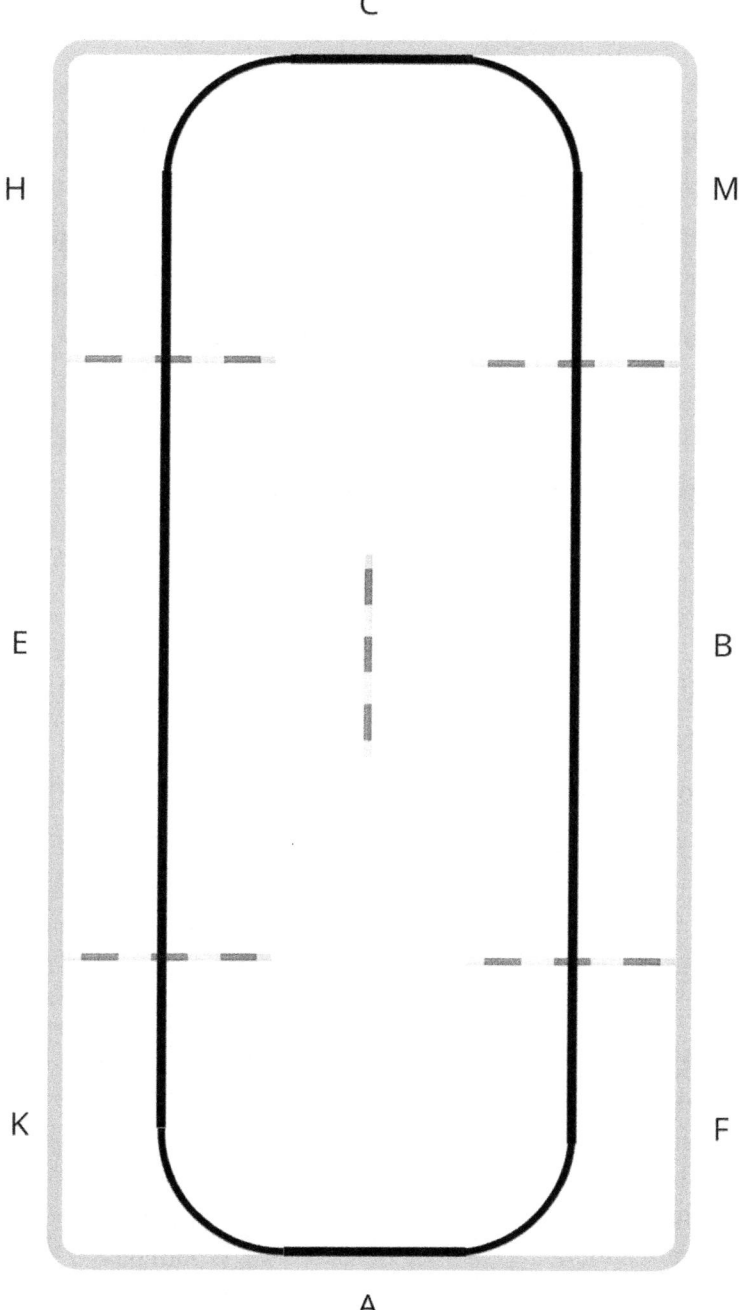

The Bedford

Add accurate and relaxed upward and downward transitions to the previous exercise. Work first at the walk. When your horse is relaxed and feels ready make upward and downward trot transitions where indicated by the stars. Pass over the centre of the poles to help yourself to ride accurately. Add canter transitions when you feel your horse is ready. Work in both directions.

Goal: Your goal is to be able to do this exercise accurately with smooth and relaxed upward and downward transitions.

Tips:

- Aim to ask for downward transitions from your body rather than relying on your reins.
- Are you still breathing regularly?

Poles: 5

Level: ★ ★

Benefits:

- ☑ Accuracy
- ☑ Rhythm
- ☑ Impulsion
- ☑ Straightness
- ☑ Suppleness & bend
- ☐ Lateral movement & collection

Gaits:

- ☑ Groundwork
- ☑ Walk
- ☑ Trot
- ☑ Canter

Movements:

- ☐ Backup
- ☐ Leg yield
- ☐ Sidepass
- ☐ Shoulder in

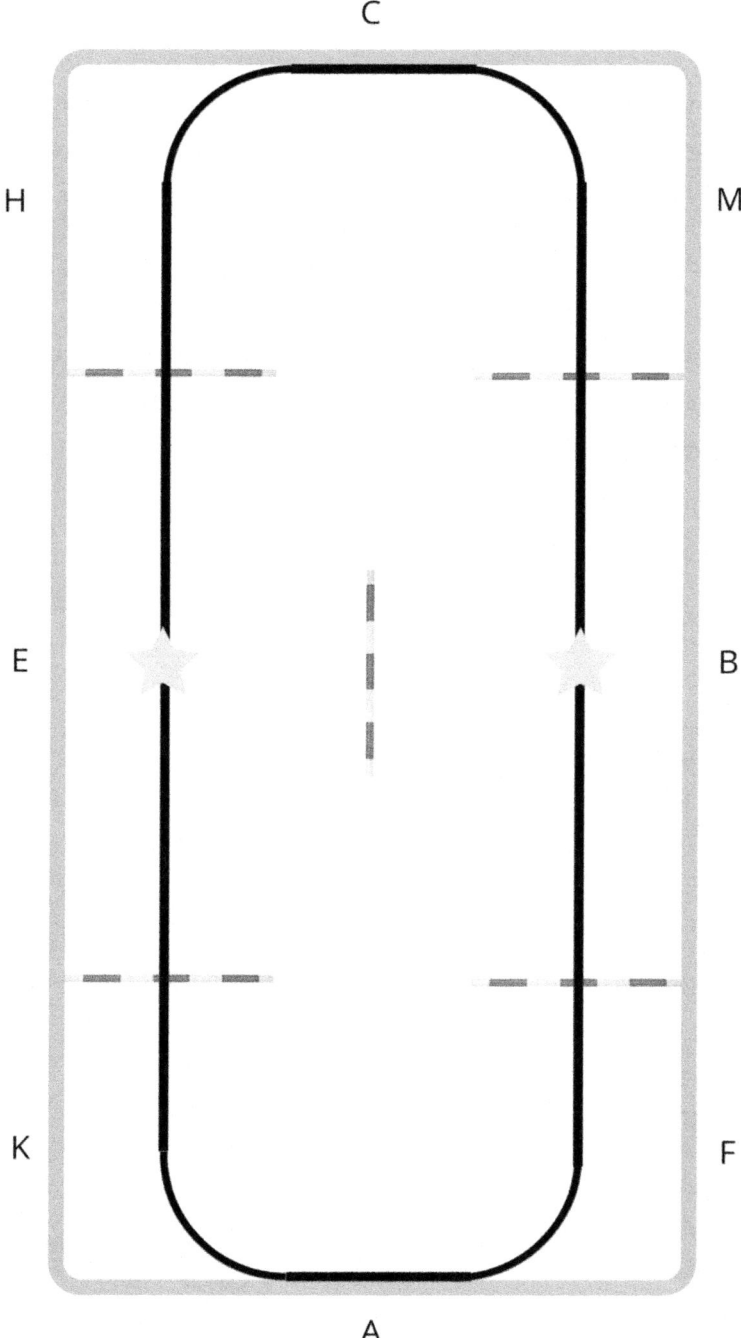

The Canterbury

Ride at the walk, passing accurately over the middle of the poles. Change direction in the centre of the arena by riding over the middle of the pole. Pay attention to your horse maintaining an even and relaxed walk.

Goal: Your horse should be able to complete the pattern accurately with consistent gait and rhythm and soft bend on the turns. You should be riding mostly from your body without an over-reliance on the reins.

Tips:

- Keep your head up and look to where you want to go.
- Is your lower back relaxed and moving with the swing of your horse's body?

Poles: 5

Level: ★ ★ ★

Benefits:

- ☑ Accuracy
- ☑ Rhythm
- ☑ Impulsion
- ☑ Straightness
- ☑ Suppleness & bend
- ☐ Lateral movement
  & collection

Gaits:

- ☑ Groundwork
- ☑ Walk
- ☑ Trot
- ☑ Canter

Movements:

- ☐ Backup
- ☐ Leg yield
- ☐ Sidepass
- ☐ Shoulder in

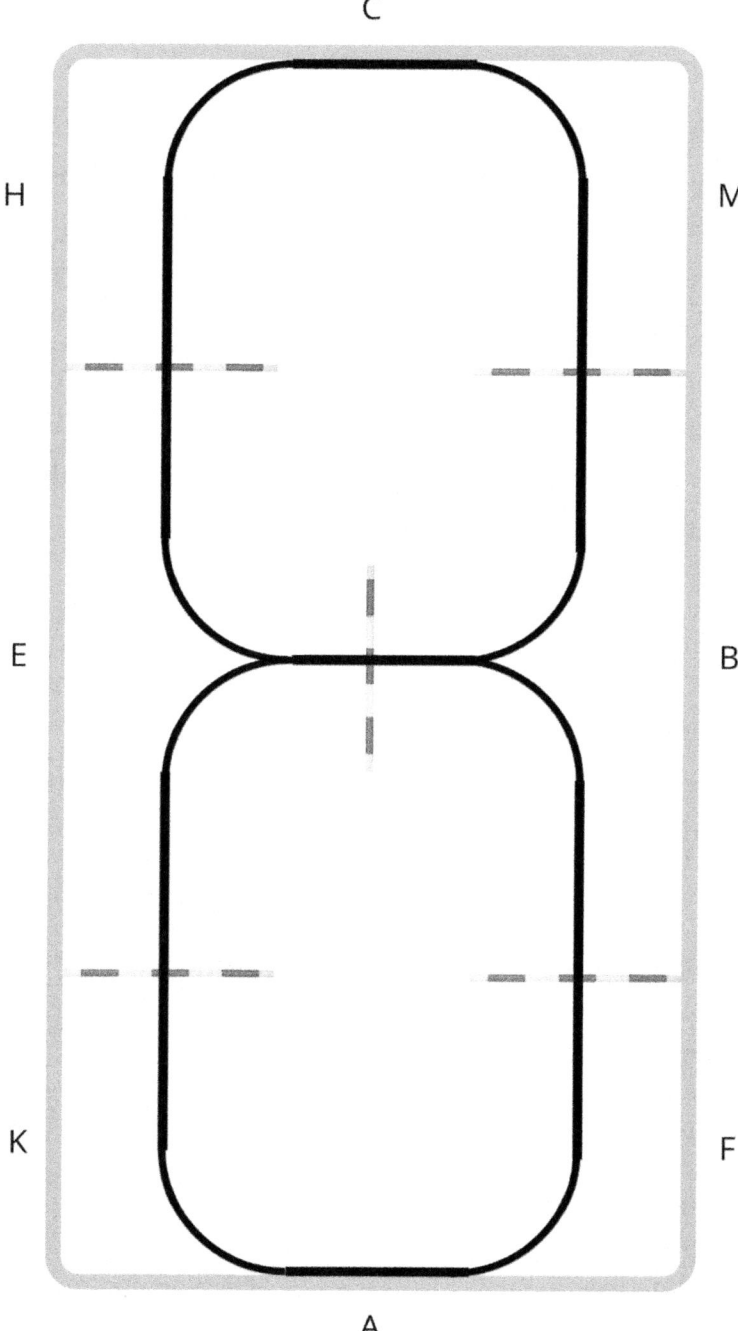

C

H

M

E

B

K

F

A

The Oxford

Add upward and downward transitions to the previous exercise, using the stars as markers. Change direction as you cross over the pole in the centre and pass over the middle of the outside poles. Transition from walk to trot and make sure your horse is relaxed before attempting canter transitions.

Goal: To be able to ride the pattern accurately with relaxed transitions in both directions. Your goal is to be riding mostly from your body without relying heavily on your hands.

Tips:

- Remember to smile.
- Change the bend in your horse's body before you change direction.

Poles: 5

Level: ★ ★ ★

Benefits:

- ☑ Accuracy
- ☑ Rhythm
- ☑ Impulsion
- ☑ Straightness
- ☑ Suppleness & bend
- ☐ Lateral movement
  & collection

Gaits:

- ☑ Groundwork
- ☑ Walk
- ☑ Trot
- ☑ Canter

Movements:

- ☐ Backup
- ☐ Leg yield
- ☐ Sidepass
- ☐ Shoulder in

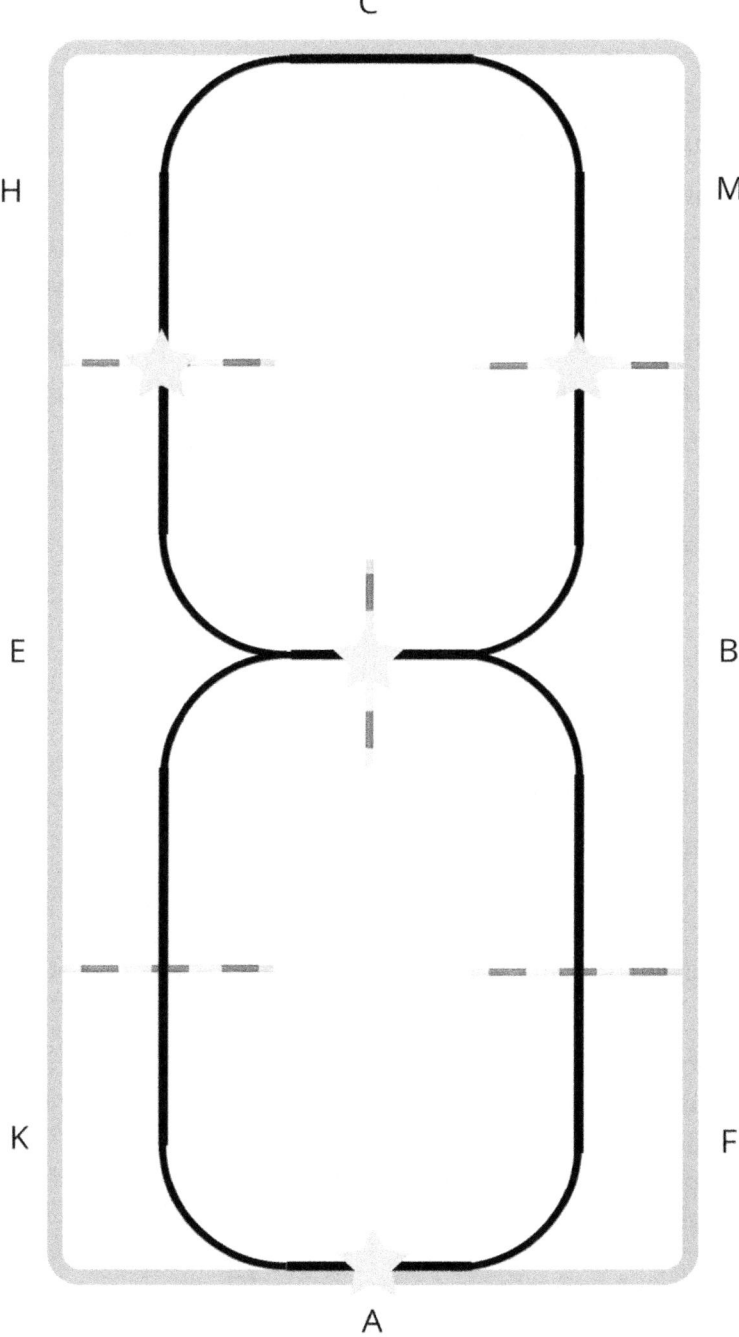

The Nottingham

This exercise uses poles to encourage you to ride your horse accurately and practise straightness. The two poles in the middle will encourage focus. Work at a walk in both directions. Think about straightness and use your inside leg to ask your horse to move his body into the corners. Encourage the bend by slightly lifting the weight off your outside seat bone. Avoid trying to pull your horse into the corners with the reins. When you ride it should be 90% seat and 10% reins.

Goal: Your goal is to be able to do this exercise accurately with a happy horse.

Tips:

- Lift your outside hip bone a little to ask for bend on the corners.

Poles: 2

Level: ★ ★ ★

Benefits:

- ☑ Accuracy
- ☑ Rhythm
- ☑ Impulsion
- ☑ Straightness
- ☑ Suppleness & bend
- ☐ Lateral movement
        & collection

Gaits:

- ☑ Groundwork
- ☑ Walk
- ☑ Trot
- ☑ Canter

Movements:

- ☐ Backup
- ☐ Leg yield
- ☐ Sidepass
- ☐ Shoulder in

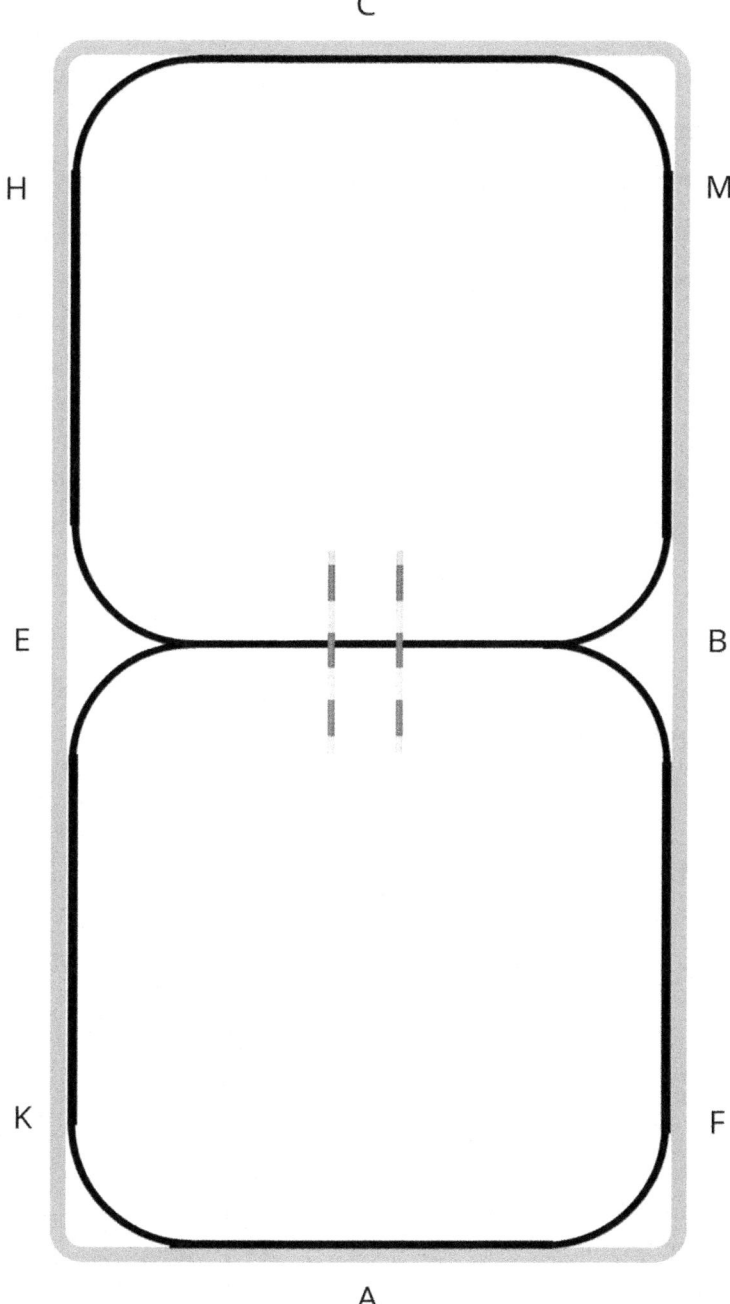

The Bath

This exercise develops the previous one by introducing upward and downward transitions. Make the transitions where indicated by the stars, with upward transitions as you move away from the poles and downward transitions as you approach them. Try first at trot in both directions, then in canter.

Goal:

Your goal is to be able to complete the exercise with relaxed and accurate transitions.

Tips:

- Keep your head up and look to where you want to be.
- Are your shoulders relaxed and level?

Poles: 2

Level: ★ ★ ★

Benefits:

- ☑ Accuracy
- ☑ Rhythm
- ☑ Impulsion
- ☑ Straightness
- ☑ Suppleness & bend
- ☐ Lateral movement
  & collection

Gaits:

- ☑ Groundwork
- ☑ Walk
- ☑ Trot
- ☑ Canter

Movements:

- ☐ Backup
- ☐ Leg yield
- ☐ Sidepass
- ☐ Shoulder in

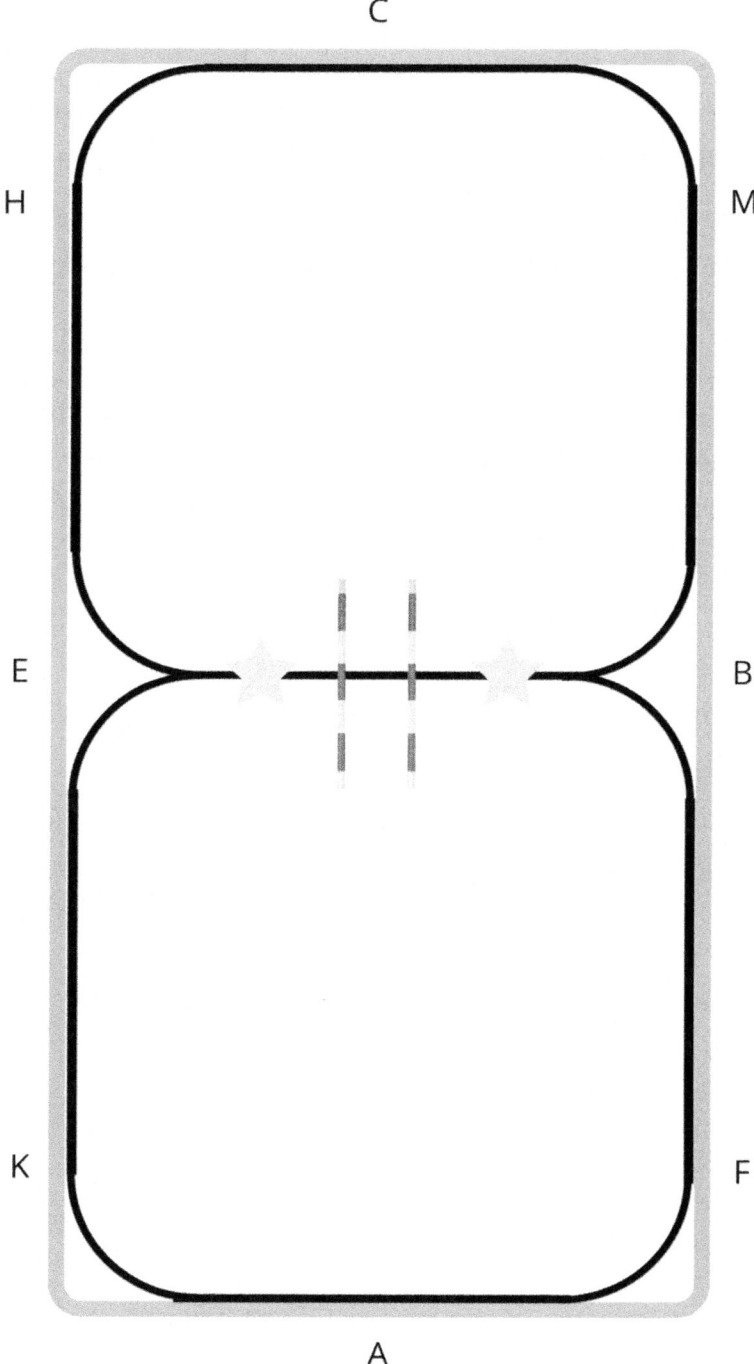

The Cambridge

In this exercise you will use the poles as guides to ride accurate circles. Do the exercise at the walk, thinking about working in a soft bend and a good rhythm. Start at one end of the arena, ride a circle. Change direction in the middle of the arena while riding over the centre of the poles.

Goal: Your goal is to be able to complete the exercise accurately while your horse stays relaxed and maintains a rhythmic gait. Your horse should be passing over the poles without touching them.

Tips:

- Lift your outside seat bone slightly to encourage bend.
- Don't forget to breathe. Can you count your breaths?
- Keep your hands close together at the pommel. No one should be able to see them move.

Poles: 2

Level: ★ ★ ★

Benefits:
- ☑ Accuracy
- ☑ Rhythm
- ☑ Impulsion
- ☑ Straightness
- ☑ Suppleness & bend
- ☐ Lateral movement
     & collection

Gaits:
- ☑ Groundwork
- ☑ Walk
- ☑ Trot
- ☑ Canter

Movements:
- ☐ Backup
- ☐ Leg yield
- ☐ Sidepass
- ☐ Shoulder in

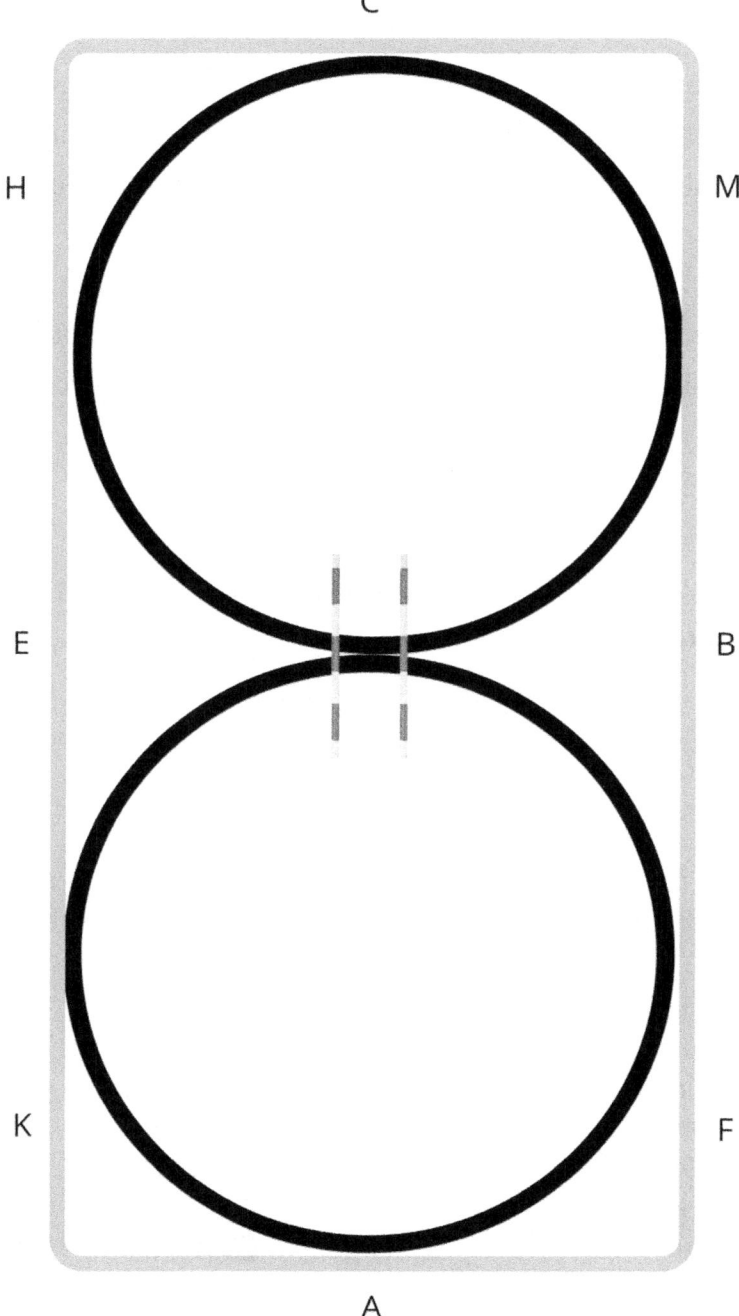

The Heathrow

Develop the previous exercises by introducing upward and downward transitions where indicated by the stars. Make sure that you are established in consistency and bend before moving to a faster gait.

Goal: To be able to complete this pattern in both directions with relaxed transitions while maintaining gait, soft bend and relaxation.

Tips:

- Aim to ask for downward transitions from your body rather than relying on your reins.
- Allow your hips to move side to side with the swing of your horse's barrel.

Poles: 2

Level: ★ ★ ★

Benefits:

- ☑ Accuracy
- ☑ Rhythm
- ☑ Impulsion
- ☑ Straightness
- ☑ Suppleness & bend
- ☐ Lateral movement
  & collection

Gaits:

- ☑ Groundwork
- ☑ Walk
- ☑ Trot
- ☑ Canter

Movements:

- ☐ Backup
- ☐ Leg yield
- ☐ Sidepass
- ☐ Shoulder in

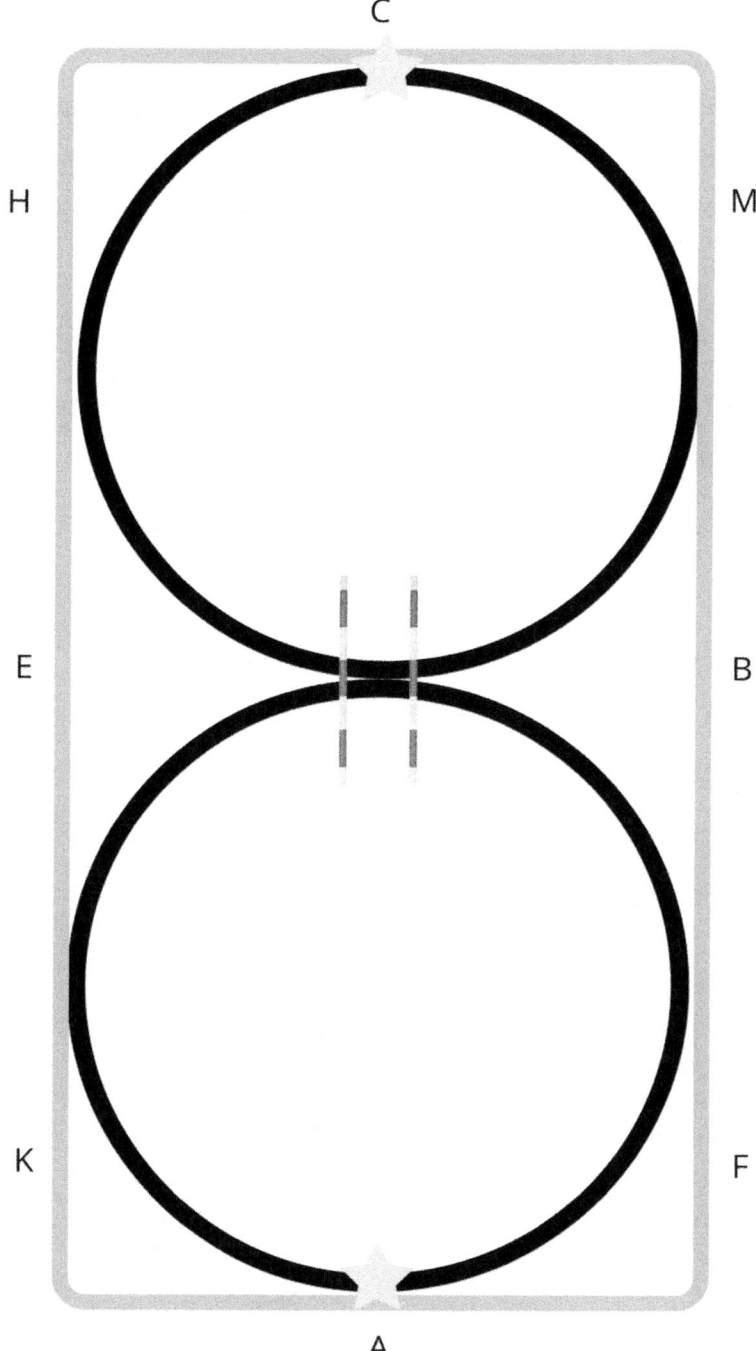

The Bristol

In this exercise you will work on accuracy, straightness and soft bend. Aim to steer with your body rather than your hands. Keep your turns soft and consistent and your lines straight.

Goal:

To be able to complete this pattern accurately in both directions with your horse moving with relaxation and soft in your hand.

Tips:

- Keep your head up and look to where you want to be.
- Relax your shoulders and breathe.
- When you ride you should use 90% seat and 10% reins.

Poles: 2

Level: ★ ★ ★

Benefits:

- ☑ Accuracy
- ☑ Rhythm
- ☑ Impulsion
- ☑ Straightness
- ☑ Suppleness & bend
- ☐ Lateral movement
  & collection

Gaits:

- ☑ Groundwork
- ☑ Walk
- ☑ Trot
- ☑ Canter

Movements:

- ☐ Backup
- ☐ Leg yield
- ☐ Sidepass
- ☐ Shoulder in

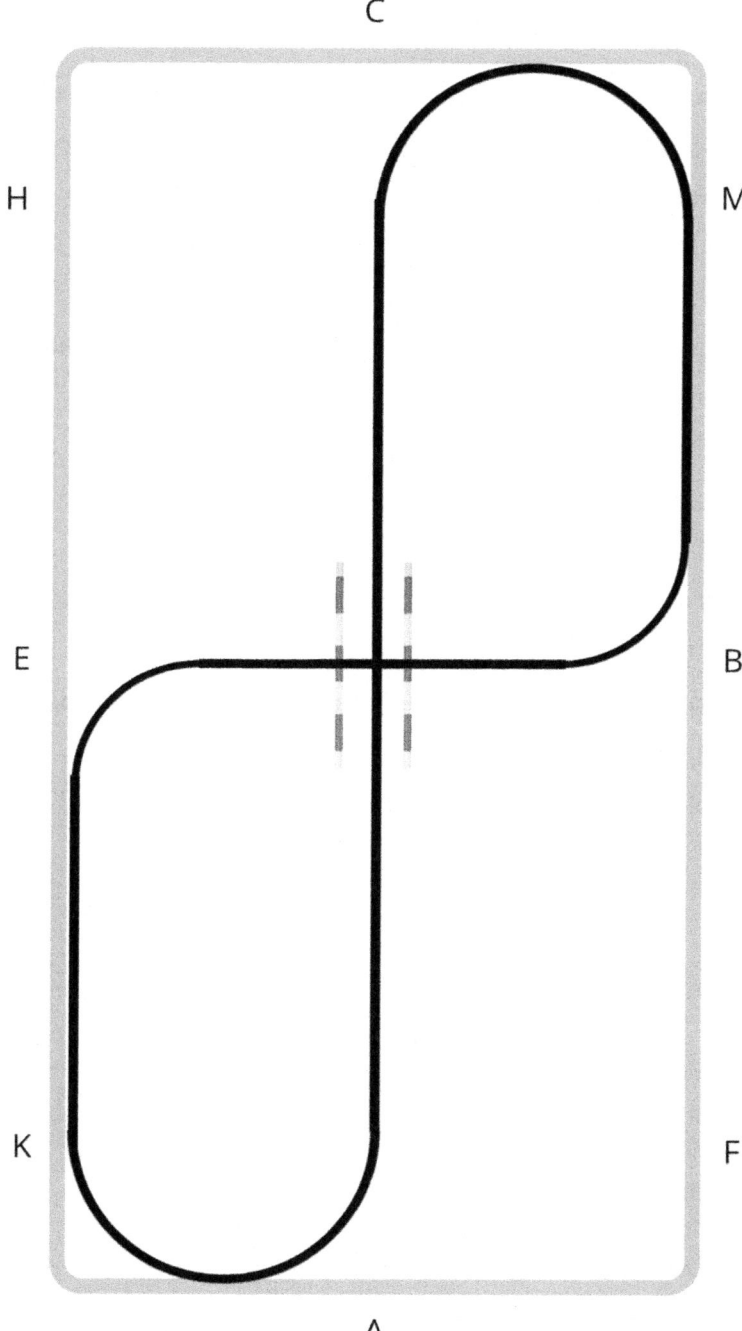

C

H

M

E

B

K

F

A

The Ashbourne

In this exercise you will develop the previous exercise to add transitions up and down. Make your transitions where indicated by the stars. Your horse should feel relaxed and forward before you go up a gait.

Goal: Your goal is to complete this pattern in both directions with relaxed and accurate transitions.

Tips:

- Experiment with how small and subtle your cues for transitions can be.
- Ask for downward transitions through your body rather than relying on your hands.
- Smile!

Poles: 2

Level: ★ ★ ★

Benefits:

- ☑ Accuracy
- ☑ Rhythm
- ☑ Impulsion
- ☑ Straightness
- ☑ Suppleness & bend
- ☐ Lateral movement
      & collection

Gaits:

- ☑ Groundwork
- ☑ Walk
- ☑ Trot
- ☑ Canter

Movements:

- ☐ Backup
- ☐ Leg yield
- ☐ Sidepass
- ☐ Shoulder in

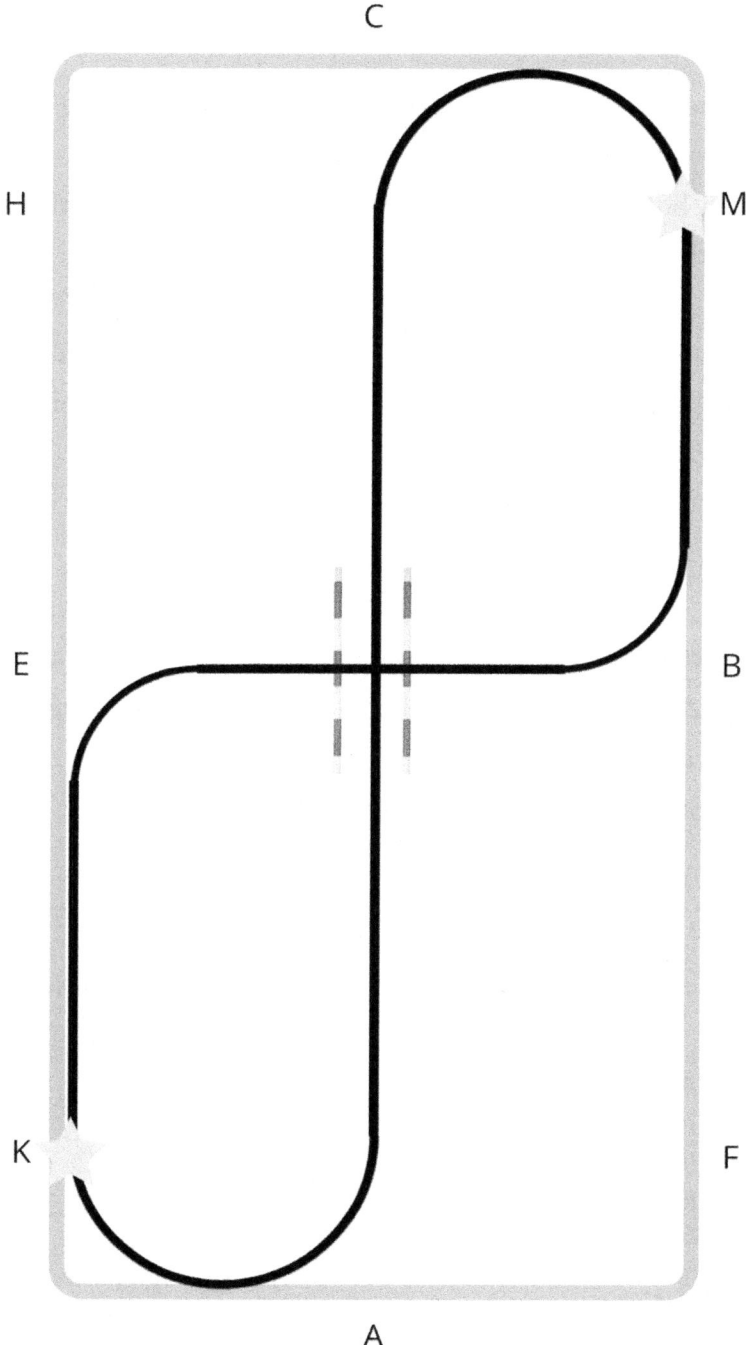

The Liverpool

Work at the walk and use the poles to guide you in making accurate turns and riding straight to the other side of the arena. Remember to work in both directions. Try to use your body rather than your hands for the turns.

Goal: Your goal is to be able to complete this exercise accurately with your horse working softly with rhythm and keeping out on the track and corners.

Tips:

- If your horse starts to wander off the outside track think about pushing with your inside leg rather than using the rein to correct them.
- Look up and focus where you want to go.

Poles: 4

Level: ★ ★ ★

Benefits:

- ☑ Accuracy
- ☑ Rhythm
- ☑ Impulsion
- ☑ Straightness
- ☑ Suppleness & bend
- ☐ Lateral movement
  & collection

Gaits:

- ☑ Groundwork
- ☑ Walk
- ☑ Trot
- ☑ Canter

Movements:

- ☐ Backup
- ☐ Leg yield
- ☐ Sidepass
- ☐ Shoulder in

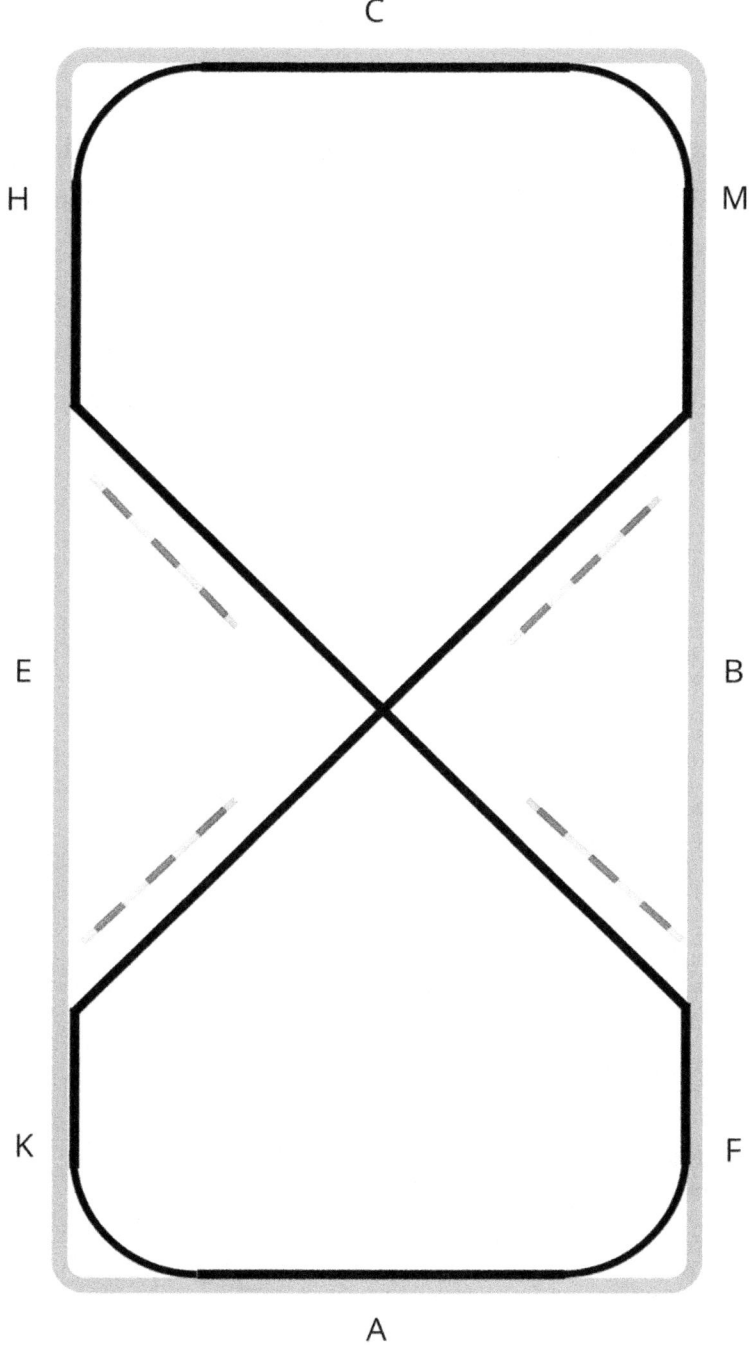

The Manchester

This exercise develops the previous one by introducing upward and downward transitions. Make the transitions where indicated by the stars. Practise walk to trot transitions in both directions, then when your horse feels relaxed and forward go for canter.

Goal: When working with transitions your goal is always for them to be smooth and relaxed. Your horse will be consistent and rhythmic in the gaits.

Tips:

- Quit on a good note, even if you haven't managed to canter yet.
- Relax your shoulders.
- Look where you are going.

Poles: 4

Level: ★ ★ ★

Benefits:

- ☑ Accuracy
- ☑ Rhythm
- ☑ Impulsion
- ☑ Straightness
- ☑ Suppleness & bend
- ☐ Lateral movement
      & collection

Gaits:

- ☑ Groundwork
- ☑ Walk
- ☑ Trot
- ☑ Canter

Movements:

- ☐ Backup
- ☐ Leg yield
- ☐ Sidepass
- ☐ Shoulder in

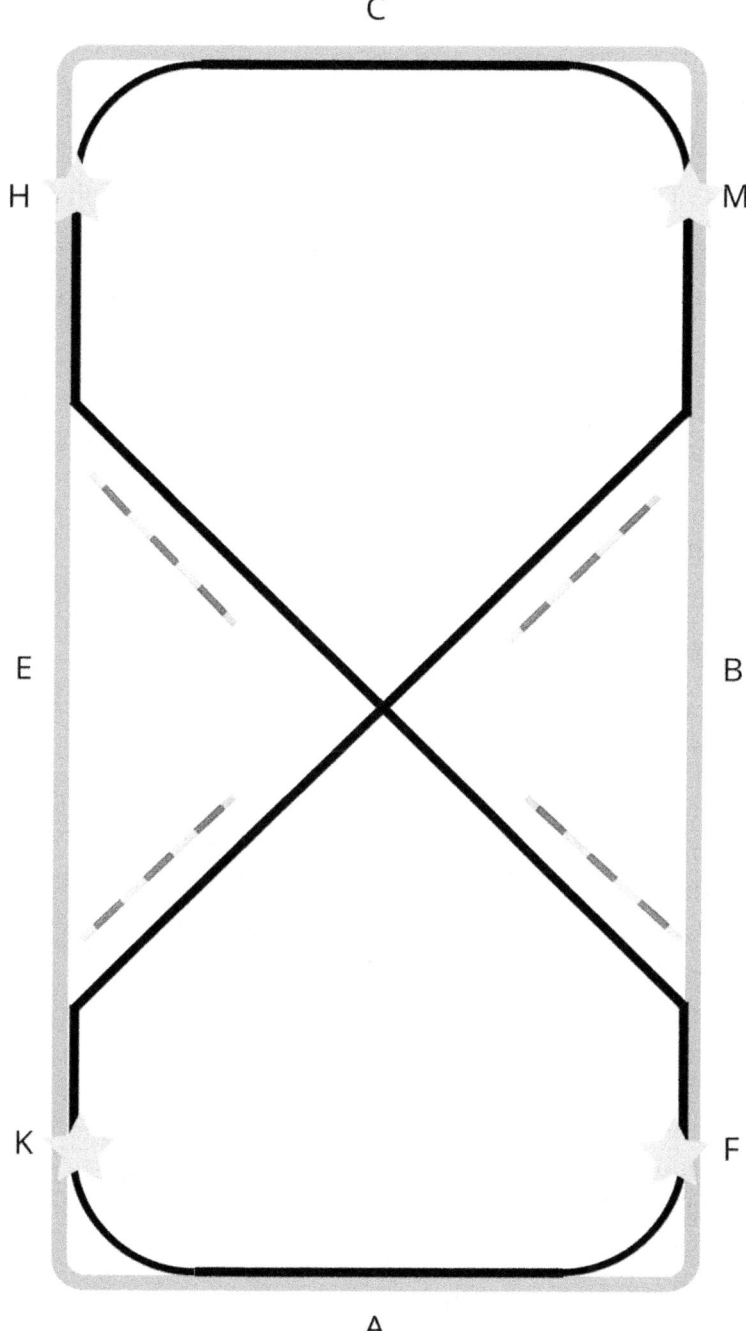

The Preston

Ride this exercise in walk in both directions. The placement of the poles will help you to work away from the fence and maintain straight lines. They will also encourage your horse to lift their feet.

Goal: To complete the pattern with your horse staying relaxed and in a rhythmic and consistent gait.

Tips:

- Feel the movement of your horse barrel through your legs to encourage a rhythmic walk.
- Keep your head up and look where you want to be.
- Relax your lower back.

Poles: 4

Level: ★ ★ ★

Benefits:

- ☑ Accuracy
- ☑ Rhythm
- ☑ Impulsion
- ☑ Straightness
- ☑ Suppleness & bend
- ☐ Lateral movement
  & collection

Gaits:

- ☑ Groundwork
- ☑ Walk
- ☑ Trot
- ☑ Canter

Movements:

- ☐ Backup
- ☐ Leg yield
- ☐ Sidepass
- ☐ Shoulder in

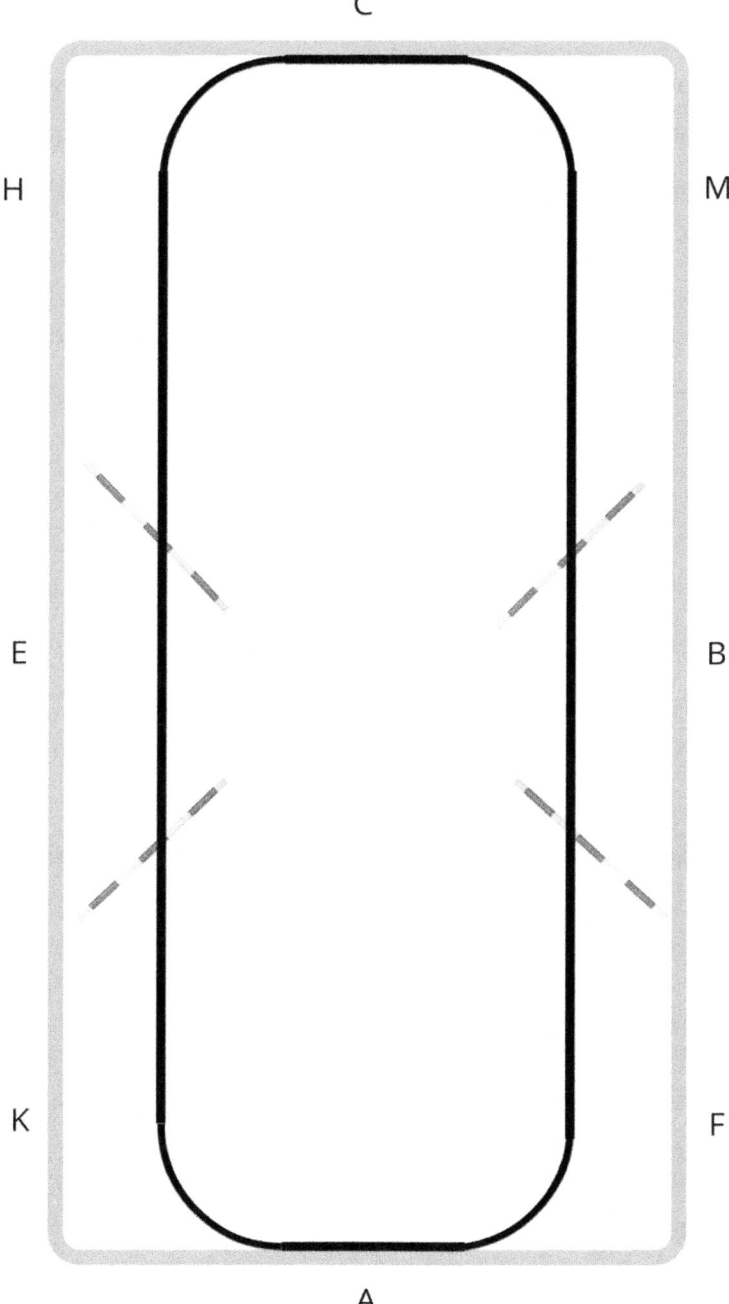

The Southhampton

Develop the previous exercise by introducing upward and downward transitions, accurately where indicated by the stars. Start at the walk and work up to trot and canter when your horse feels relaxed and ready.

Goal: When working with transitions your goal is always for them to be smooth, accurate and relaxed.

Tips:

- Keep your hands close together at the pommel. No one should be able to see them move.
- When you ride you should use 90% seat and 10% reins.

Poles: 4

Level: ★ ★ ★

Benefits:

☑ Accuracy
☑ Rhythm
☑ Impulsion
☑ Straightness
☑ Suppleness & bend
☐ Lateral movement
       & collection

Gaits:

☑ Groundwork
☑ Walk
☑ Trot
☑ Canter

Movements:

☐ Backup
☐ Leg yield
☐ Sidepass
☐ Shoulder in

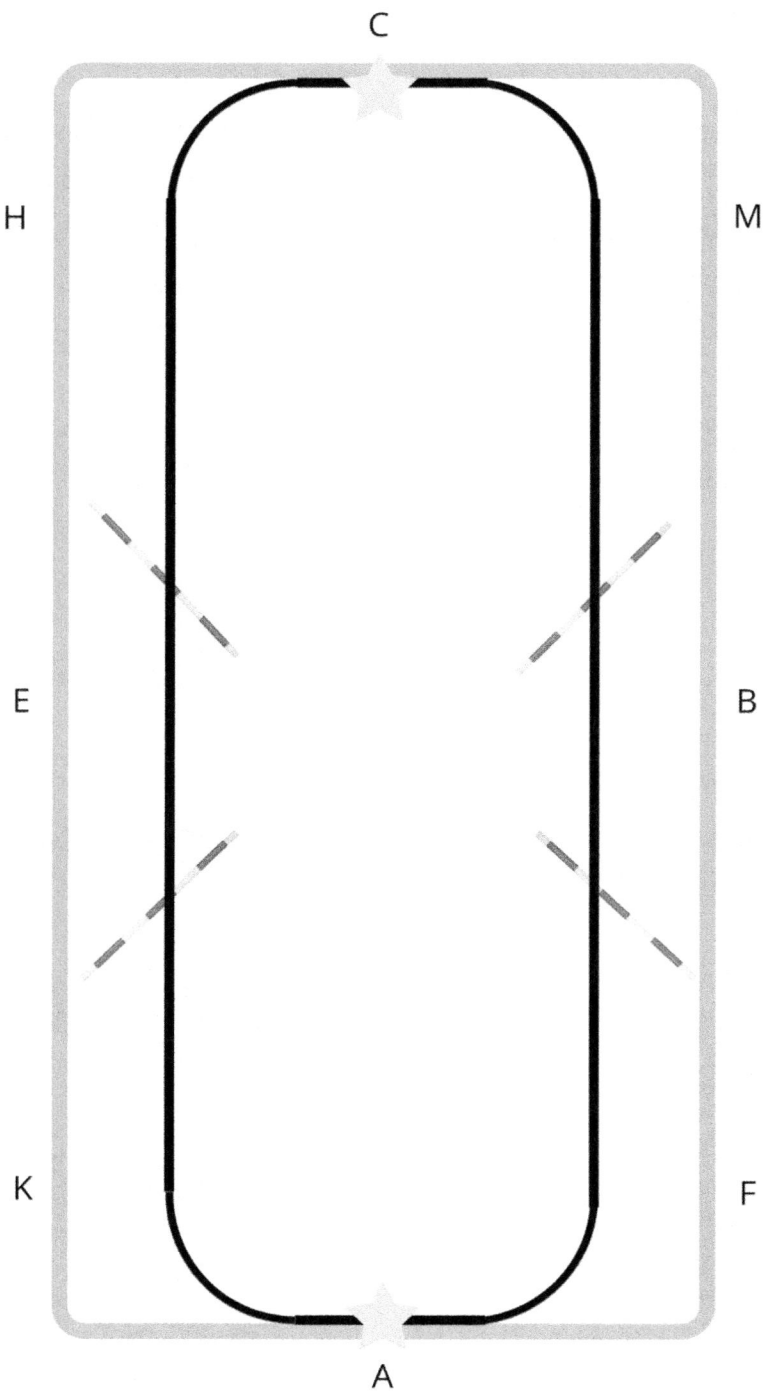

The Westminster

This exercise is similar to the previous one, but you will be working further away from the ends of the arena. This might mean that your horse will find it more difficult to keep to a consistent pattern, so be aware of that and make sure that your feel through your body is clear. Work at a walk in both directions first.

Goal: To complete the pattern with your horse staying relaxed and in a rhythmic and consistent gait.

Tips:

- Lift your outside hip slightly to encourage your horse to bend through his body.
- Keep your shoulders level.
- Look ahead and prepare for the turns, this will help you to be accurate.

Poles: 4

Level: ★ ★ ★

Benefits:

- ☑ Accuracy
- ☑ Rhythm
- ☑ Impulsion
- ☑ Straightness
- ☑ Suppleness & bend
- ☐ Lateral movement
  & collection

Gaits:

- ☑ Groundwork
- ☑ Walk
- ☑ Trot
- ☑ Canter

Movements:

- ☐ Backup
- ☐ Leg yield
- ☐ Sidepass
- ☐ Shoulder in

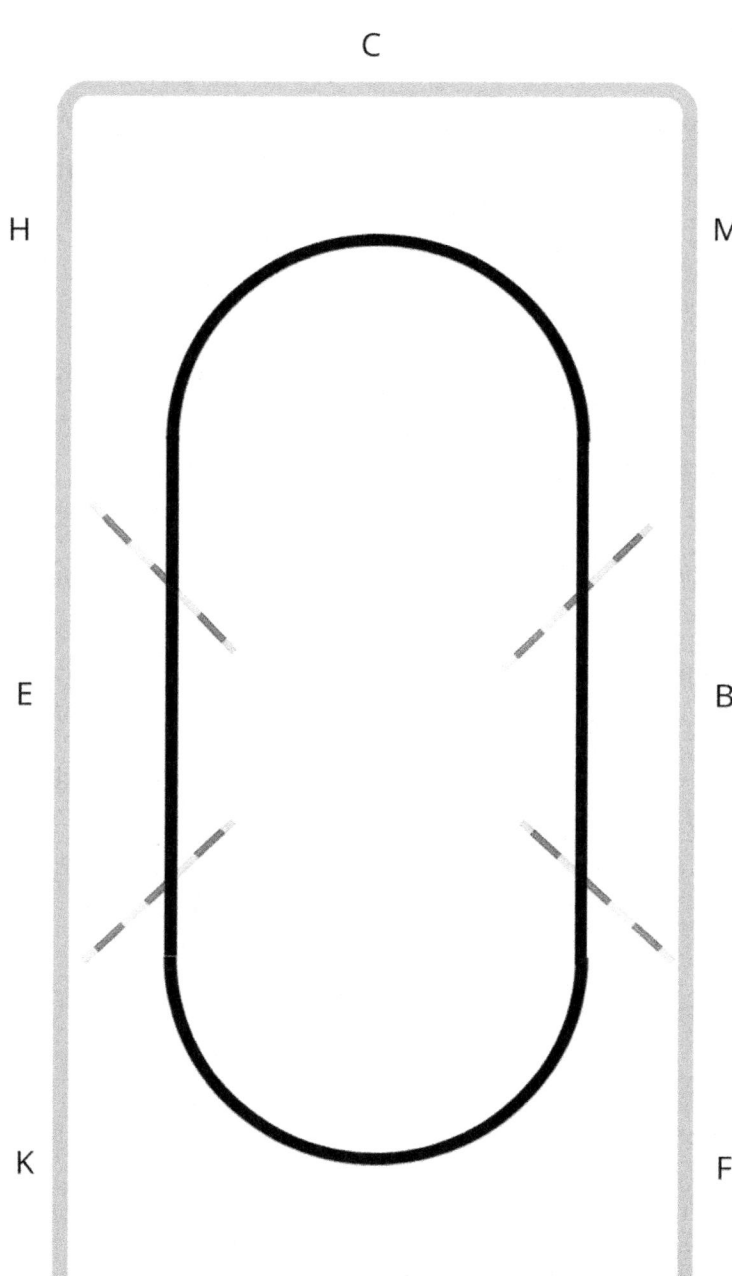

The York

Develop the previous exercise by introducing upward and downward transitions, accurately as indicated by the stars. Start at the walk and work up to trot and canter when your horse feels ready. Your horse should feel forward and relaxed before you go up a gait.

Goal: When working with transitions your goal is always for them to be smooth and relaxed. Your horse will be consistent and rhythmic in the gaits.

Tips:

- Aim to make downward transitions from your body rather than relying on your hands.
- Is your breathing regular and consistent when changing gaits?

Poles: 4

Level: ★ ★ ★

Benefits:

☑ Accuracy
☑ Rhythm
☑ Impulsion
☑ Straightness
☑ Suppleness & bend
☐ Lateral movement
      & collection

Gaits:

☑ Groundwork
☑ Walk
☑ Trot
☑ Canter

Movements:

☐ Backup
☐ Leg yield
☐ Sidepass
☐ Shoulder in

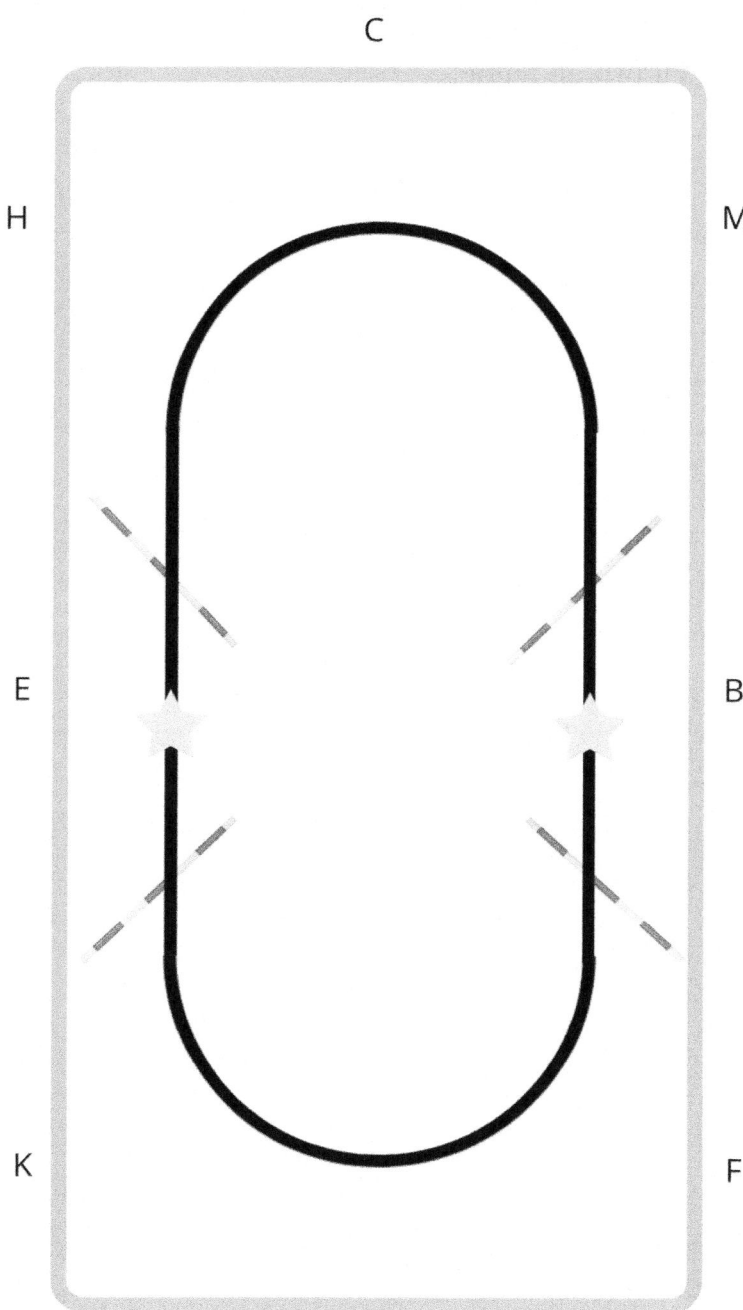

C

H

M

E

B

K

F

A

Create your own flatwork floorplan

Floorplan name: _____

....

....

....

....

....

....

....

....

....

....

....

....

....

....

Notes:

_____

_____

_____

_____

_____

_____

Create your own flatwork floorplan

Floorplan name: _____

....

....

....

....

....

....

....

....

....

....

....

....

....

....

Notes:

_____

_____

_____

_____

_____

_____

Create your own flatwork floorplan

Floorplan name: _____

....

....

....

....

....

....

....

....

....

....

....

....

....

Notes:

_____

_____

_____

_____

_____

_____

C

H

M

E

B

K

F

A

Walk, trot and canter Dressage Tests

Doing dressage tests at home, whether they're walk only tests, walk and trot tests, or walk, trot and canter tests, can be really beneficial for both you and your horse.

Walk only tests are great to begin with, and are perfect to try out a dressage test, for young horses, green horses or just to have some fun with your horse and complete a new goal, while developing your partnership together.

You can focus entirely on your connection with your horse without the stress of a competition, travel drama, or the presence of a judge,. Practicing these tests in a familiar environment allows you to enjoy the process and take your time working on specific movements and transitions that need a little extra attention. You can skip the stress of dressing up in white jodhpurs or worrying about whether your horsebox has a flat tire. It's just you and your horse enjoying the ride!

What you will need: A 20m x 40m area in an arena, paddock or field.

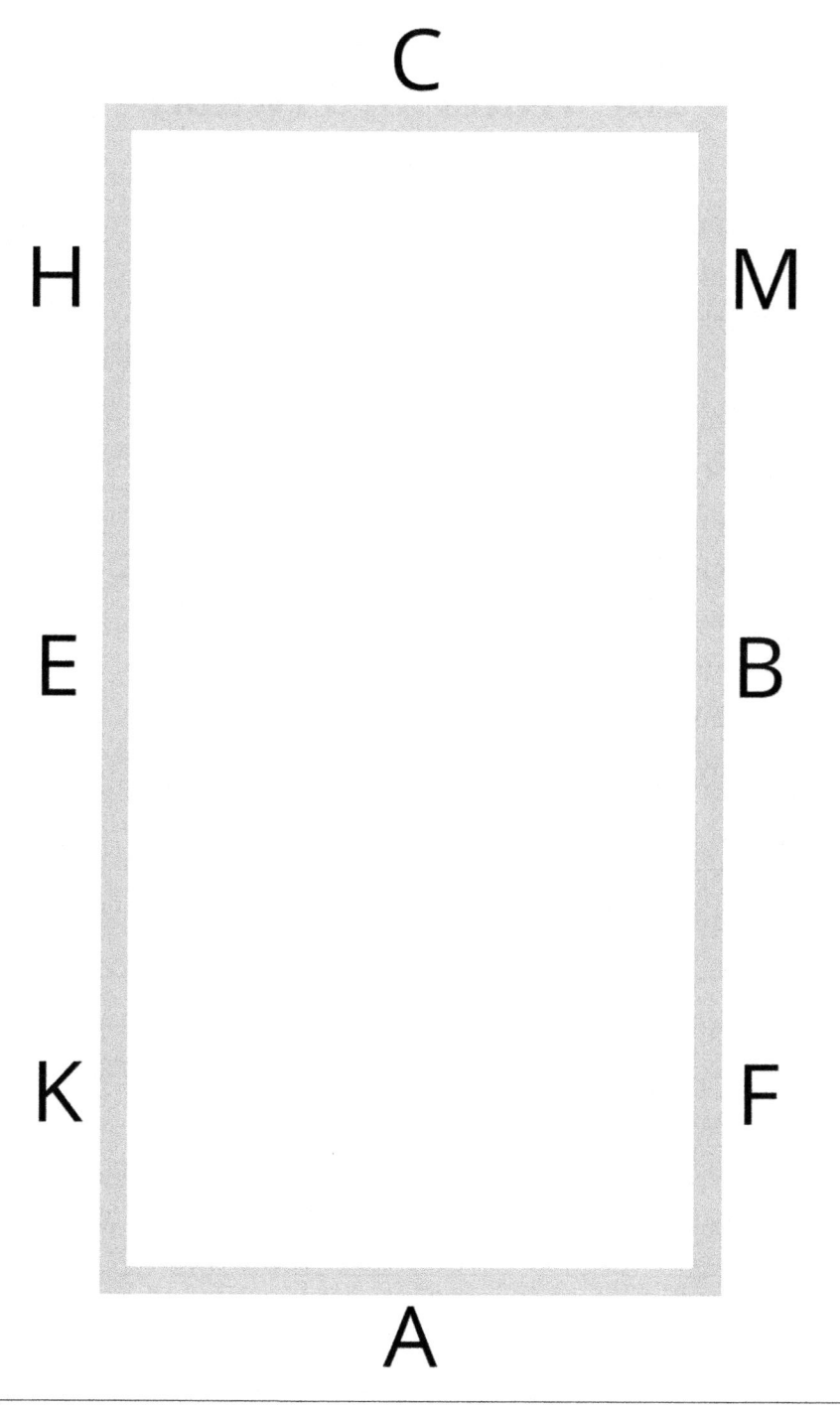

C

H

M

E

B

K

F

A

The Waterford (walk)

AX: Medium walk

X: Halt & salute

X to C: Working walk

C: Turn left

CEA: Medium walk

A: Circle left 20 metres

AFHC: Medium walk

C: Circle right 20 metres

CBF: Free walk on a loose rein

FAX: Medium walk

X: Halt, salute

From X, leave arena at A in free walk on a long rein

Notes:

_____

_____

_____

_____

_____

_____

_____

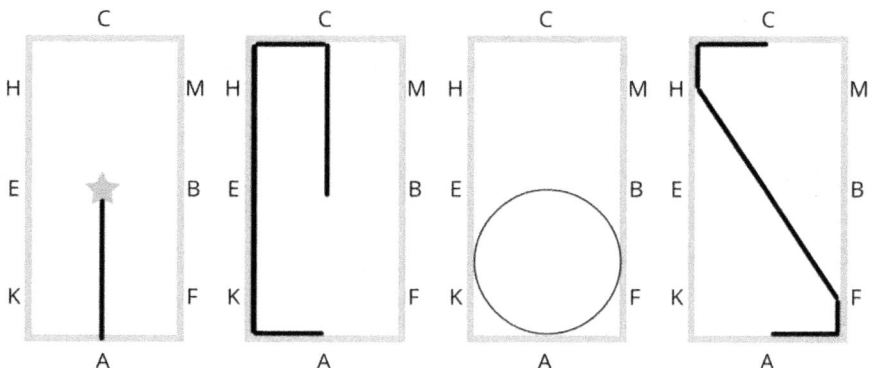

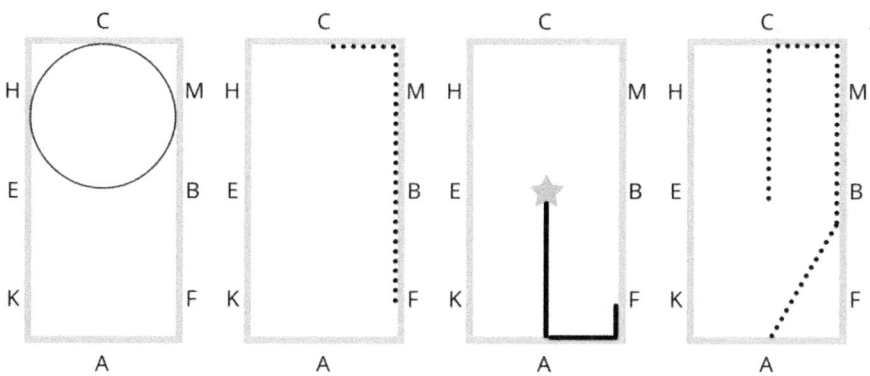

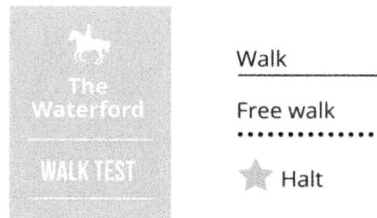

Walk _____

Free walk
•••••••••••••

⭐ Halt

The Kilkenny (walk)

AXC: Medium walk

C: Turn right

CMB: Medium walk

B: Circle right 20 metres

BAK: Medium walk

KXM: Free walk on a loose rein

MCHE: Medium walk

E: Circle left 20 metres

EKA: Medium walk

AX: Medium walk

X: Halt, salute

From X, leave arena at A in free walk on a long rein

Notes:

_____

_____

_____

_____

_____

_____

_____

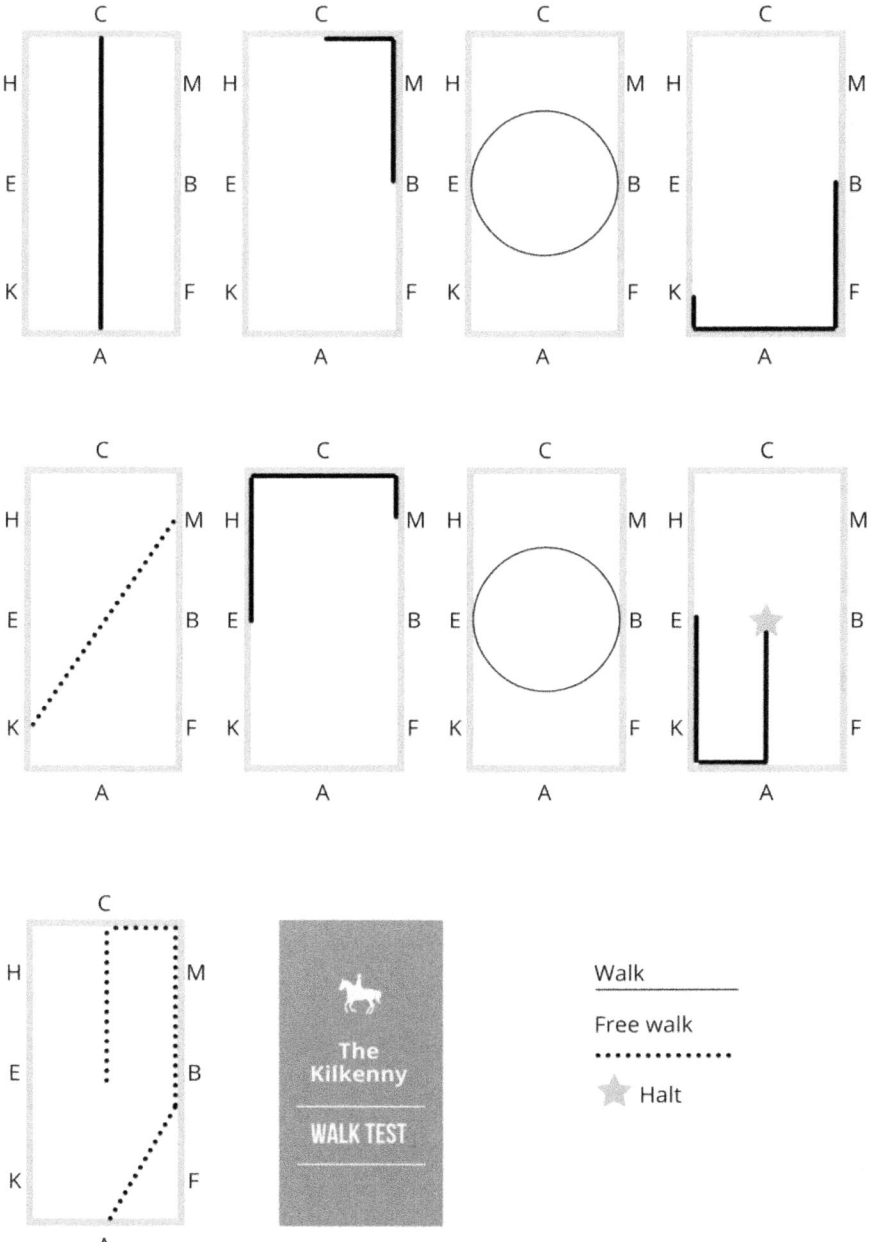

The Wexford (walk)

AXC: Medium walk

C: Turn right

CBA: Medium walk

AC: 3 serpentine loops

C: Circle right 20m

CM: Medium walk

MXK: Free walk on a loose rein

KA: Medium walk

AC: 3 serpentine loops

C: Circle left 20m

CEA: Medium walk

AX: Medium walk

X: Halt, salute

From X, leave arena at A in free walk on a long rein

Notes:

_____

_____

_____

_____

_____

_____

_____

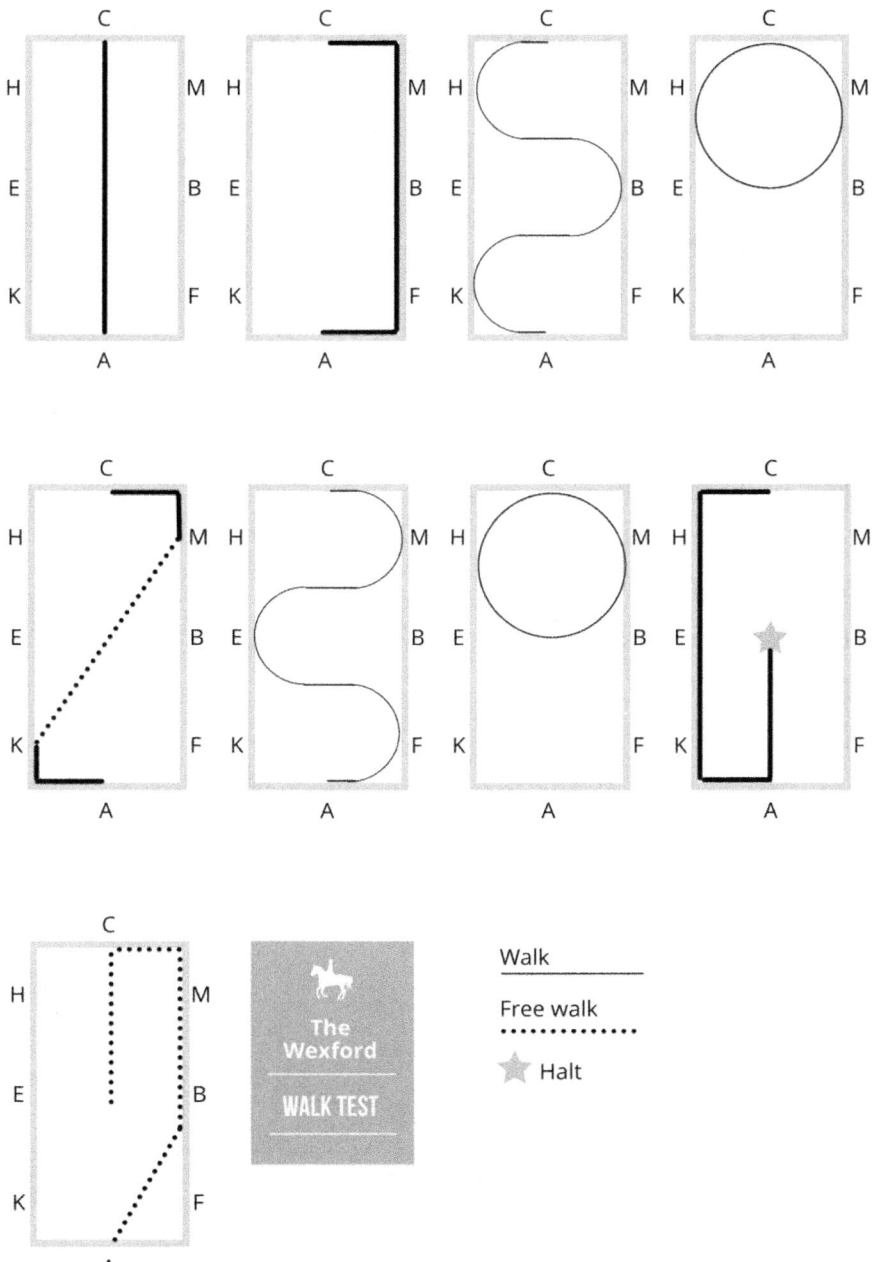

Walk

Free walk

⭐ Halt

The Tipperary (trot)

AXC: Medium walk

C: Turn right

CBA: Medium walk

A: Circle right 20m, working trot

A: Medium walk

AEBC: Medium walk

C: Circle left 20m, working trot

C: Medium walk

CEBF: Medium walk

FAX: Medium walk

X: Halt, salute

From X, leave arena at A in free walk on a long rein

Notes:

_____

_____

_____

_____

_____

_____

_____

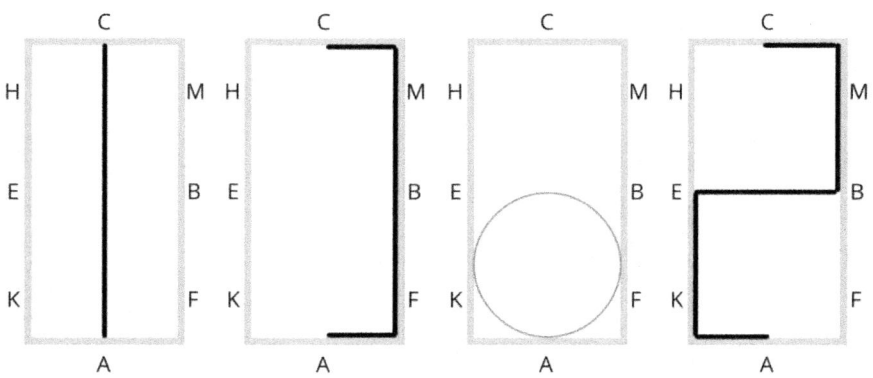

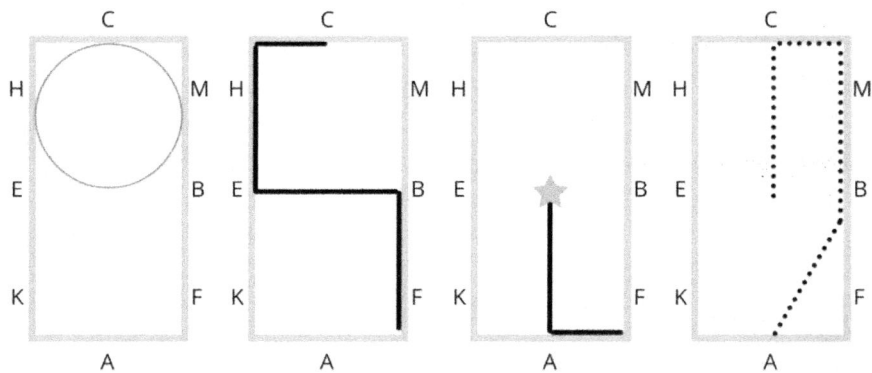

Walk _____

Free walk ··············

Trot _____

⭐ Halt

The Mayo (trot)

AX: Medium walk

X: Halt & salute

X to C: Working walk

C: Turn left

CE: Medium walk

E: Circle 20m left, working trot

EK: Working trot

K: Medium walk

KAB: Medium walk

BEC: Medium walk

CMB: Medium walk

B: Circle 20m right, working trot

BF: Working trot

F: Medium walk

FAX: Medium walk

X: Halt, salute

From X, leave arena at A in free walk on a long rein

Notes:

_____

_____

_____

_____

_____

_____

_____

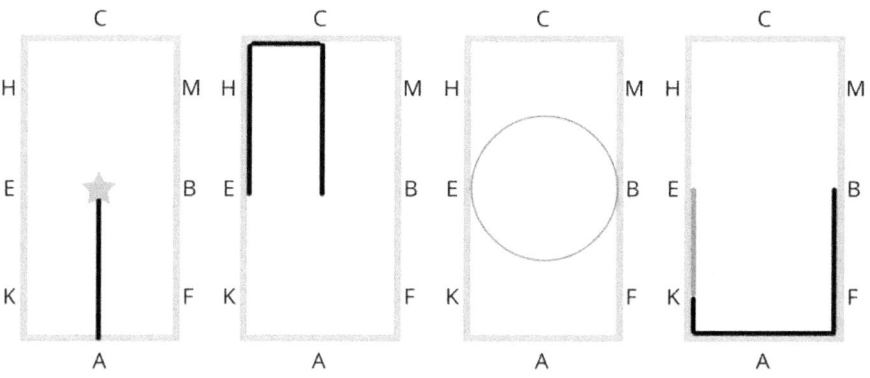

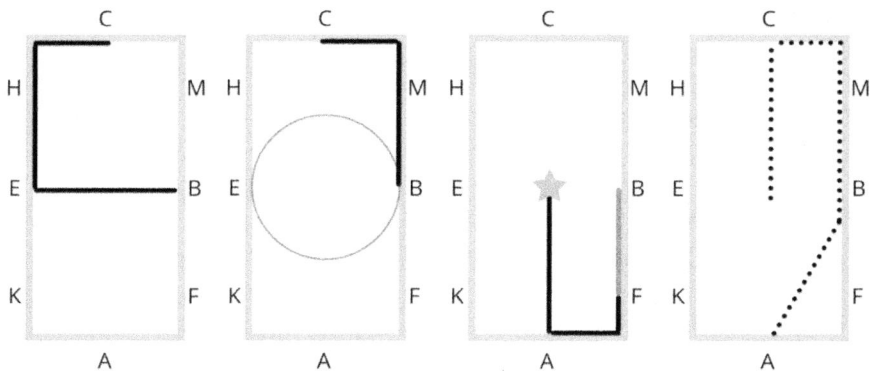

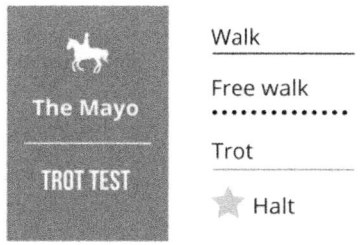

Walk ──────

Free walk ··············

Trot ──────

⭐ Halt

The Sligo (trot)

AX: Medium walk

X: Halt & salute

X to C: Working walk

C: Turn left

CH: Medium walk

HFA: Working trot

A: Circle 20m right, working trot

A: Medium walk

AKM: Medium walk

MC: Working trot

C: Circle 20m left, working trot

C: Medium walk

CEB: Medium walk

BFAX: Working trot

XG: Medium walk

G: Halt, salute

From G, leave arena at A in free walk on a long rein

Notes:

_____

_____

_____

_____

_____

_____

_____

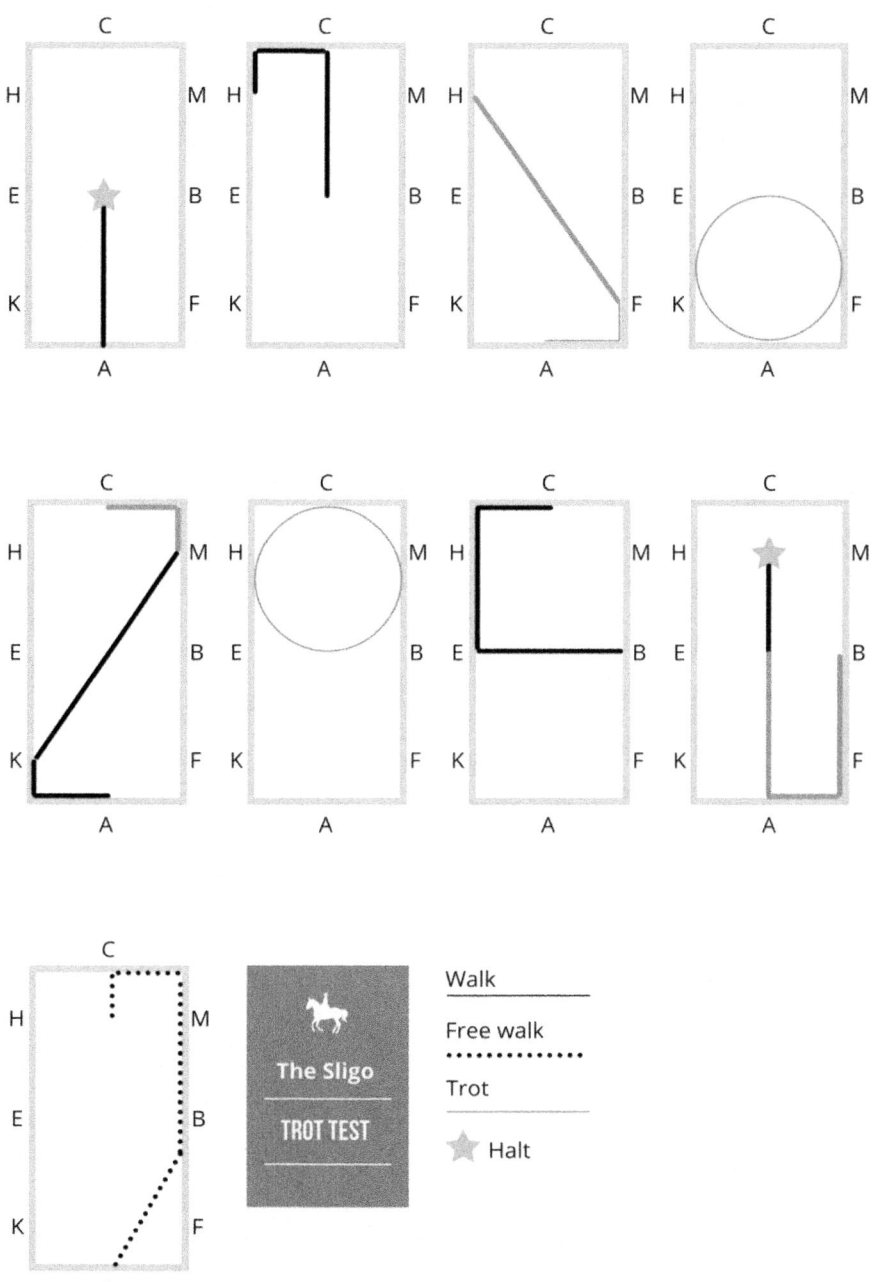

Walk

Free walk

Trot

Halt

The Sligo

TROT TEST

The Meath (canter)

AXC: Medium walk

C: Turn right

CM: Medium walk

M: Working trot

MB: Working trot

B: Circle right 10m, working trot

BFA: Working trot

A: Circle right 20m, canter

A: Working trot

AK: Working trot

KXM: Free walk on a loose rein

M: Medium walk

MCH: Medium walk

HE: Working trot

E: 10m circle left, working trot

EKA: Working trot

A: 20m circle in canter

A: Working trot

AFB: Working trot

B: Medium walk

BE: Medium walk

EKAX: Medium walk

X: Halt, salute

From X, leave arena at A in free walk on a long rein

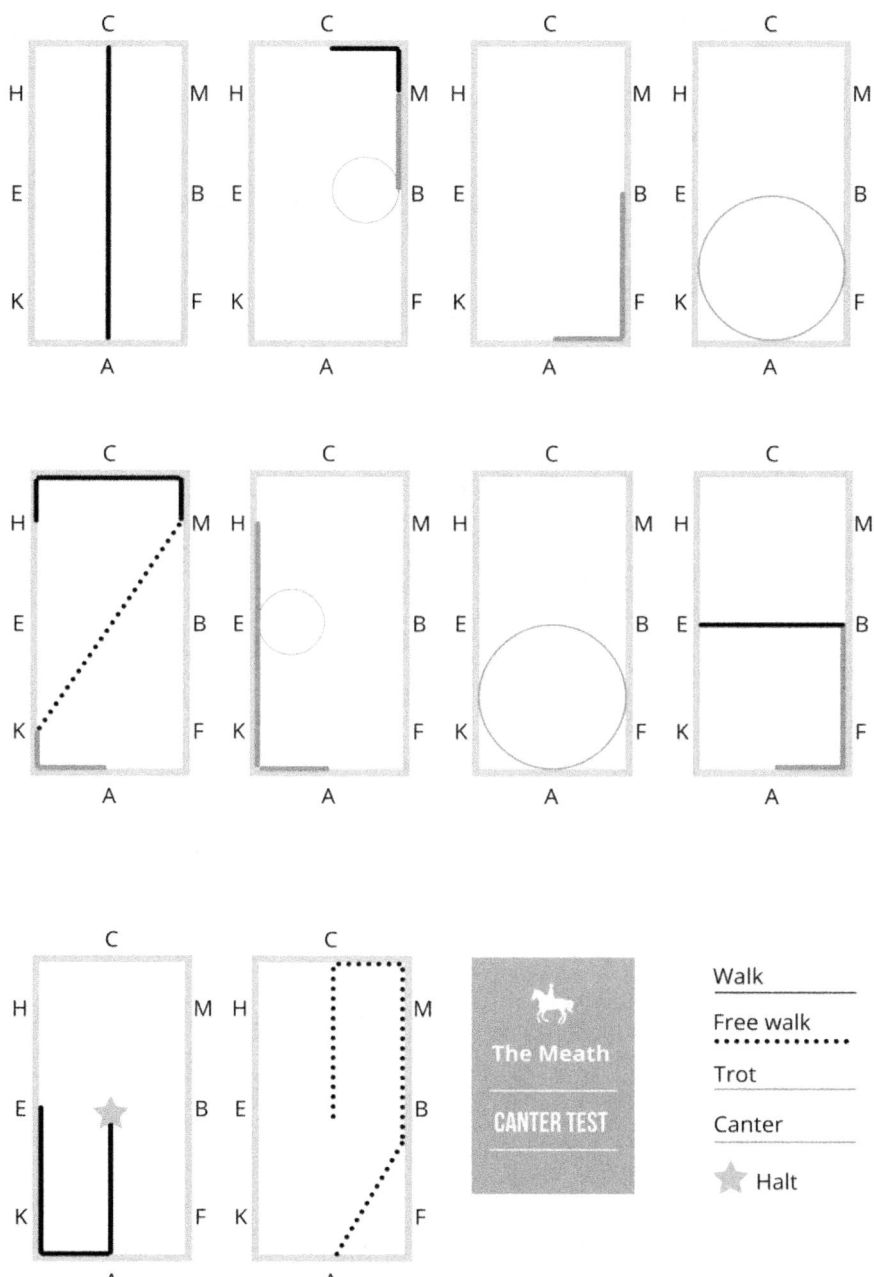

Walk

Free walk

Trot

Canter

⭐ Halt

The Meath

CANTER TEST

The Donegal (canter)

AXC: Medium walk

C: Turn right

CMBF: Medium walk

F: Half circle right 10 metres

DMC: Working trot

C: 20m circle left, canter

C: Working trot

CHEK: Working trot

K: Medium walk

K: Half circle left 10 metres

DH: Medium walk

HC: Working trot

C: Circle right 20m, canter

C: Working trot

CMBF: Working trot

F: Medium walk

FAX: Medium walk

X: Halt, salute

From X, leave arena at A in free walk on a long rein

Notes:

_____

_____

_____

_____

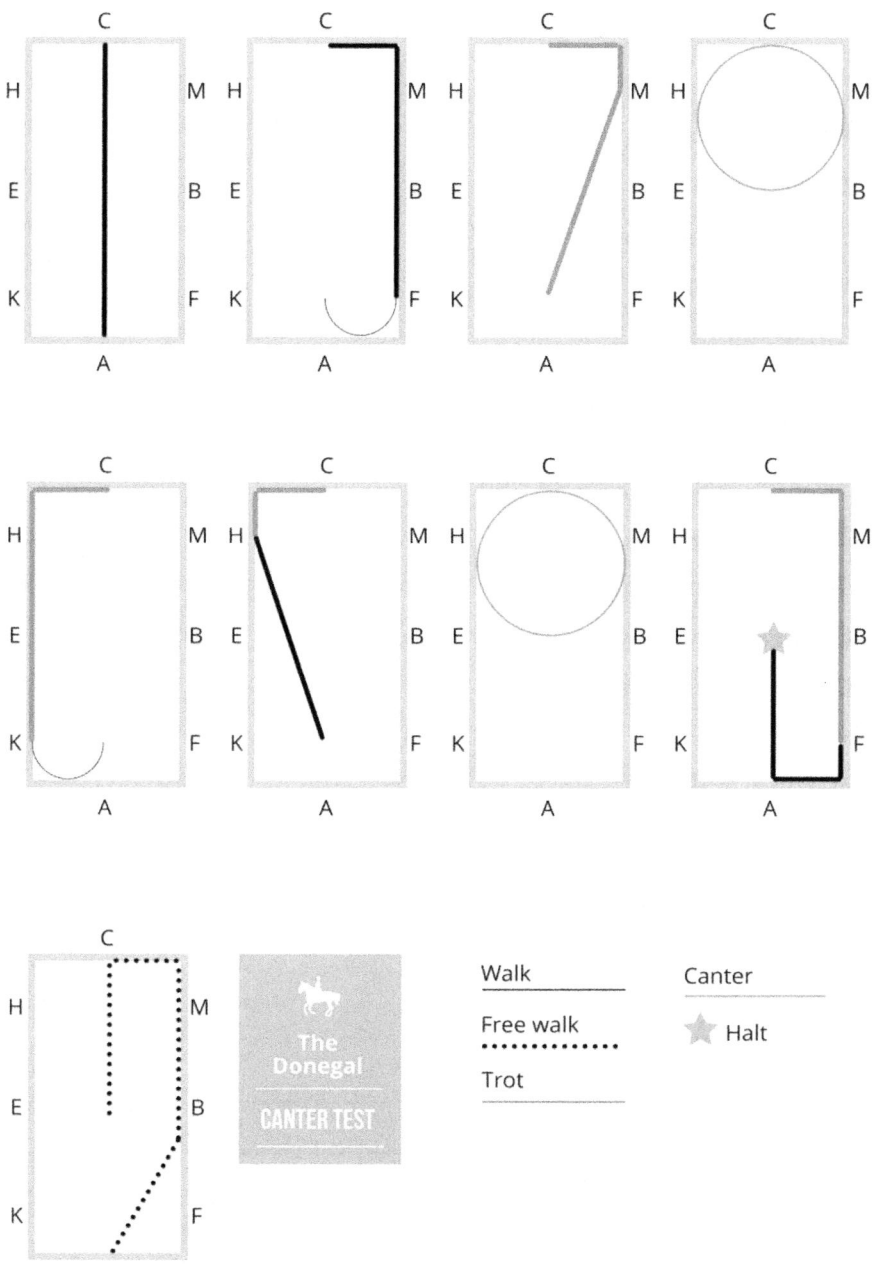

The Donegal

CANTER TEST

Walk ——————
Free walk ••••••••••••
Trot ——————

Canter ——————
⭐ Halt

The Galway (canter)

AXC: Medium walk

C: Turn right

CA: 3 serpentine loops

A: Working trot

A: Circle right 10m

A: Circle right 20m canter

AK: Working trot

KXM: Free walk on a loose rein

MC: Medium walk

CA: 3 serpentine loops

A: Circle 10m, left, working trot

A: Circle left 20m canter

ABC: Working trot

C: Medium walk

CEAX: Medium walk

X: Halt, salute

From X, leave arena at A in free walk on a long rein

Notes:

_____

_____

_____

_____

_____

_____

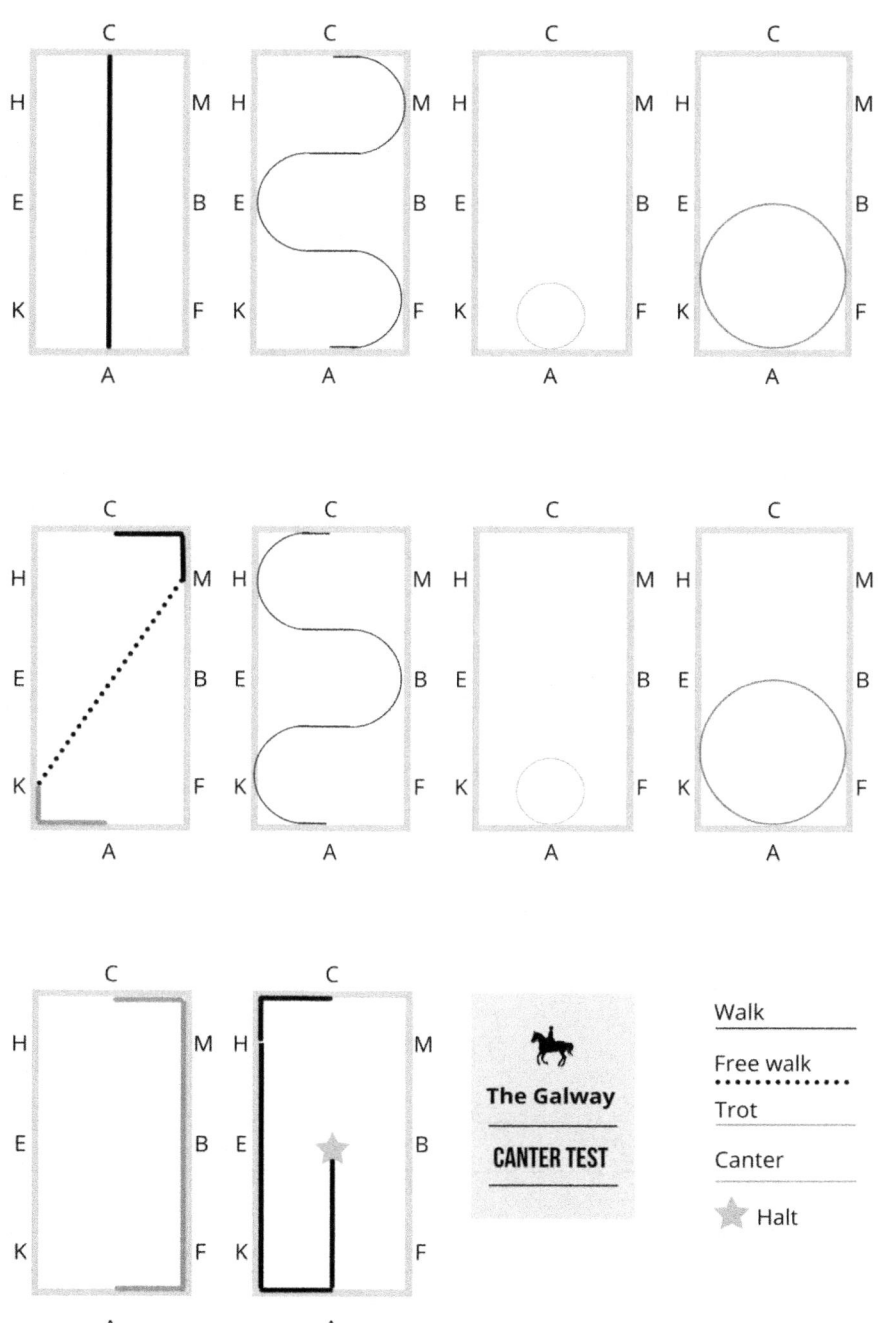

The Galway

CANTER TEST

Walk	———
Free walk	••••••••
Trot	———
Canter	———
⭐	Halt

Create your own dressage test

Test name: _____

....

....

....

....

....

....

....

....

....

....

....

....

....

....

....

Notes:

_____

_____

_____

_____

_____

_____

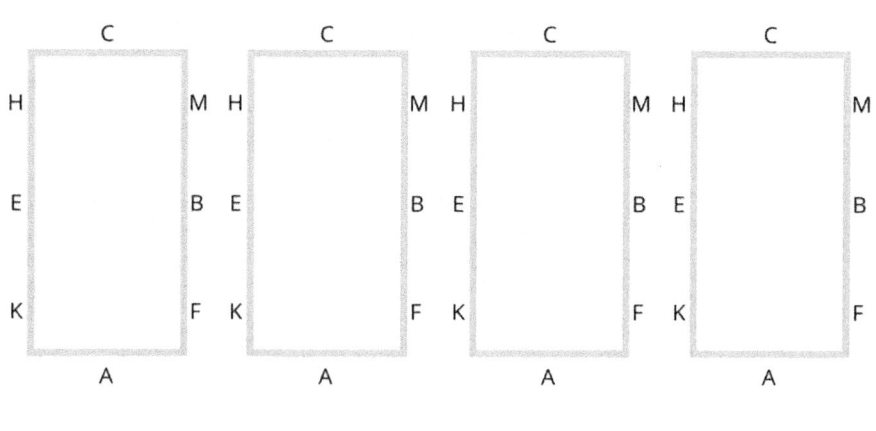

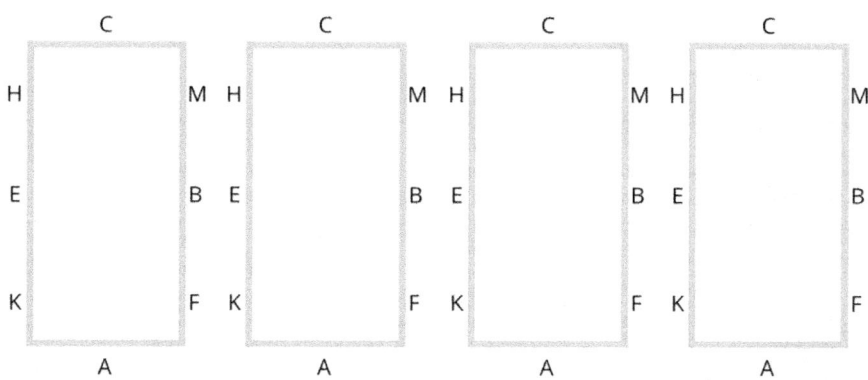

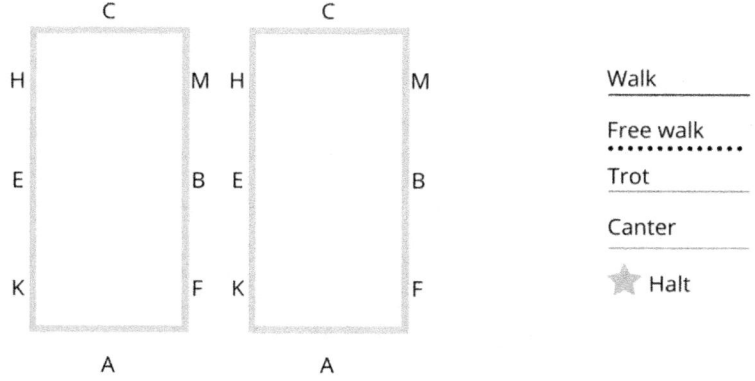

Walk

Free walk
••••••••••••

Trot

Canter

⭐ Halt

Create your own dressage test

Test name: _____

....
....
....
....
....
....
....
....
....
....
....
....
....
....

Notes:

_____

_____

_____

_____

_____

_____

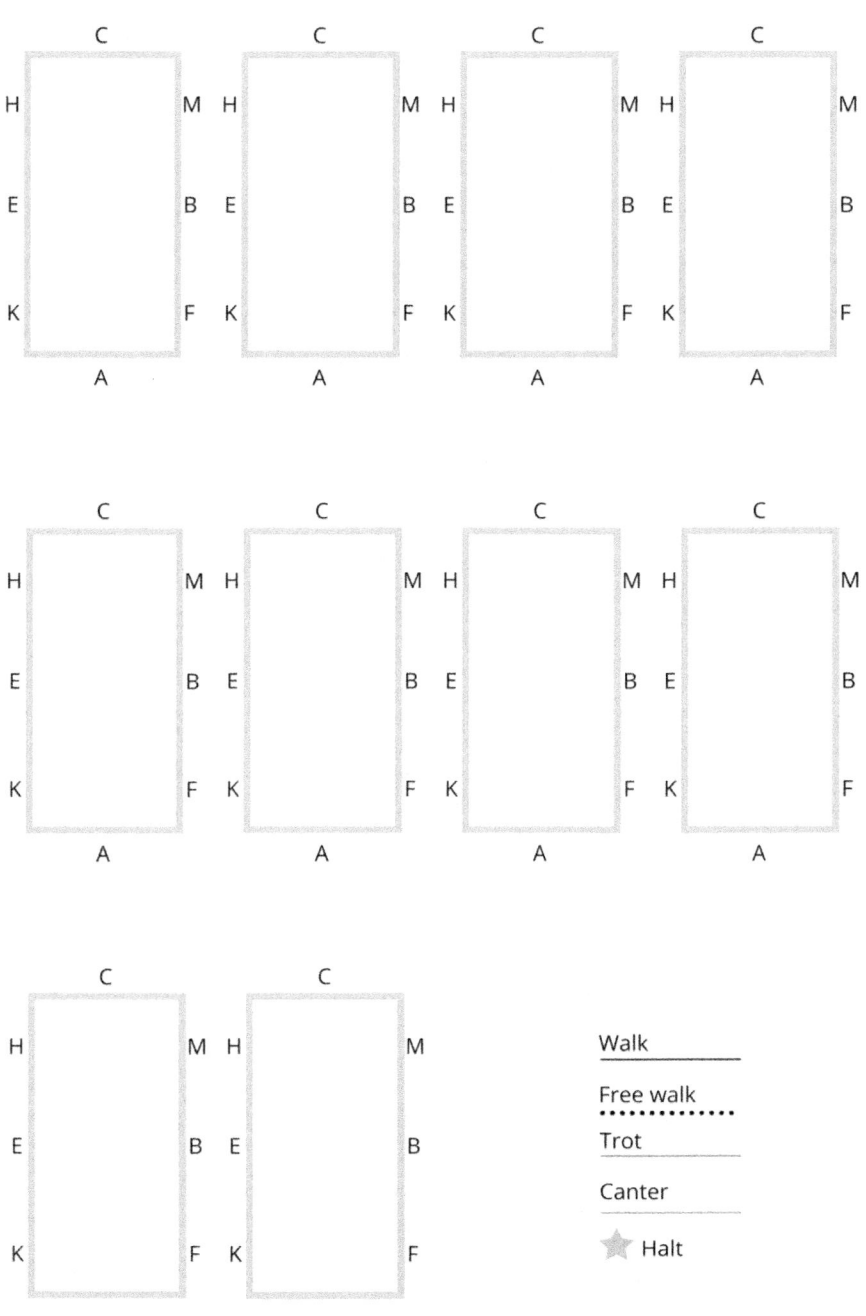

Walk ——————
Free walk ••••••••••••
Trot ——————
Canter ——————
⭐ Halt

Create your own dressage test

Test name: _____

....

....

....

....

....

....

....

....

....

....

....

....

....

....

Notes:

_____

_____

_____

_____

_____

_____

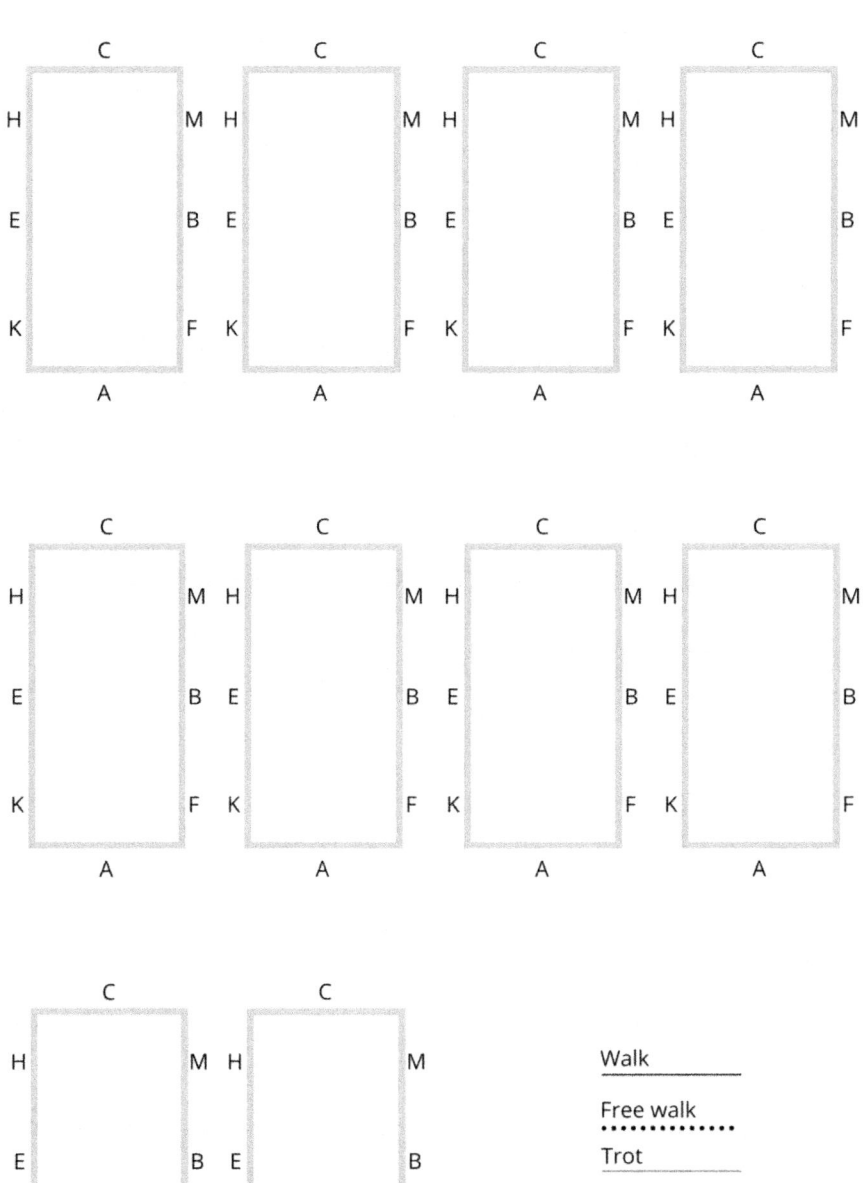

Walk ———————

Free walk •••••••••••••

Trot ———————

Canter ———————

⭐ Halt

Track & celebrate your new skills with your horse!

Date: _____   **Horse's Name:** _____

Milestone Achieved: Exercise completed, improved transitions, maintained straightness over poles, etc.

_____

_____

Breakthrough Moment: Describe what clicked for you and your horse. What change made the difference?

_____

_____

Challenges Overcome: What obstacles did you face, and how did you work through them?

_____

_____

Next Steps: How will you build on this progress? What's the next goal?

_____

_____

Celebrate Your Success! What did you enjoy most about reaching this milestone?

_____

Date: _____ **Horse's Name:** _____

Milestone Achieved: Exercise completed, improved transitions, maintained straightness over poles, etc.

_____

_____

Breakthrough Moment: Describe what clicked for you and your horse. What change made the difference?

_____

_____

Challenges Overcome: What obstacles did you face, and how did you work through them?

_____

_____

Next Steps: How will you build on this progress? What's the next goal?

_____

_____

Celebrate Your Success! What did you enjoy most about reaching this milestone?

_____

Date: _____   **Horse's Name:** _____

Milestone Achieved: Exercise completed, improved transitions, maintained straightness over poles, etc.

_____

_____

Breakthrough Moment: Describe what clicked for you and your horse. What change made the difference?

_____

_____

Challenges Overcome: What obstacles did you face, and how did you work through them?

_____

_____

Next Steps: How will you build on this progress? What's the next goal?

_____

_____

Celebrate Your Success! What did you enjoy most about reaching this milestone?

_____

Date: _____ **Horse's Name:** _____

Milestone Achieved: Exercise completed, improved transitions, maintained straightness over poles, etc.

_____

_____

Breakthrough Moment: Describe what clicked for you and your horse. What change made the difference?

_____

_____

Challenges Overcome: What obstacles did you face, and how did you work through them?

_____

_____

Next Steps: How will you build on this progress? What's the next goal?

_____

_____

Celebrate Your Success! What did you enjoy most about reaching this milestone?

_____

Date: _____   **Horse's Name:** _____

Milestone Achieved: Exercise completed, improved transitions, maintained straightness over poles, etc.

_____

_____

Breakthrough Moment: Describe what clicked for you and your horse. What change made the difference?

_____

_____

Challenges Overcome: What obstacles did you face, and how did you work through them?

_____

_____

Next Steps: How will you build on this progress? What's the next goal?

_____

_____

Celebrate Your Success! What did you enjoy most about reaching this milestone?

_____

_____

Create your own flatwork floorplan

Floorplan name: _____

....
....
....
....
....
....
....
....
....
....
....
....
....
....

Notes:

_____
_____
_____
_____
_____
_____
_____

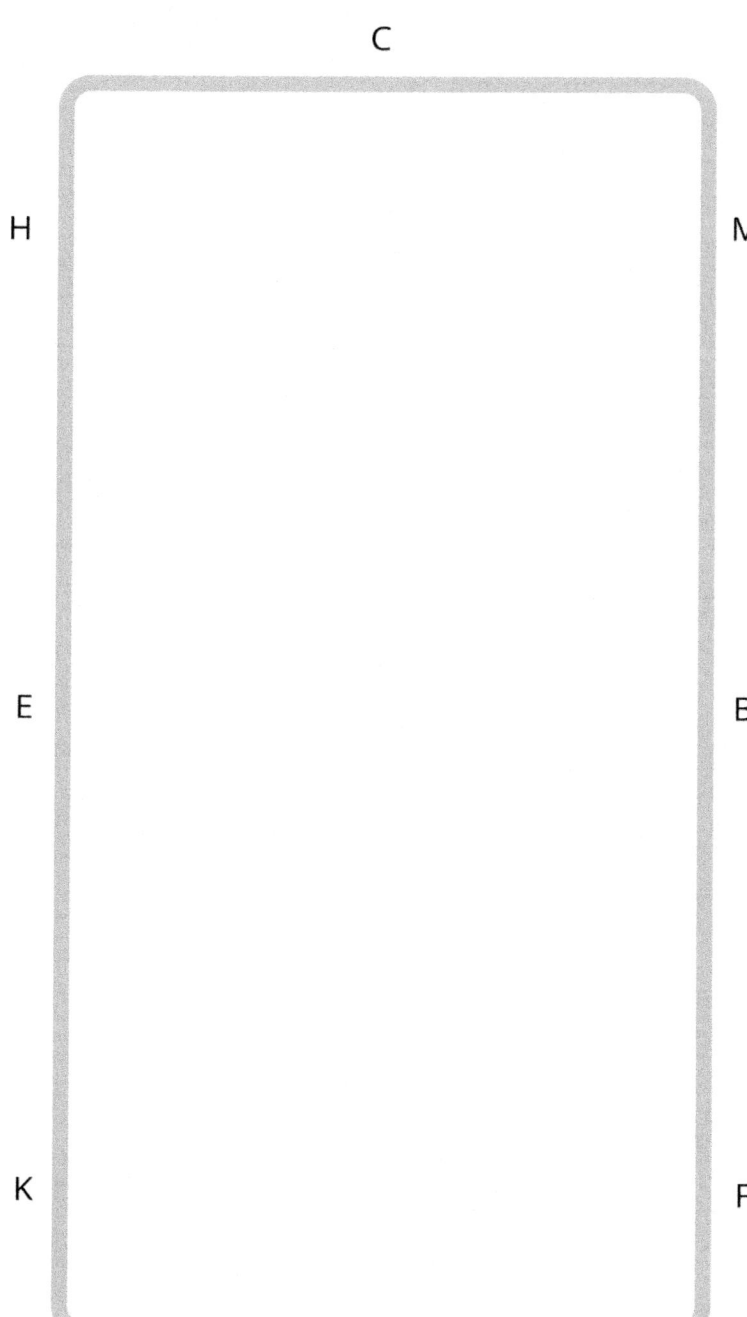

Create your own flatwork floorplan

Floorplan name: _____

....

....

....

....

....

....

....

....

....

....

....

....

....

....

Notes:

_____

_____

_____

_____

_____

_____

C

H

M

E

B

K

F

A

Create your own flatwork floorplan

Floorplan name: _____

....

....

....

....

....

....

....

....

....

....

....

....

....

....

Notes:

_____

_____

_____

_____

_____

_____

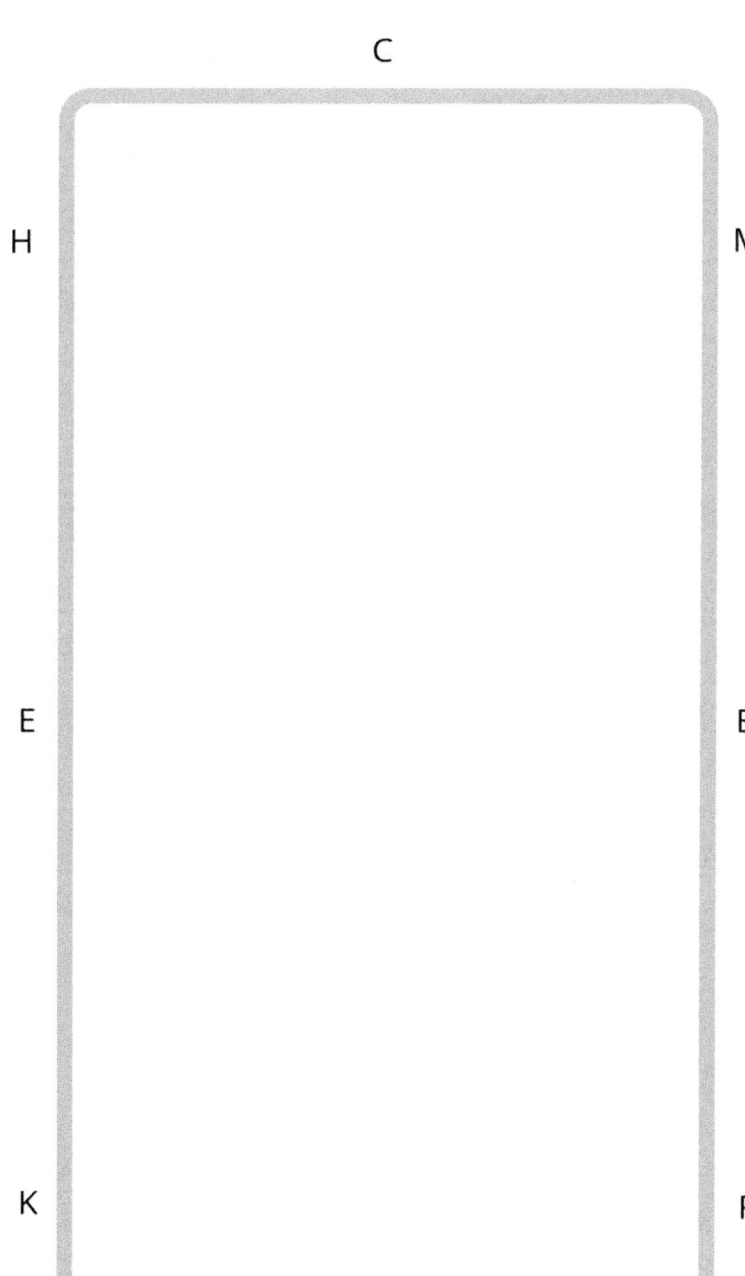

C

H

M

E

B

K

F

A

Create your own dressage test

Test name: _____

....

....

....

....

....

....

....

....

....

....

....

....

....

....

....

Notes:

_____

_____

_____

_____

_____

_____

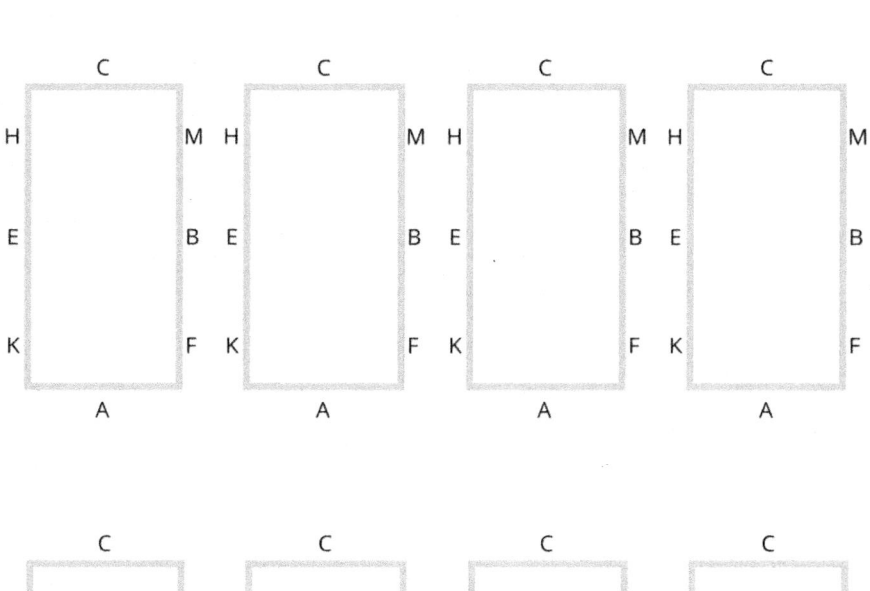

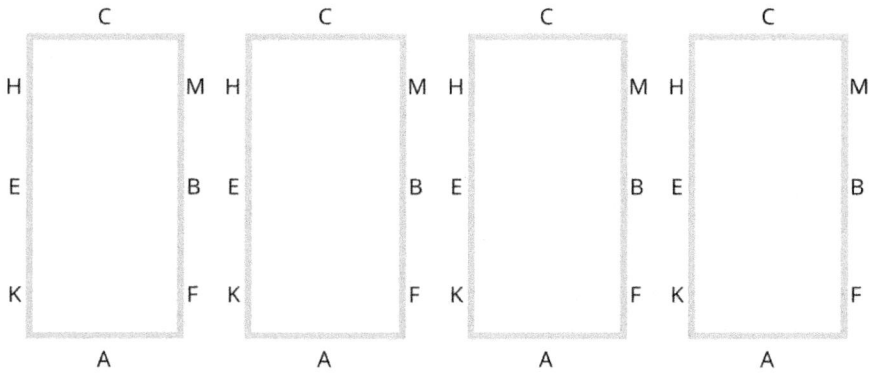

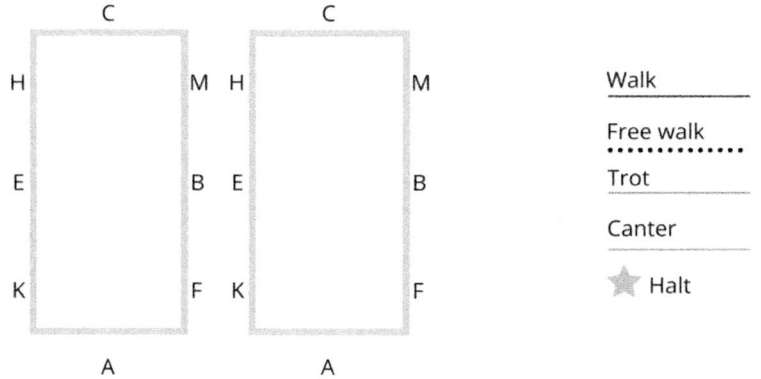

Walk ————————

Free walk ••••••••••••••

Trot ————————

Canter ————————

⭐ Halt

Create your own dressage test

Test name: _____

....
....
....
....
....
....
....
....
....
....
....
....
....
....

Notes:

_____
_____
_____
_____
_____
_____
_____

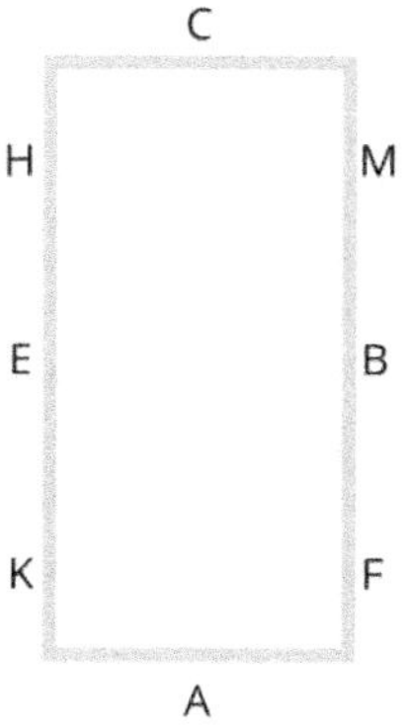

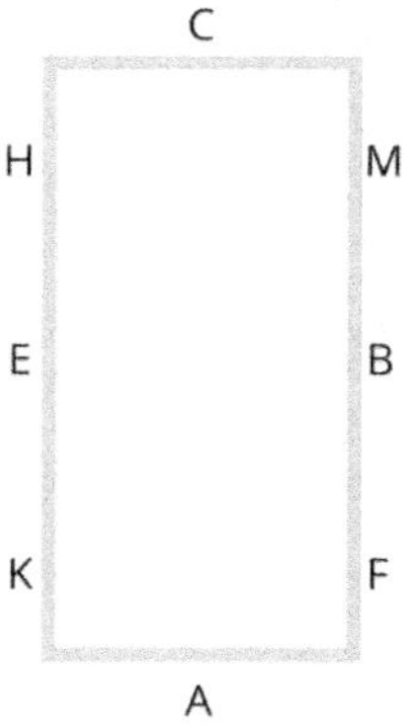

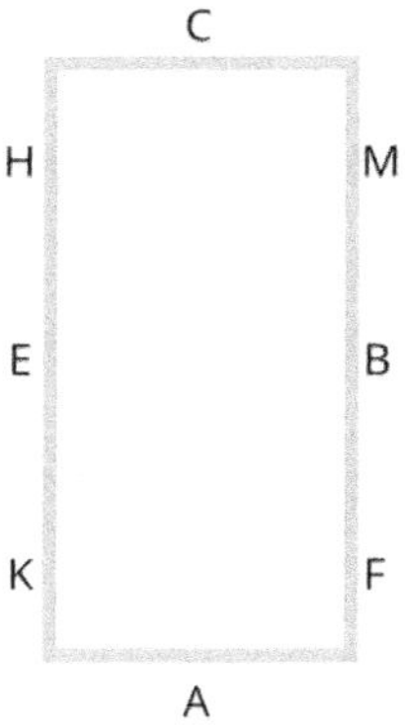

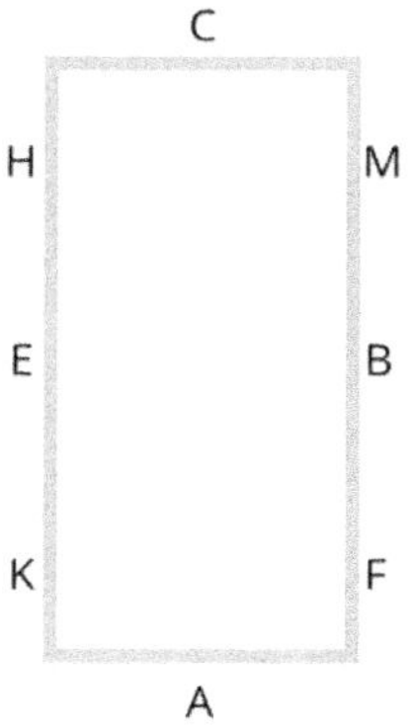

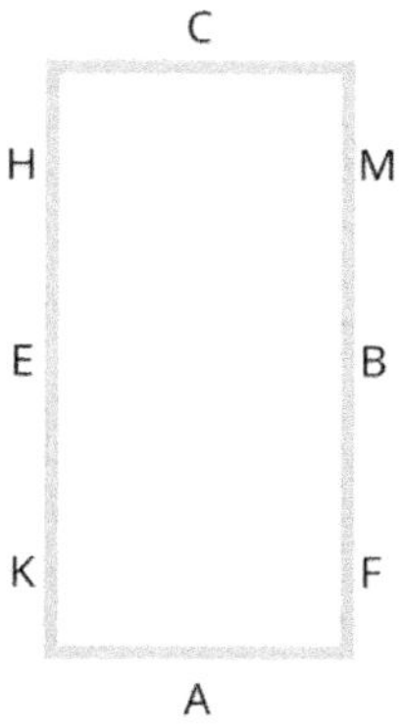

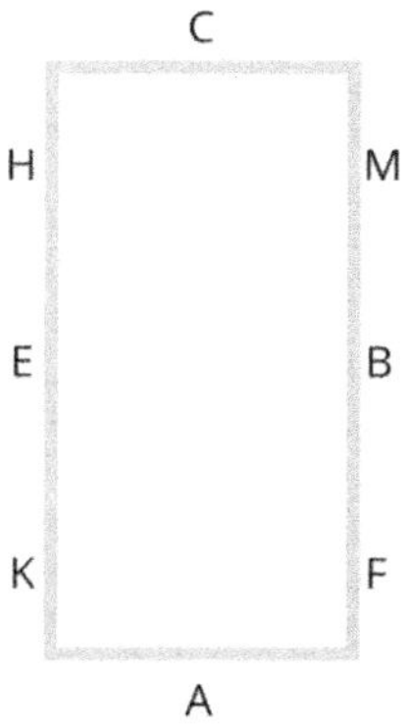

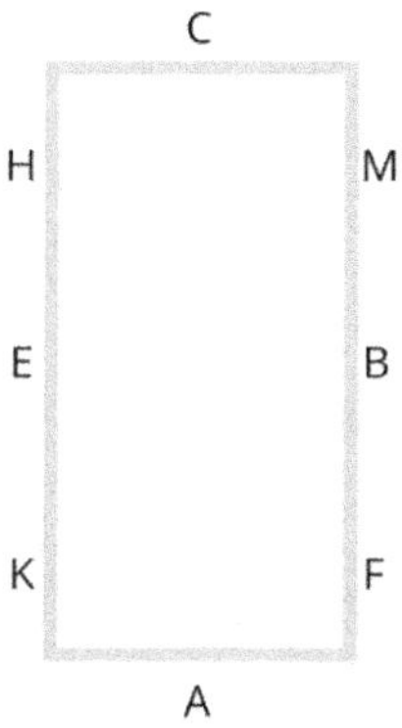

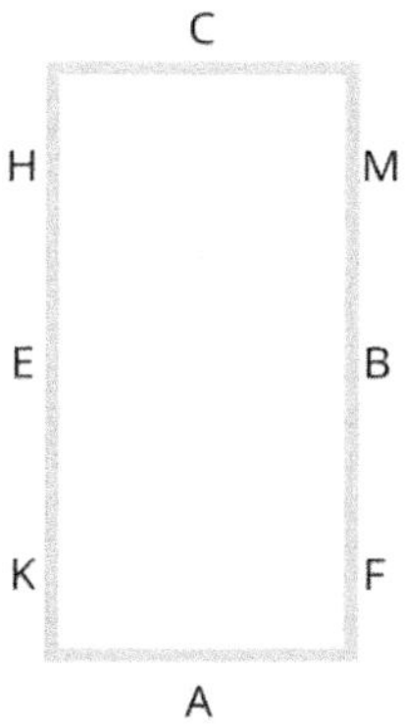

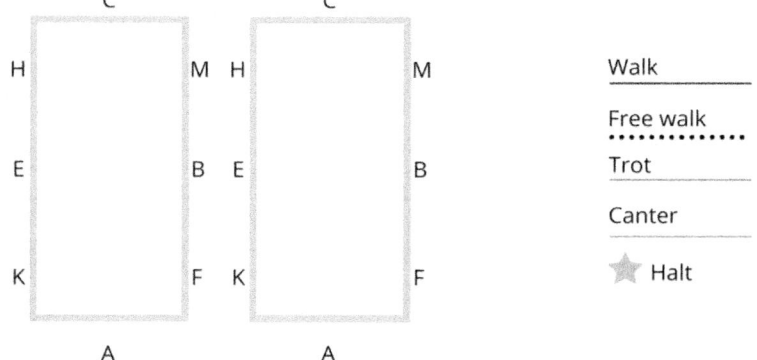

Walk ─────────

Free walk ••••••••••••

Trot ─────────

Canter ─────────

⭐ Halt

Create your own dressage test

Test name: _____

....

....

....

....

....

....

....

....

....

....

....

....

....

....

Notes:

_____

_____

_____

_____

_____

_____

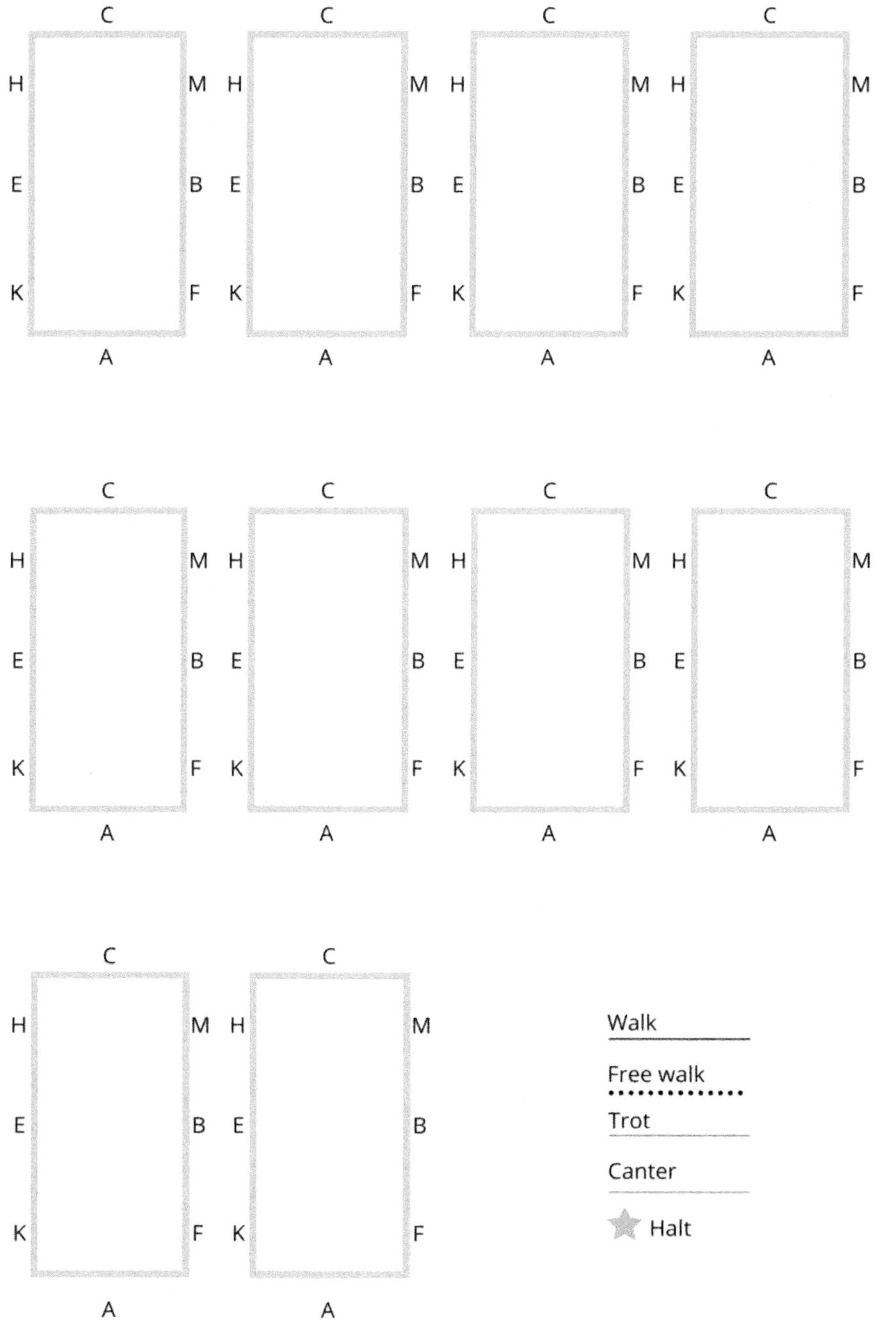

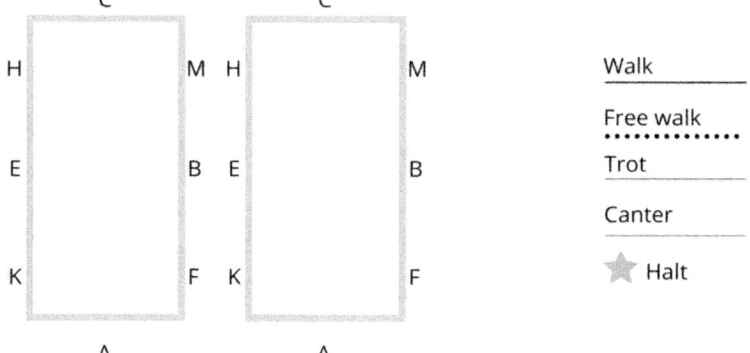

Arena 1: C / H M / E B / K F / A

Arena 2: C / H M / E B / K F / A

Arena 3: C / H M / E B / K F / A

Arena 4: C / H M / E B / K F / A

Arena 5: C / H M / E B / K F / A

Arena 6: C / H M / E B / K F / A

Arena 7: C / H M / E B / K F / A

Arena 8: C / H M / E B / K F / A

Arena 9: C / H M / E B / K F / A

Arena 10: C / H M / E B / K F / A

Walk ——————

Free walk •••••••••••••

Trot ——————

Canter ——————

⭐ Halt